The Evolution of an International Actor

Western Europe's New Assertiveness

The Evolution of an International Actor

Western Europe's New Assertiveness

EDITED BY
Reinhardt Rummel

with the assistance of Colette Mazzucelli

Westview Press
BOULDER, SAN FRANCISCO, & OXFORD

Westview Special Studies in West European Politics and Society

This Westview softcover edition is printed on acid-free paper and bound in library-quality, coated covers that carry the highest rating of the National Association of State Textbook Administrators, in consultation with the Association of American Publishers and the Book Manufacturers' Institute.

Published in 1990 in the United States of America by Westview Press, Inc., 5500 Central Avenue, Boulder, Colorado 80301, and in the United Kingdom by Westview Press, Inc., 36 Lonsdale Road, Summertown, Oxford OX2 7EW

Library of Congress Cataloging-in-Publication Data
The Evolution of an international actor : Western Europe's new
assertiveness / edited by Reinhardt Rummel.
p. cm.—(Westview special studies in West European politics
and society)
ISBN 0-8133-7534-7
1. Europe—Politics and government—1945- . 2. Europe—Defenses.
3. Europe—Economic conditions—1945- . I. Rummel, Reinhardt.
II. Series.
D1053.E94 1990
320.94—dc20 90-12282
CIP

Printed and bound in the United States of America

The paper used in this publication meets the requirements of the American National Standard for Permanence of Paper for Printed Library Materials Z39.48-1984.

10 9 8 7 6 5 4 3 2 1

Contents

Preface

This volume is the result of a joint effort on the part of European and American scholars to describe and analyze the nature and the role of the European Community on the threshold of the 1990s.

The 1980s stood witness to a significant change in West Europe from "Eurosclerosis" to close European cooperation in the fields of security, foreign policy and trade. This newly won "assertiveness" on the part of the West Europeans will be put to a test in the next decade, as, in addition to the progressing West European integration process, a new dynamic is likely to preoccupy the 1990s - the ongoing reform process in East Europe.

West European integration implies major challenges for the West European nations as well as for the transatlantic relationship. The following chapters concentrate on various aspects of West European assertiveness. Part One discusses how the theme of "national" versus "global" needs intersects with that of the struggle to define a nascent West European "identity." Part Two deals with the growing European cooperation in defense matters and the inherent challenges for the West European nations as well as for NATO. Finally, Part Three provides case studies of European assertiveness in the context of European-American relations.

Given the scope of the project and the number of contributors, drafts of each chapter were initially submitted to the editor. Colette G. Mazzucelli, M.A.L.D., (Tufts University - The Fletcher School of Law and Diplomacy), Ph.D. candidate (Georgetown University), was responsible for subsequent academic research, English language editing and the organization of the documents in the Annex. Barbara Bläsing and Karen Murphy, research assistants at Stiftung Wissenschaft und Politik, Ebenhausen, contributed to the editing as well.

The editor is grateful for the support by the members of the International Security Studies Program of The Woodrow Wilson International Center for Scholars, Washington, D.C., where he was granted a fellowship during 1989.

Reinhardt Rummel

1

Preparing West Europe for the 1990s

Reinhardt Rummel

But Who Wants a Big Europe, Anyway?
Stephen Low[1]

Stephen Low's question is as much a provocation as a concern. Europe is, in fact, growing and moving toward center stage and nobody can help it - not even the Europeans. The surprise may be real, but the worry seems unjustified. Europe is much better prepared for the new role than ten years ago. During the 1980s, West Europe's assertiveness reached for, and achieved, new heights in the overall process of West European integration. Yet, to cope successfully with the challenges of the 1990s, the West Europeans will need to enhance, and expand, the influence of their assertive behavior.

The revolutionary changes in Eastern Europe and the Soviet Union have modified the traditional systemic antagonism between East and West and are about to dismantle the postwar political architecture of Europe. This is not "the end of history" and the beginning of a period of political dullness.[2] At least not for the peoples, policy makers and policy analysts in Europe. West Europe

---

1 *International Herald Tribune*, 2-3 December 1989, p. 10.

2 In the Summer of 1989 a heated debate took place among Western scholars on the question whether or not the ideological change in the Soviet realm meant the end of the ideological antagonism between East and West, and, therefore, the end of history. The debate was launched by the following article: Francis Fukuyama, The end of history? in *The National Interest*, No. 16, Summer 1989.

has to synchronize its own dynamics of the 1992 Internal Market project with its support for a successful reform in the East. Furthermore, it has to digest the reconciliation of the two German states and has to cope with the next EC enlargement round. These adaptations, in turn, will demand a substantive modernization of the transatlantic alliance.[3]

Assertiveness is a quality which is neither freely granted nor easily acquired. This is especially the case for a grouping of states which do not have a common or central political authority, and which depend heavily on others for supplies of energy and raw material as well as for crucial support in trade and defense matters. More concretely, how could such asssertiveness be developed at the beginning of the 1980s when the Persian Gulf conflict and a souring of Soviet-American relations demonstrated the full array of West European weaknesses including the obstacles of diversity in the domestic policies of the individual member states and a subsequent lack of international influence? Yet, for some in West Europe, like EC Commissioner Christopher Tugendhat, the Community's problem was not of a structural nature. West Europe's difficulty was clearly not a question of a deficiency of authority and resources, but rather a psychological issue rooted in a lack of self-confidence.[4] In fact, as West Europeans developed new strategies of their own to deal with domestic as well as international questions in the 1980s, they experienced increasing self-confidence. By the end of the decade, West Europeans had come full circle from the days of "Euro-sclerosis" to a period of "Euro-phoria."

How did this impressive change come about? Was it mostly due to West European courage or ingenuity? In what way has the evolving international environment contributed to the success story? Will the newly acquired optimism endure in West Europe? Is it strong enough to meet the tasks of the new decade? In short, is West Europe going to challenge the superpowers at the end of the century by establishing the Community as a leading world power? In the

---

3 For suggestions to restructure transatlantic relations on the background of major changes in the international system see Samuel F. Wells, Jr., A New Transatlantic Bargain, in *The Washington Quarterly*, Vol. 12, No. 4 (Autumn 1989), pp. 53-60.

4 Christopher Tugendhat, Europe's Need for Self-Confidence, in *International Affairs*, Vol. 58, No. 1 (Winter 1981-82), pp. 7-12.

following pages, some tentative answers will be given to these questions which all revolve around West Europe's assertiveness.

THE 1980s: A DECADE OF CHANGE WITHIN AND AROUND WEST EUROPE

Inside the European Pillar

In the first half of the decade, while the superpowers reached a new peak in the arms race and global confrontation, West Europe remained in a relatively gloomy and pessimistic stage, incapable of shaping either its domestic fabric or its political environment. Structural problems seemed to hinder any substantive progress in cooperation and integration among the West European countries. Yet, pooling of resources among the group of West European countries continued to be the only viable avenue to redress the power balance. The European Community's budget remained uncertain for many years. The distortion of the budget due to disproportional expenditures for the Common Agricultural Policy (CAP) continued, leaving badly needed technology programs with only minor funds. Greece's accession as an unusually troublesome member country of the Community complicated the EC and the European Political Cooperation (EPC) bargaining process,[5] while the "British problem" was still occupying the agenda of the Council of Ministers. The West European integration process seemed to have reached its limits.[6] Almost all of the member countries suffered due to economic and social problems which where aggravated by the second energy crisis. This produced an increasing unemployment rate. In comparison to Japan and the United States, West Europe seemed to be constantly losing ground in terms of economic growth rates and technological competitiveness.

---

5 Philippe de Schoutheete, *La coopération politique européenne* (Brussels: Editions Labor 1986), p. 199 f.

6 It had become fashionable among integration practitioners and academic researchers alike to point at the limits of the West European integration process. Ulrich Everling, Possibilities and Limits of European Integration, in *Journal of Common Market Studies*, Vol. 18, No. 3, 1980, pp. 217-228. Paul Taylor, *The limits of European integration* (London: Croom Helm 1983).

In the area of defense and security, West Europe also entered a difficult period of its development. In view of the fact that military affairs were not part of the multilateral integration and cooperation efforts, West European nations were in trouble whenever a common reaction to security related issues was required. The most difficult problem was the stationing of intermediate range nuclear missiles (INF) in five West European countries following a NATO decision of 1979. A large portion of the population in West Europe felt that these weapon systems should not be deployed on the continent. The Reagan administration urged West European governments to demonstrate strength vis-à-vis the Soviets. The INF question drove wedges into the security consensus of many a European nation and put a strain on intra-European as well as transatlantic relations. Washington, using the term "Finlandization," continuously criticized the West Europeans for displaying an acommodating attitude toward the Soviets, and for doing "business as usual" with Moscow during negotiations on the big natural gas/pipeline deal with the Soviet Union. Moreover, in response to crises and terrorist actions originating from some of the Middle Eastern countries, specifically Libya, West European countries did not share the sometimes tough American reactions.

It is true that West European nations had started to consult on economic and political aspects of security. However, plans to go beyond those consultations and to link the EC nations together for the establishment of a common security policy failed. The 1983 Stuttgart Declaration of the Heads of State and Government fell short of this goal mainly due to the reservations expressed by Greece, Ireland, and Denmark. Other more audacious plans for integration, such as the Spinelli Project for a European Union[7] which was launched by the European Parliament, achieved some political momentum in the first half of the 1980s, but encountered stiff opposition from national governments when the question of implementation arose.

Yet, it seemed obvious to the West Europeans that in order to overcome some of the above mentioned problems a renationalization, or a retreat from the clumsy process of European unification, was not a viable alternative. Certainly, some of the problems had to

---

7 Otto Schmuck, "The European Parliament's draft treaty establishing the European Union (1979-1984)," in Roy Pryce (ed.), *The dynamics of the European Union* (London: Croom Helm 1987), pp. 188-216.

be solved within member countries and, ultimately, decisions taken in Brussels had to be implemented in the national framework as well. Yet, the main potential for confidence, growth and power was clearly to be found only by pooling West European resources and by coordinating policy instruments on a European level.

This perspective started to gain momentum toward the mid-1980s when the West European Heads of State and Government, together with the new EC Commission President Jacques Delors, embarked on a new course of political decisions.[8] Among the decisions taken were the conclusion of the negotiations with two new EC member candidates, namely Spain and Portugal, the launching of the 1992 Internal Market project and the adoption of the Single European Act (SEA). Some of these decisions must be recalled in more detail in order to understand this period of change. The historical record shows that progress in European integration was achieved by incremental steps rather than by big leaps.

The fact that the Community, despite its internal problems, remained attractive for newcomers, helped to maintain interest in the development of the European Union. From the time of their accession, in January 1986, Spain and Portugal, unlike Greece when it joined the EC in 1981, displayed a positive and constructive attitude toward EC and EPC policies and decision-making procedures. This eased the internal transformation of the EC, which the southern enlargement of the Community produced, and created additional optimism which was badly needed for the more complex and diversified Europe of the Twelve. Certainly, the prospects of the enlargement had put additional pressure on the older member countries to overcome some of the accumulated problems on the EC agenda and to unbloc the institutional stalemate which the growing habit to avoid majority voting in the Council of Ministers implied.

At the European Council meeting of Fontainebleau in June 1984, special agreements on the main questions pending approval were reached. These agreements paved the way for structural reform two years later. In spite of opposition from certain member states, the European Council, meeting in Milan in June 1986, authorized the Intergovernmental Conference to draft what was later to become the Single European Act. This act, the first constitutional reform of the

8 Jacques Delors, "Europe: Embarking on a new course," in D. Bell and J. Gaffney (eds.), *1992 and After* (Oxford: Pergamon Press 1989), pp. 15-28.

Rome Treaty, ratified by the Parliaments of the member states, came into force on July 1, 1987. Thus, within three years, the twelve West European states managed to overcome their "Euro-pessimism" in order to tackle a series of disruptive issues which seemed to bring the West European integration process to a disasterous deadlock. According to the then Secretary General of the EC Commission, Emile Noël, "a sudden burst of political energy prevented the disaster."[9]

The ratification of the SEA by the national parliaments of the EC member states implied three major institutional breakthroughs. First, for a number of decisions made by the Council of Ministers (the EC institution which represents the interests of the member states) the previous requirement of unanimity in voting procedures has been replaced by that of a qualified majority. This is especially important for directives concerned with the realization of the Internal Market. In practice, this means that the "Special Agreement" of Luxemburg, the so-called Luxemburg Compromise of 1966, which introduced the concept of voting until unanimity was reached, is not being questioned. However, most of its effects are being corrected, such as the slowing down of the Community decision-making. Secondly, the SEA reorganized the distribution of power among the EC institutions. The European Parliament acquired decisive influence in the external relations of the Community and its role in the legislative process, albeit still restricted, is somewhat more concrete. The Community decision-making system shifted toward a triangular pattern - Commission, Council, Parliament. Thirdly, the SEA incorporated those parts of the *acquis communautaire* of the last twenty years which were achieved by intergovernmental cooperation at the fringes of the supra-national Community (such as the European Monetary System), or outside the EC framework (such as the European Political Cooperation). Even though these policy sectors continue to evade the obligations of the Rome Treaties, such as the Court of Justice, they are now an integral part of the SEA. Thus, the SEA constitutes a bridge between the Rome Treaties and any subsequent constitutional modifications which would be a necessary step toward European Union. Except for the areas of security and defense, the Twelve now dispose of a unified common

9 Emile Noël, "The Single European Act: Meaning and Perspectives," in D. Bell and J. Gaffney (eds.), *1992 and After*, op. cit., p. 95.

constitutional framework for all of their government activities. It is up to the political will of the West European political elites to use the legal basis. The legal preconditions for major qualitative developments toward political union in West Europe are better than ever.

A parallel to the institutional breakthrough is the establishment of the 1992 project which provides the Community with a dramatic new frontier. West Europeans, still guided by their national thinking, tend to underestimate the impact of the project on their mind-sets and on their socio-economic environment. Non-Europeans, like the pioneer oriented Americans, are inclined to overestimate the international consequences of the endeavor. The 1992 project amounts to less than the creation of the United States of Europe, but is more than just a wider single market of 320 million consumers. The concept provides for a package of new policies which, taken in its entirety, will create an integrated economic West Europe in the realms of environmental, monetary, social and technological policy as well as in fiscal harmonization.

External Federators

These policies are not simply an answer to domestic problems in West Europe. They are also designed to keep West Europe on a competitive level of economic performance with the United States and Japan. West Europe is taking up the challenge of the two economic and technological superpowers by developing, in spite of obstacles, a huge program of countermeasures making use of its growth potential as a result of further political and economic integration. West Europe is trying to avoid the "costs of non-Europe."[10] In this context, it is of secondary importance to consider the extent to which, or whether in fact, this external challenge was real. The relevant point is that the West Europeans perceived an American and a Japanese threat which they were determined to counter.

---

10 *Completing the Internal Market.* White Paper from the Commission to the European Council, Brussels: COM (85) 310, 14 June 1985. Paolo Cecchini, *The European Challenge 1992* (Adlershot: Wildwood House 1988). *Research on the Costs of Non-Europe. Basic Findings.* 16 Volumes (Luxembourg: Office for Official Publications of the European Communities 1988).

Some of the incentives for the change in direction from a stagnant to a dynamic West Europe in the mid-1980s were a direct response to specific policy initiatives of the Reagan administration. A case in point was the creation of Eureka as an answer to President Reagan's Strategic Defense Initiative (SDI).[11] The way in which SDI was launched, without any prior consultation with the Europeans, and the type of strategic and technological implications it presented were perceived as a provocation which demanded a joint reply by West European nations. This reply came from 23 European nations and the EC. It was a demonstration of the wider West Europe beyond the EC-Twelve. The same holds true for the boost which the programs of the European Space Agency (ESA), which forms part of another powerful West European organization outside the EC establishment, received at mid-decade. In this case, the motivation derived from a series of failures in the US space program that affected all West European nations which previously had relied on American space launching capabilities.

But SDI had also security implications for the Europeans. The program and its philosophy seemed to be directed toward US defense interests alone, it hampered progress in arms reduction talks with the Soviet Union and it seemed to overburden the US budget which was already in critical condititons Among West Europeans, the impression was growing that the US might not have the potential to meet both its traditionally extensive threat perception and its ambitious plans for high-tech solutions to defense problems. Moreover, SDI and the INF treaty seemed to convey the message that Washington was gradually sneaking out of some of its European commitments. Western Europe had to prepare for the day of more substantial withdrawal than just a few soldiers as repeatedly proposed in the US Congress. The United States seemed to be incapable and unwilling to carry on the same level of protection for all its allies. The academic debate of the delinists, such as Paul Kennedy, and the devolutionists, such as David Calleo, delivered the conceptual background for possible major changes in US foreign and security policy.

Not surprisingly, a new attitude on the part of West European nations toward security and defense cooperation started to grow

---

11 For the record of Eureka see Knut Reintz, Eureka - 3 years already! Results so far and future outlook, in *European Affairs*, Vol. 3, No. 1 (Spring 1989), pp. 112-114.

since the mid-1980s. This started with the revitalization of the West European Union (WEU) in October 1984 and the transformation of this organization into a framework for consensus building on security related issues. The institution was reorganized as a consultative body, and its procedures were modeled after the EPC infrastructure. While decisions on INF had been taken in the national and in the NATO context, part of the opinion forming on new issues like SDI, the Reykjavik summit, the Gulf crisis, or the negotiations on the Conventional Forces in Europe (CFE) were the result of discussions within the circle of the WEU member states. WEU also elaborated a platform of common security interests[12] identified by the core West European countries, which is something that the EPC has been unable to accomplish. Certainly, the reform of WEU was facilitated by a new higher level of Franco-German defense cooperation which began gradually at the end of 1983 and reached maturity with the establishment of the joint Defense Council in 1988.[13]

Some of the motivation for intensified West European security cooperation originated in drastic changes within both the United States and the Soviet Union as well as in a subsequent change in East-West relations. These changes affected the European NATO members (including France). To some extent, they also had consequences for the European neutrals and non-aligned countries and for the member states of the Warsaw Pact. In fact, all of Europe, East and West, as it was structured in the last forty years is about to change. At the beginning of the 1980s, the Soviet military invasion of Afghanistan, and the American reaction to it, reinforced the classical mold of superpower antagonism and confrontation. The picture at the end of the decade has been redrawn to delineate the new expression of détente and East-West cooperation on the continent. But this is not an era to sit back and relax, instead, the West Europeans are faced with an unprecedented panoply of challenges which gradually emerged from Gorbachev's revolution.

West Europe which charted a steady course during stormy years has achieved a profile of opposing the East-West confrontation at its

---

12 See the text of the WEU Platform in the Annex (Documents).

13 For an assessment of the most recent development in Franco-German defense cooperation see Peter Schmidt, The Franco-German Council for Defense and Security, in *Außenpolitik (English Edition)*, Vol. 40, No.4 (Summer 1989), pp. 370-381.

height and lending support to the first initiatives of politico-military détente. Yet, West Europe has not been instrumental to any of these changes. It can claim some moral advantage, however, thanks to the fact that East-West relations have finally developed in a direction the West Europeans originally favored. And it can claim the Community's attractiveness in terms of a model for a political system: a civilian power image, a socially based market economy, a solidarity-oriented cooperation among states. Most of the additional prestige which West Europe has gained during the 1980s is relative to the loss of influence of both Moscow and Washington. In an overall atmosphere of détente, and declining Soviet and American empires, West Europe can bring its assets to bear and strengthen its assertiveness.

To continue along the line of argumentation, it seems obvious that a substantial part of the success story of West European assertiveness in the 1980s must be attributed to the change in the international environment. The new West European take off, the *relance européenne*, would not have been possible, and would appear to be less extensive, without such favorable changes.

WEST EUROPEAN ASSERTIVENESS: FACT OR FICTION?

West Europe has yet to consolidate the obvious strength which it has recently aquired. What will happen if East-West relations sour again, if Moscow, like China in June 1989, decides that it cannot cope with international interdependence, or if Washington suddenly feels that it must renew its dominant world position? How stable is the newly acquired West European self-confidence in the face of major problems in the integration process such as: an economic recession similar to the one in the 1970s; a re-emergence of the financial difficulties of the early 1980s; an unaccomplished 1992 project? What are the positive changes in West Europe's stature which are of a durable, structural nature? Where are the areas of stabilization and further growth in West European assertiveness?

Some indication of the durability of West Europe's assertiveness can be drawn from the state of maturity of the "Political System West Europe" as well as from an analysis of some of the key events of the decade in which the West Europeans displayed such assertiveness.

Political System: West Europe

For the state of the art in West European integration, it is highly indicative that the political and administrative experts inside as well as outside West Europe dispose of no commonly agreed notion to describe the Political System West Europe, just as social scientists have no commonly accepted analytical tool to analyse and evaluate the political entity West Europe as a regional and international actor.[14] This entity was easily definable twenty years ago, when the West European integration consisted of the six founding countries of the European Economic Community. Meanwhile, the Community has grown into the "EC/Twelve," dominating but not monopolizing the integration process in West Europe. Other specialized multilateral organizations inside or outside the Community contribute to a large network of mutually overlapping institutions. Transnational, non-governmental processes, such as interparty relations and multinational companies, add to the picture.

Not all of the Twelve participate in monetary cooperation, Great Britain forming the significant exception. Only five EC member states signed the Schengen Agreement of 1985 to remove state borders among them.[15] Franco-German cooperation, including the creation of a joint Defense and Security Council and a Council for Economics and Finance, is regarded as the most effective engine of West Europe's integration. The nine member states of the WEU are trying to shape a West European viewpoint in security matters.[16] The Independent European Program Group (IEPG) includes all those countries which are working to rationalize military procurement, while Eurogroup consists of the European NATO

---

14 The difficult task of describing and evaluating the present state of the West European integration process is the focus of a research project conducted during 1988/1989 by William Wallace (Chatham House, London) under the title of "The Dynamics of West European Integration." The results of this research enterprise will be published in early 1990.

15 In 1987, Italy considered joining the Schengen group (consisting of Belgium, France, Germany, Luxembourg and The Netherlands).

16 For a short, informative survey on the main West European organizations which deal with security matters see the Annex (Institutions).

member countries and tries to promote a European stand in transatlantic defense. In the sector of technology, organizations such as ESA and Eureka are attempting to coordinate and integrate national efforts in highly specialized and extremely costly research projects. The Council of Europe with its 24 member countries working together in political, social and human rights questions is stressing yet another realm of European understanding and harmonization. Some of these organizations are open to further European membership and offer observation status for neutral, nonaligned, and East European countries.

This list of West European collaboration agencies inside, at the fringes, and outside the Community could be easily extended. But the above enumeration already hints at the complexity of today's European integration system. The fabric of this system is further shaped by the varying levels of cooperation among these organizations, some of them based on international treaties, some on intergovernmental agreements, some on business contracts. Only the EC has supranational elements which allow for a genuine standpoint of its own on a European level. In some fields (Common Market, Common Agricultural Policy, Commercial Policy) EC law takes precedence over national law. The Court of Justice creates and enforces European law via interpretation of the Treaties and their amendments, such as the SEA. However, most of the West European joint policies and organizations are not supra-national, but intergovernmental, such as the European Monetary System, the coordination of national economic policies, and the European Political Cooperation.

This mixture of federal and confederal components in West Europe enriched by a vast transnational texture was not developed by a grand design. It rather represents the current appearance of a multitude of integration processes each of which started at a different time, follows different purposes, and applies different strategies. This amorphous entity West Europe continues to be in flux. Its final development stage may be called the European Union or the United States of Europe, but the particular quality of statehood of this entity is still undetermined. The wording of the treaties and the agreements among West European countries are surprisingly vague in this regard. For the time being the entity is characterized by the coexistence and interaction of the nation states of West Europe and of a multitude of European frameworks. This system of overlapping networks of organizations seems to be Community-centered but powers are separated between various levels and locations of decision-making. No central authority is established and almost none of the traditional legitimation mechanisms known from nation states are at work, not even for the EC which has a directly elected Parliament.[17] While it is a fact that the Community disposes of many components of a state, it is a fiction to believe that these elements form a state-like, democratic composition.

The weakness of the Political System West Europe, therefore, might not be its institutional heterogeneity and its unorganized authority, but its lack of democracy in terms of representation of interests and pluralistic control of political power. Whether this type of democratic underdevelopment will turn out as a decisive deficiency of the system as a whole must remain an open question until more is known about the ingredients and the functioning of this entity, especially when unprecedented challenges are testing the system. Recent trends in the Community, especially the SEA, have attributed more influence to the European Parliament, in relation to the Council and the Commission.[18] On the other hand, Council and Presidency have developed toward a collective authority, at least inside the Community.[19] Yet, these are changes at the margin of the Political System West Europe, which do not correct its unbalanced structure, governed by a technocratic management rather than by political, Europe-wide responsibility.

The election of a European President, as suggested by former French President Giscard d'Estaing, is politically not in reach. The European Council will probably continue to take on some of the

---

17 The European Parliament elections do not affect the "executive branch" of the EC. See Vernon Bogdanor, The June 1989 European elections and the institutions of the Community, in *Government and Opposition*, Vol. 24, No. 2 (Spring 1989), pp. 199-214. Lord Plumb, Building a democratic Community: the role of the European Parliament, in *The World Today*, Vol. 45, No. 7 (July 1989), pp. 112-117.

18 Emile Noël, *Working Together. The institutions of the European Community* (Luxemburg: Office for Official Publications of the European Communities 1988).

19 Guy de Bassompierre, *Changing the guard in Brussels. An insider's view of the EC presidency* (New York: Praeger 1988).

"presidential functions."[20] Yet, too many organizations and cooperative groupings in West Europe remain outside the coordination and guidance of the twelve Heads of State and Government. West Europe will continue to look like a whirlpool of actors which is as confusing for the citizens within West Europe as it is for those who want to deal with it from the outside.

The European Parliament will most likely increase its influence along with the 1992 process and during the upcoming decisions on a further enlargement of the EC. The applications for membership of Turkey (1987) and Austria (1989) are on the table of the EC institutions in Brussels. However, a decision will not be taken before December 1992; even negotiations in this regard are excluded. And after this magic date, the need for a further period of consolidation of the Community is more likely than the desire for its enlargement, especially if the reform and stabilization of the German Democratic Republic becomes a responsibility of the Community as the the Strasbourg European Council in December of 1989 has implied. The political and economic digestion of two quasi-confederated German states, the completion of the Internal Market, and the more far-reaching program of an Economic and Monetary Union will require a further improvement of the decision-making procedures and the external powers of the Community as well as new institutions and more democratic control. If this new stage of integration is not prepared in time, the asymmetries and inconsistencies of the Political System West Europe could increase dramatically. Part of West Europe's assertiveness gained at the end of the 1980s might thus be lost in the first half of the 1990s.

Experience with West European Assertiveness in the 1980s

The 1980s have seen a large number of show cases for either West European assertive behavior or the lack thereof. The following chapters in this volume analyze some of these cases. Assertiveness, in all of these examples, has its particular features, depending on the issues and sectors in which it occurs, depending on the counterpart

---

20 Simon Bulmer and Wolfgang Wessels, *The European Council - Decision-making in European politics* (London: Macmillan Press 1987).

to whom assertiveness is demonstrated, and depending on the question by whom of the many West European actors it is developed. In each of these cases, however, assertiveness means one or several of the following ways of behavior:

- to develop more of a common West European viewpoint and position,
- to adapt effectively to new internal or external challenges,
- to take care of West Europe's problems without relying on the help of others,
- to resist domination by others, especially the superpowers, and to oppose other international actors' views, if necessary,
- to take on new responsibilities beyond West Europe,
- to increase West Europe's influence on international events.

Many analysts of West Europe's international behavior in the last decade have claimed that West Europe was more effective in conducting collective foreign policy toward the Third World than in engendering much of a common position in the relations with the two world powers. In the 1980s, in fact, West Europe as a civilian power with economic, conciliatory and moral strength seemed to be more attractive to Third World nations than the interventionist and politically polarizing superpowers. But despite its external attractiveness and its relative high degree of common ground in the relations with Third World nations, West Europeans did not have much influence in most of the many regional instabilities and crises: Afghanistan, the Persian Gulf, Lebanon, Namibia, Central America. The soft approach to countries which support terrorism was not effective. Gadhdhafi was tamed only after Washington's raid on Libya. Argentina retreated from the seizure of the Falklands only after the massive British counterattack was supported by the United States.

West European nations have deplored the spillover of the Soviet-American rivalry into all corners of the world, which reduces their chances for a non-confrontational and non-military approach. On the other hand, the superpowers, too, had only very limited influence on some of the regional events as demonstrated during the Iran-Iraq war. Yet, the very fact of their increasingly military rivalry caused a deterioration of East-West relations in the first half of the 1980s which would not allow to bring West European assets of an economic-political dialogue to bear. Likewise, when détente between Reagan and Gorbachev broke out in the mid-1980s, the West Europeans were largely isolated from major steps of disarmament and East-West security talks. Only toward the end of the decade when negotiations on conventional forces made a participation of the allies indispensable, were the West Europeans able to set a foot in the East-West negotiation door. Their influence is likely to grow with the decline of the super-empires, the increase of cooperative elements in bloc to bloc diplomacy and the expansion of economic and political reform in Eastern Europe and the Soviet Union. West Europe can now bring its comparative advantages into play.

In the 1980s it was neither the East-West nor the North-South relations, but primarily the West-West relations which formed the playground for West European assertiveness. On the one hand the West Europeans were provoked by the American and Japanese technological challenge to increase their international competitiveness - a provocation which they tried to meet by launching their 1992 project. On the other hand the West Europeans' assertiveness grew when they learned to cope with the challenges of Reaganism. The fluctuation between staunch confrontation in East-West relations during President Reagan's first term and the erratic turn to détente in his second term made him a serious puzzle for the West Europeans.

During the decade of the 1980s, US administrations have come full circle from an assertive hegemonic power of the Western alliance to a partner in leadership, which even submits to the lead of West Europe in specific tasks of the West's relations with the East. In the early 1980s West Europe was confronted with economic sanctions by an American president who tried to deny the Yamal pipeline deal and to impose his view of the Soviet Union on his reluctant allies. The INF deployment was pushed in a way that it became co-responsible for the toppling of the Schmidt government in the FRG. In Reykjavik, the American president, in one stroke, questioned all the major defense elements of West Europe. The West Europeans hastily tried to develop defense cooperation among themselves in order to take a larger part of their destiny into their own hands. Only by the end of the decade had the American administration achieved a level of understanding where President Bush gave credit to his European allies and - accepting most of their interpretation of the "Gorbachev challenge"[21] - entrusted them with the coordination of Western aid programs for Poland and Hungary.

This most recent American turn is more than a change of diplomatic style from Reagan to Bush. It illustrates the relative decline of the US as a global power and the beginning of its gradual retreat from an overcommitment in the world, including Europe. It also represents the view that West Europe is about to grow up and to develop beyond the position of a junior partner. The fact that the West European integration process has accelerated contributes to this assumption. The concessions which the EC has made in GATT are not as important as the 1992 project, or the plans for an economic, monetary and social union. But for the first time since its inception, the CAP may become subject to reform discussion within a multilateral trade forum. While the "corn war" in the mid-1980s showed technical as well as political limits of West European assertiveness in transatlantic trade, the EC now seems prepared to drop a taboo. It should be recalled that the CAP represented the centerpiece of the EC for the majority of European integrationists.

Yet, the major sector of West European struggle for assertiveness was neither economic nor foreign relations but defense and security policy. In each decade after World War II, the West Europeans have tried to develop a more advanced security identity of their own. Most of these attempts ended in failure and frustration. The 1980s are no exception to this rule. West European security cooperation was not a total flop, but it did not progress much either. Certainly, a number of selective facts, institutional changes (restructuring of WEU, Franco-German Defense Council) as well as policy actions (Gulf mine sweeping, WEU platform) may be mentioned which have broadened the basis for a future development toward a European pillar in NATO. But, as the British commentators would say, this did not add one soldier to the West defense forces. Moreover, contrary to the economic and foreign policy sector, the defense sector has not been made a systematic area of integration in West Europe. No integration strategy has been worked out, no attempts were made to develop a genuine West European threat assessment, no 1992 project for a defense union was launched. Instead, the Genscher/Colombo initiative of 1981 to

---

21 European Strategy Group, *The Gorbachev Challenge and European Security* (Baden-Baden: Nomos Verlagsgesellschaft 1988).

include security in the policy-making process of EC and EPC was rejected by some of the member countries and, by the end of the decade, Genscher himself rejected his own proposal. Under the impression of the reformative changes in Eastern Europe and the Soviet Union the German Foreign Minister now favors a civilian EC/EPC in order to remain attractive and accessible for eastern countries.

While the European pillar did not materialize, it became obvious that the Franco-German defense cooperation - admittedly the only genuine nucleus for a West European security union - was only a long-term option. Kohl and Mitterrand tested it. Between 1985 and 1988, the Kohl government asked for more explanation of France's nuclear strategy and its intention to include German interests. This followed a growing German uncertainty concerning US nuclear guarantees and a shift in French strategy. In those years, Paris and Bonn reached the optimum of rapprochement. It shows the present structural limits (consultation, but no guarantees) as well as the potential in case of a further American decoupling from West Europe's strategic defense (a French nuclear umbrella for the Federal Republic). Yet, Ullman's recent study[22] on the American dependence of French nuclear weapons technology made it crystal clear: there is no genuine military alternative for the West Europeans to US strategic defense. Nuclear deterrence is not an area of West Europe's assertiveness.

On some occasions, individual statesmen acted assertively on behalf of West Europe. Margaret Thatcher had some influence on the American arms control position in November 1986, immediately after the Reykjavik summit. She was respected, almost adored, by President Reagan. All WEU member states had supported her mission to Washington. In another case, President Bush yielded to the German position on short range nuclear forces in late spring of 1989. This was not a concession of friendship, nor was Chancellor Kohl supported by all the WEU members, but Bonn had decided to adopt a new assertive role. It had become a key player in both West European integration dynamics and the all-European cooperation boom. Washington could not afford to offend Bonn. This is not to say that the Federal Republic will stay in the offensive, rather the

22 Richard H. Ullman, Ending the Cold War, in *Foreign Policy*, No.72 (Fall 1988), pp. 130-151.

West Germans continue to be puzzled by new American initiatives, as was the case with SDI. They are not yet in a position, where they would meet such American initiatives with benign neglect and trust in the self-destructive mechanisms of the US policy machine which eventually will reduce its own initiatives to a moderate size.

Although part of West Europe's assertiveness was gained by strong policies of individual governments, most of it stemmed from collective action of the West Europeans. Certainly, West Europe continued to be stronger in designing theoretical solutions of problems than in providing the substance for policy implementation. To the extent, however, that European problems (such as technological competitiveness, environment standards, anti-terrorist policies, economic relations with East European countries) are identified and tackled, West Europe has gone beyond promise and has delivered. In these instances, the West European actor has moved from a diplomatic *quantité négligeable* to an *interlocuteur valable*. The last proof for this qualitative shift was provided at the very end of the decade, when François Mitterrand as the European Council President invited the Heads of Government of the member countries to a summit meeting in Paris in late November 1989 devoted exclusively to the dramatic changes in East Europe.This gethering was scheduled to take place before the non-summit summit of Bush and Gorbachev at Malta in early December of 1989.

CHALLENGES OF THE NEXT DECADE

While the 1980s were characterized by the struggle for West Europe's assertiveness, the 1990s are likely to become a decade of overcommitment for West Europe. At a time, when the newly acquired level of assertiveness is not yet consolidated, West Europe has to cope with several issues of a truly tall order: the consolidation of the European Union, the ending of the division of Europe and the modernization of European-American relations.

Consolidating the European Union

In the 1990s, the West Europeans will have to deal with a new round of intensification and enlargement of the Community, while considering the political landslide of changes in Eastern Europe and in East-West relations. A number of integration projects have been launched towards the end of the 1980s and have to be concluded early in the 1990s, such as the Internal Market program, or are up for revision, such as the provisions for EPC in Title III of the SEA. The SEA and the subsequent decisions of the European Council, especially in Hannover (June 1988), in Madrid (June 1989) and in Strasbourg (December 1989) have set the stage for the development of the Economic and Monetary Union (EMU) in the last decade of this century. Compared to the attempts of the early 1970s it seems that, this time, the EMU plans are projected in a more favorable economic and political environment. This does not mean it will be easy to implement the three stages layed out in the Delors Report.[23] The task reaches way beyond the diffusion of Margaret Thatcher's objection to a monetary union and also beyond meeting the 1992 deadline for the Internal Market. Rather, the challenge will derive from the vast practical adaptation process of the twelve economies to the EMU, from the creation of new EC policies (monetary, technology, environment), and from the indispensable institutional innovations, such as a European Central Bank and other bodies of policy-making.[24]

As in the 1970s (northern enlargement) and the 1980s (southern enlargement), the European Community will have to enter a new enlargement or association round in the next decade. After accommodating first British, then French and Italian demands, it is now West Germany asking for priority of "its" geopolitical region of interest within the West European integration activity. In principle, London, Paris and Rome should be keen in following the West German lead toward the East, while simultaneously tying down West Germany to the multilateral process of decision-making in West European fora. The motivation for the UK, France and Italy is certainly enhanced by the increasingly realistic perspective of a stronger Germany, West and East. With NATO's relative declining importance in a détente oriented world, West European organizations will have to take over part of its functions to balance the size

---

23 Committee for the Study of Economic and Monetary Union, *Report on Economic and Monetary Union in the European Community*, Brussels 1989 (Delors Report).

24 See the speech of Jacques Delors at the College of Europe in Bruges, 17 October 1989. (*Europe*, Documents, No. 1576, 21 October 1989).

and the energies of the German nation in Europe. The Strasbourg European Council in December 1989 has made a first step in this direction by committing the Twelve to both the establishment of the EMU and the support of German unification.[25]

The perspective of an eastern enlargement of the Community (GDR as member, other countries associated) rivals not only with the still undigested Mediterranean expansion, but clashes with the regional and social consolidation of post-1992 West Europe. Investment in West Europe's economic efficiency is indispensable in order to keep up with American and Pacific economic innovation and productivity.When, in the mid-1980s, the rerouting of the West European integration engine to the economic track occurred, the dynamics of the East European reforms had not yet unfolded its full bloom. In the 1990s, the originally Western oriented dynamics of union-building have to take on an eastern perspective, too. West Europe will have to meet the needs of the transition from the postwar order in Europe to a new structure of East-West interaction (European House, European Peace Order).

It seems that West Europe has no choice. There is demand to shoulder all of these responibilities: towards the West for economic-technological reasons; towards the East for political-security reasons; towards the South for reasons of internal cohesiveness and social stability. This may be a too heavy burden for West Europeans to bear.

Ending the Division of Europe

During the 1980s, West Europe has gradually shifted from an object of superpower rivalry to an active force of stability and change in Europe, recognized as such by both Moscow and Washington. Except for the suspicion of a renewal of some sort of condominium ("from Yalta to Malta"), West Europe's task is eased by a genuine Soviet attempt to reduce East-West antagonism and to overcome the division of Europe. Ending the division of Europe is

25 The Heads of State and Government attached two strings to their support for a possible German unification: it has to be inserted in the perspective of further West European integration toward the European Union and must be based on the principles of the Helsinki Final Act which allows the change of frontiers by peaceful means.

the goal of a lengthy process which began with the rise of Gorbachev in the Soviet Union in the mid-1980s and continued with the fall of Honecker in East Germany at the end of the 1980s. West Europe has long been asking for this change. Now the situation has arrived, now West Europe must act.

With some of the East European countries turning toward pluralistic democracies and market economies the systemic divide of Europe is increasingly blurred. The military blocs, while under major review, are still in existence, but have lost much of their thrust. How to manage the upcoming transitional period, the ending of the division of Europe, the switch from an ideologically and militarily antagonistic Europe to a Europe of economic regions, ethnic groupings, cultural spaces and political spheres of influence all of which competing with eachother?

The transition process consists of military and nonmilitary components. Despite the relatively high speed of negotiations on nuclear, chemical and conventional disarmament, the matter is loaded enough to preoccupy East and West for many years. Moscow needs at least the whole decade of the 1990s to push its economic and political reform to a point of no return. To succeed, it needs both the help of the western world and an environment of change in Eastern Europe. Gorbachev is as much forced to accept change in Eastern Europe as he himself is the propelling force for such a change. Yet, there are strategic, economic and political boundaries for the westward orientation of this change that West Europe will have to observe.

The complicated task for the West will be to keep up the stabilizing balance of strategic deterrence, albeit on a lower level, while opening up new avenues for East-West cooperation. To keep deterrence intact and to manage disarmament requires, after all, the proper functioning of the two military blocs. They will certainly change their character (and the Warsaw Pact is not the same after Gorbachev dropped the Breshnev doctrine, and Krenz dismantled most of the Berlin Wall), but will remain an important element during the transitional phase. If the system of alliances is rapidly becoming obsolescent, preparations must be made for an alternative framework of security for the entire continent. Even East European countries, despite their neutralist drive, will understand that they need a framework in which to articulate their security interests and with which to manage the military downgrading.

For West Europe, the questions to solve will relate to new forms of burden sharing as well as burden shedding with regard to reducing and modernizing forces. What should the post-CFE structure of West Europe's defense look like? It will certainly comprise more features of a regional identity, but it will have to supplement Washington's deterrence role. How should the post-CFE defense posture of the West look like? Major elements of the Western defense strategy appear as anachronistic (such as forward defense, follow-on forces attack, short range nuclear forces) on the conceivable background of a confederated Germany and EC associated Poland, Hungary and CSSR. How should the post-CFE solidarity among West European nations look like? In a Single Market West Europe, it may no longer be feasible to distinguish economic gains, political risks and military challenges by means of nationalistic calculations.

In the 1980s, West European security cooperation helped to articulate European views in the Atlantic Alliance. In the 1990s, a "pillar" will be needed for the European House in order to organize a West European *Ostpolitik*, to carry the hopes of the reform process in the East, and to take over major responsibilities in the new all-European peace order. The constellation to prepare for is combining a continued, but reduced, military threat with new instabilities of a socio-political as well as politico-ethnic nature. As the stabilization function of the alliances is decreasing, it has to be supplemented by East-West interaction. This will have to support socio-economic progress and political reform in Eastern Europe and should create a wider network of East-West interdependence. The texture of this network will have to set the guidelines for the solution of the German question. In other words, "Europe is the issue, not German union."[26] Any German confederal or federal structure will have to be inserted in the new all-European architecture in addition to its insertion in the European Union.

The task for West Europe is predominantly non-military, but of a strategic dimension. It will be more difficult than West Europe's assistance for political change of the rightest dictatorships in Southern Europe during the 1970s. It will imply much more than the mere unleashing of the gravitational forces of the European

---

26 George F. Kennan, Europe is the issue, not German union, in *International Herald Tribune*, 15 November 1989, p. 4.

Community. The attractiveness of the West European integration process is both a guiding factor for the market and technology related reform process in Eastern European countries and a misleading temptation for the economies of these countries which continue to be structurally linked with the Soviet Union. Therefore, part of the West European *Ostpolitik* should be designed to create incentives for regional cooperation among the Council of Mutual Economic Assistance (CMEA) countries, also because this organization has become an empty shell.

It is likely that the economic-political reform processes in the East will end in failure. But there seems to be no alternative to reform. Therefore, the relations between the EC/Twelve, the EFTA countries and the European CMEA member states need to be organized for a longer term. Stimulated by the 1992 project the West Europeans have started to think of a market area including both EC and EFTA. Both organizations will have to extend offers for cooperation to all countries of the East, including the Soviet Union and extending beyond the economic sphere. To separate Moscow from Europe would mean to impede the Europeanization of a Soviet Union which is about to reorganize its relations with the Western neighbors and to find a new confederal structure for the Soviet Union itself. To concentrate only on economic interaction would underestimate the interdependence of the security, political and economic elements of East-West relations. West Europe has to make sure that the embryonic framework of the CSCE is pushed upward to a new quality of cooperation and institutionalization constituting as well an *Ersatz* peace treaty for Germany as a new European system of security.[27] This imperative might well be asking too much of West Europe, but the ending of the division of Europe will not be granted cheaply.

Adapting Transatlantic Relations

If the West European integration process leaps on to the substantive level of a real European Union, and if the structure of East-West relations is undergoing a fundamental transition, what

---

27 Elements of such a system could be developed during the CSCE summit meeting later in 1990 as suggested by Gorbachev during his state visit to Italy early in December 1989.

about the Atlantic alliance? The answer is, of course, that NATO and European-American relations have to be adapted to the new environment. The political constellation is new to both the United States and West Europe. In the last 40 years, Washington has hardly been in a position where it had to react to constructive dynamics in Europe. Certainly, West Europe has become the world's largest trading bloc, but this occurred over a long time. The challenges now are of a different nature. The United States, while being confronted with revolutionary changes in Europe, East and West simultaneously and abruptly, is not the master of these changes. It is in many respects a bystander. This is an unusual role for Washington to play. Conversely, West Europe has been moved to an unusual position of taking initiative and responsibility. The 1990s will demand considerable energies from both sides of the Atlantic to excercise these new roles in a constructive manner.

The preponderance of the US in the transatlantic defense setup will continue, but has to be balanced with a new assertive West Europe and its security cooperation. To the extent that such cooperation develops and is backed up by the wider context of the West European integration process, it should be represented in NATO and in other security related transatlantic fora. Given the changes in progress in West and in East Europe, NATO must tackle the subject of its own structural change. While the West Europeans have used the 1980s to prepare for this task under the heading of a "European pillar," Washington has hardly begun to shift roles. The US must admit that the business of running NATO is becoming more complicated. Washington has less leverage to discipline the allies and cannot deal any longer with the "simple" alliance of 16 nations, it must deal with the policies of a grouping of West European institutions working on aspects of defense and security.

The redressing of the power balance in NATO and in transatlantic relations at large will have to take into account that the common military threat from the East is deemphacized and that West Europe after 1992 might become economically stronger, while the United States will either continue its relative decline or will move on to a period of renewal.[28] The pressures for devolution have constantly increased in the 1980s, but it remains rather unclear how

---

28 Youri Devuyst, The United States and Europe 1992, in *World Competition*, Vol. 13, No. 1 (September 1989), pp. 29-42.

far future American administrations will go beyond the claim of burden-sharing in order to accept a power-sharing as well. President Bush has made a start,[29] Congress has been more reluctant in this regard. The West Europeans will have to lobby hard in order to convince the political elites in the US that security cooperation in West Europe and West European *Ostpolitik* are important elements of their assertiveness *and* of the transatlantic burden-sharing balance.[30]

Under the conditions of a both less militarily based East-West relations and the rise of new challenges from change in the East, the West's military establishment has voiced the goal to shift NATO to a more politically oriented alliance.[31] In fact, to support political change in the East, the Western alliance must initiate and coordinate a broader range of non-military East-West relations, ranging from managerial help for economic reform to non-governmental political relations. If NATO can be instrumental for this type of a western *Ostpolitik*, the group of West European states should be a part of it. If NATO is deemed not to be well suited to take on the missions of economic and political interaction with the East, then it has to be complemented with a specific transatlantic dialogue on East-West relations, with EC/EPC as the counterpart to Washington. In both cases, West Europe will need a much higher level of self-confidence than in the 1980s. It will have to take and carry on the initiative for the modernization of transatlantic relations.[32]

Modernizing European-American relations and ending the division of Europe can only be achieved on the bases of a

---

29 See President Bush's foreign policy speeches in the first few months of his term: 17 April 1989 at Hamtramck City Hall in Hamtramck, Michigan; 12 May 1989 at Texas A&M University in College Station, Texas; 21 May 1989 at Boston University in Boston, Massachusetts; 24 May 1989 at Coast Guard Academy in New London, Connecticut; 29 May 1989 at NATO Headquarters in Brussels, Belgium; 31 May 1989 at Rheingoldhalle in Mainz, West Germany; 17 July 1989 at the Pieterskerk in Leiden..

30 Kenneth Moss, The next step in US - European relations, in *The Washington Quarterly*, Vol. 11, No. 2 (Spring 1988), pp. 103-107.

31 Stanley R. Sloan (ed.), *NATO in the 1990s* (Washington, D.C.: Pergamon-Brassey's 1989).

32 Reinhardt Rummel, Modernizing transatlantic relations: West European security cooperation and the reaction in the United States, in *The Washington Quarterly*, Vol. 12, No. 4 (Autumn 1989), pp. 83-92.

consolidated European Union. If West Europe successfully copes with all three issue areas, then it has definitely overcome its long postwar agony and struggle for emancipation among the leading powers in the world. Thanks to an innovative method of policy-making which combines the Community with national interests, West Europe will then have proved the high degree of flexibility and, indeed, efficiency of a new type of political system. But many impediments are in the cards and it may well be that Samuel Huntington is totally wrong in predicting that West Europe could be the leading power at the beginning of the next millenium.[33]

---

33 Samuel Huntington, The US - Decline or Renewal? in *Foreign Affairs*, Vol. 67, No. 2 (Winter 1988/89), pp. 76-96.

PART I: West Europe between National Interests and Global Needs

Part I highlights the creative tension which exists between the pursuit of individual interests by nation-states, and the fulfillment of the needs of the international system by the European Community (EC), a regional actor with a global conscience. Three chapters explore the extent to which, given the internal constraints of the integration process and the external constraints of the existing international situation, the EC can establish a separate identity vis-à-vis the superpowers. In the spheres of European foreign, trade and security policy, the difficulties inherent in the harmonization of divergent national interests provide a striking contrast to the needs and responsibilities of the Community which compel it to "speak with one voice."

As *Christopher Hill* concludes in his chapter, the Community has the unique opportunity to demonstrate that civil relations can extend into the realm of relations marked by suspicion, as in the case of Franco-German reconciliation. *Roy Ginsberg's* analysis of European trade policy illustrates the tension which exists between the triumph of state interests in the form of non-tariff barriers and the Common Agricultural Policy (CAP), and evidence of a global conscience in trade through the nonreciprocal tariff cuts which are provided to LDC beneficiaries of the Lomé Convention and the Mediterranean Policy. *Reinhardt Rummel's* chapter explains the desire of West Europeans to explore ways to reconcile national interests with regional cooperation while responding to global security needs. The economic and political stabilization of the Mediterranean, as Greece, Spain and Portugal acceded to the EC, is a positive step in this direction.

The EC's influence in world affairs is unprecedented and, thus, it cannot be evaluated solely by the criteria which realists use to assess the power capabilities of nation-states. In the decades ahead, as the Community achieves economic, and perhaps monetary, unification, it will respond further to the internal dynamics of the integration process and to global pressures and expectations.

2

European Foreign Policy: Power Bloc, Civilian Model - or Flop?

Christopher Hill

INTRODUCTION

Insofar as states have a long historical consciousness of a global role, the states of West Europe may claim it. Spanish and Portuguese navigators blazed the trail to the New World in the 15th and 16th centuries, as the Vikings had done 6OO years before. English and Dutch sailors were not far behind them, and by 17OO the Americas and Indies were opened up, with knowledge even of Japan and China vastly increased. Australia and Africa were to hold out a little longer, but inevitably succumbed given the unfavorable circumstances for the peoples of those continents to reverse the flow of influence.

The twentieth century, however, has seen one of the most speedy and remarkable dissolutions of an empire in history, as the world role of the West European states has been dismantled. Yet the legacy of the Europeans is profound: they have brought a global awareness, and globalized international system (for good or ill) to the successor states of imperialism, and they have retained in themselves a deep concern for the world outside the circuit of Rome, Brussels, Paris, London, and the rest. At the heart of this concern, however, is a natural ambivalence. Europeans know that they are wholly imbedded in the world system, but they are unsure how far they wish to take on responsibility for its arrangement - particularly at the political level. Decolonisation was a trauma, leaving a vein of sensitivity over the inappropriateness of intervening in the affairs of peoples still rejoicing in their freedom from European rule. Compounding this reticence is the knowledge of the large gap that has opened up on the indicator of military strength between the superpowers and the individual states of Europe, and, of course, the still bright scar of war. It would, indeed, now be surprising if there were widespread enthusiasm in Europe for a forceful global role.

Yet Euro-isolationism is equally unavailable as an option in the late twentieth century. The development of an integrated (if patchy) world economy means that the rich, trade-intensive states of the European region have a serious involvement in global patterns of production, exchange, debt, and migration. Telecommunications, and their comparative advantage in the information and education industry make sure that European voices are heard on almost all the major issues of inter-state relations, even in areas where the physical presence of diplomats, soldiers, or investors might be thin on the ground.

Thus China has turned increasingly toward the universities of West Europe (as of the United States) in the pursuit of expertise which will help her shorten the long development process. One hundred and ten years ago the Chinese official Liu Hsi-Hung informed the English Ambassador, who was pressing the case of modernization upon him: "We Chinese base our culture on the pursuit of righteousness rather than the pursuit of profit, preferring to suit the taste of the people rather than disturb them."[1] Now British power over China is non-existent, as the 1984 negotiations on Hong Kong demonstrated, but its intellectual influence, its ability to "disturb" the people of China (jointly with other Western states), is probably rather greater than in the days of the unequal treaties.

Thus, in the 1980s, the Europeans are still important actors at the global level. Whether they thereby fulfill *global needs*, or just pursue, more or less effectively, *state interests* is the question that this chapter must address, with particular reference to foreign policy. Perhaps the dichotomy is a false one, with interests being pursued which are not wholly at odds with the needs of the wider system, insofar as anyone is capable of confidently judging what

---

1 Journal of Liu Hsi-Hung, "On a Voyage to England," in J. D. Frodsham, ed., *The First Chinese Embassy to the West: the Journals of Kuo Sung-Tao, Liu Hsi-Hung and Chang Te-Yi* (Oxford: Clarendon 1974), p. 11O.

they are. This point will be returned to. But one distinction which does need maintaining is that between two kinds of "state interests." On the one hand, there is the familiar set of national interests contained within the activities of the European Community (EC) in the world (for "European foreign policy" is now universally taken to refer to the political activities of the European Community, led by European Political Cooperation, or EPC). It is clear that at the very least there is still a substantial residuum of what are perceived locally as distinctive national concerns in foreign policy, especially among the older or larger states.

On the other hand, we ought also to think of "state interests" in terms of the embryonic European state, and its collective interests. These will go in many of the same directions as the present national preoccupations, but will be more than the sum of the separate parts. To the extent, as some argue, that the Community is in the process of becoming a "union of states" along confederalist lines, it is doing so precisely because there exist certain perceptions (going beyond short-term calculations about the advantages of a temporary coalition), of unique European concerns. If these are, or are becoming, genuinely common interests, then they will be protected as such. It would be going too far to predict an upsurge of Euro-nationalism, but there is no doubt that there is a circular relationship among European interests, the machinery for identifying them, and the capabilities with which to assert them. We have to take into account the possibility that the European Community is approaching the point where it will act on the international stage with some of the characteristics and assertiveness of a national state.

The debate about EPC, whether among politicians or academics, has so far centered on this very issue - what kind of quality as a state, if any, it denotes. This in turn has three parts. Firstly, a good deal has now been written about the relationship between national and collective concerns. We know how the former often undermine the latter, or how the latter simply provide alibis or cover for the former. Equally, there is evidence for the socializing effects which immersion in the procedures of EPC have had on the maverick tendencies of some states, or how the coordination reflex among the European Twelve tends to narrow down the range of actions envisaged by member states.

Secondly, some good literature is available on the relationship between progress in external policies, and the internal dynamics of the Community. Although it used to be argued that a common foreign policy had to wait upon the achievement of greater supranationalism in the central institutions of the Communities, it is now more plausible to argue that the demands of the international system, in a functional sense, have forced the member states to awaken from the torpor into which they had sunk during the 197Os. The Genscher-Colombo Plan, the mooted reform of the Common Agricultural Policy, the drive for a common technology policy, and the goal to create a single market can all be seen as stemming, in an essential way, from the need to cope with external parties or problems.

The third aspect of the issue of the state-like quality of the European Community is perhaps the most neglected. It is that of the relative power of this entity in the world; how far do the policies which the states collectively embark upon, particularly in the political sphere, *matter* to outsiders? If they do, then who are the other states or groups who are most affected and why? What is the nature of any influence which might be exerted, and how far is it the result of deliberate, coordinated policy, or alternatively, (rather like the Chinese example above), the mere product of reputation, history and private enterprise? It is this question which provides the central focus of this chapter. After 3O years of the European Communities, more than half of which has now also been spent in the presence of EPC (an EPC recently linked formally to the EC by the Single European Act), what can we say about the broad pattern of interaction, not just between member states and the European collective machinery, but between the states, the European collective, and the global order as a whole?

THE COMMUNITY AS A POWER BLOC

There are three broad ways of interpreting this triangular relationship, all of them ideal (or in this case, extreme) types. The first refers to the teleological process already mentioned, and is a statement about unfolding potential rather than actual reality. It is the notion of the *Community as power bloc* in the world. This is a condition which has often been predicted, usually by those like Johan Galtung who were opposed to the boost to power-politics which such a development would bring on.[2] Those who wanted to see a United States of Europe, with all the inevitable body-building which that would mean have usually been very discreet about the international consequences of such a new, major, actor appearing. But with the levelling-off into intergovernmentalism after the Luxembourg Compromise, the lack of likelihood of such a change has led to it being less discussed, and few have felt moved to note any trends in that direction.

Nonetheless, there can be little doubt that the Community already constitutes a power-bloc in certain respects - so long as one is prepared to disaggregate the notion of "power." If a bloc is a grouping of countries combined by a common interest or aim, then the European Twelve constitute such a bloc, and are capable of wielding power in several key sectors of the international economic system. Commercially, it is incontestable that the Community commands the largest share of world trade of any state or grouping, and it is also capable of behaving in a sufficiently cohesive fashion in the GATT, and in bilateral negotiations, as to make others aware of the fact. The United States, in particular, has often enough run into firm policy-stances, sophisticated tactics, and substantive damage to its interests, to move into a position of deep ambivalence about the advantages of European economic integration. Although Japan, by contrast, has effectively managed to divide and rule the Community, that is at least as much a sign of that country's own peculiar set of strengths as of European weaknesses. The Third World countries, for their part, including the Newly Industrializing Countries (NICs) in the Multi-Fibre negotiations, have consistently found the Community a formidable *interlocuteur* in the various forms of discussion. To the extent that the Community has pursued a more generous development policy than other rich states, it has not been a policy born out of weakness.

So the European Community is already an economic power-bloc, one of Kissinger's five distinctive poles of international relations. Its subsidized agricultural exports depress world prices, its markets are crucial for all the world's trading nations, its monetary policies are important (if not predominant) in determining international financial stability. Even in economics, of course, there

---

2 Johan Galtung, *The European Community: A Superpower in the Making* (London: George Allen and Unwin 1973).

are gaps. Export credits are still an intensely competitive business between nation-states, as are other forms of trade-creation like joint-ventures. A common energy policy is still conspicuous by its absence, and a technology strategy is continually falling foul of disagreements over the level of desirable interventionism. Yet, any third states which assumed that the Community was economically a paper tiger would be in for a rude shock.

The political *uses* of economic strength are, however, a rather different matter. Let us consider two areas where the Community's economic connections should give it considerable potential assets in terms of political relationships, however, subtly the game has to be played. How far, first in East Europe, and then in relations with the associated African, Carribean and Pacific states, does the EC derive political gains from the fact of its evident economic attractiveness to the groups of countries concerned?

East Europe is not one of those areas where a Community policy has dominated over the activities of the member states; the common commercial policy was not extended to the region until 1975. As a group, the Twelve have a number of instruments at their disposal which give them considerable and subtle leverage over the Soviet Union and its allies. The latter want to earn hard currency through exports to West Europe, while the Russians and East Germans are affected by the Common Fisheries Policy. Soviet consumers benefit through cheap purchases of butter and grain. Many European firms have set up industrial cooperation ventures in the East, and Poland and Romania, in particular, have relied heavily on West European loans. Technology transfers have been significant, to the alarm of the United States, as in the construction of the Urengoi gas pipeline.

What is the political value extracted from this asymetrical economic relationship? After all, the Warsaw Treaty countries would rather forego good deals than be blackmailed on other issues, as their reactions to the Jackson-Vanik Amendment of 1973, and the post-Afghanistan sanctions showed. Moreover, the Community countries have been meticulous in resisting crude linkage politics, partly because of their fear of the US adopting the same policy toward themselves. It is largely a matter of a slow-burning impact, achieved more by carrots than sticks. Although in the nature of things this proposition cannot be demonstrated irrefutably, it is reasonable to argue that the West Europeans have been relatively successful over the last decade, despite the deterioration of superpower relations, in promoting what must be their prime foreign policy objective - stability and freedom from the threat of force in the European theater. The European Community has made this aim easier to work toward, since it possesses the advantages of collective strength, together with a number of particular economic and diplomatic instruments.

All this has, of course, happened in the context of NATO and other institutions, while bilateral relations across the iron curtain continue to be extensive. Moreover we are still a long way from the relaxation of Soviet dominance in East Europe and the re-establishment of normal contacts with the West - undoubtedly the ideal state of affairs. But the multiple avenues of influence available during the Polish crisis of the early 198Os were invaluable in bringing the Soviet Union to the realization that their interests were best served by avoiding the kind of brutal intervention with which they had "succeeded" in Czechoslovakia in 1968. (Indeed the Community states may well have had some moderating effects on the United States as well.) The reliance of Poland on economic assistance from the capitalist world, together with firm but not strident diplomatic pressure, led to some of the worst excesses of repression being avoided, and the maintenance of open ties to the West. These did not exist for Prague in the 197Os, and they may now prove invaluable as new opportunities begin to appear for East-West relations in Europe. There seems little doubt, for example, that Britain's extensive diplomacy in East Europe over the last three years (Sir Geoffrey Howe has visited almost all the Warsaw Treaty countries, and Mrs. Thatcher has paid visits to Hungary and the Soviet Union) would not have been possible without the atmosphere of basic trust which has been made possible by European Political Cooperation developing in advance of American foreign policy. Furthermore, the Soviets are happy to talk to the British not just because of their supposed influence in Washington, but because they are a prime mover in what is now a cohesive West European bloc, the attitude of which will be crucial to the USSR as it faces up to the challenge of inevitable change at home and in its relationships with its allies.

This is not just a matter of rhetoric. Political Cooperation has taken consistent lines concerning Afghanistan and the Middle East over the last seven years which the Soviets have had to take account of - even if they have not changed policy as a result. Moreover the

Community proper has concluded trade agreements with Romania and Yugoslavia, which coincidentally, no doubt, are the two Balkan countries (other than the generally intransigent Albania) to have asserted their independence most strongly from Moscow. Czechoslovakia and Hungary have also sought special agreements on textiles, while it is well-known that the German Democratic Republic is partly as stable and prosperous as it is because of the special back-door access it enjoys into the European Community via the Federal Republic. In other words, while the Soviet Union dares not exploit its allies too much for fear of reactions, neither can it meet their needs alone. The other European states, in the western half of the continent, are increasingly important for both the economic and political influence they can exert in the region, which so far has been quietly and indirectly employed toward the end of teasing open the clam of Soviet hegemony. Here "European" foreign policy has started to fall slowly into place over the last fifteen years, and so far, it has proved modestly successful.

That this is so has been demonstrated not just by the avoidance of the worst in Poland, but also through the overtures which the Soviet Union felt compelled to make toward the Community in the early 197Os, and again in 1985. The Soviet bloc has in practice already accepted dealings with the Community, and is now not far from *de jure* recognition. A framework agreement between the Community and the Council on Mutual Economic Assistance (CMEA) is on the verge of being completed, so that the next decade will probably see a further leap ahead in commercial and political contacts of all kinds across the ideological divide in Europe. Major opportunities for benign influence in the East are about to present themselves to the Community and its member states.

Approaches to the Community are the surest sign that other states see it as having significant power-resources at its disposal, and it is of great interest in recent years that these have not simply come from geographical neighbors. The Lomé system, for instance, which numbered 46 African, Caribbean and Pacific (ACP) states in 1973, after the first round of enlargement in the Community, now contains 66, including all developing countries in Sub-Saharan Africa, regardless of their colonial or non-colonial past. There has been a steady queue of applicants for associate status including the two Marxist states of Angola and Mozambique, both anxious to diversify their sources of assistance. This, in turn, has fostered contacts in the Political Cooperation framework between the Twelve and the "front-line states," leading to a full-scale multilateral meeting of foreign ministers in Lusaka in February 1986.

The consolidation of the role in Africa which Lomé represents has partly been a vehicle for the old colonial states, particularly France, to exercise influence without responsibility. But influence, of a sort, it has been. Neither superpower has been able to exert itself in the continent in the way that has proved possible elsewhere, and the Community states are clearly the major external actors when it comes to the question of whether South Africa is to be subjected to meaningful sanctions. Taking the long-term perspective again, the Community has developed the Mineral Export Earnings Stabilization (MINEX) scheme within Lomé, which, while on a small-scale at present, does at least put the Europeans on the basis of permanent dialogue with key mineral-producers, just as the Euro-Arab Dialogue did for relations with OPEC. Moreover with the security of small states and the possibilities of competitive interventions against them being one of the major issues on the international agenda, the Community is well-placed to monitor, and perhaps support pre-emptively, states within its sphere of influence (the term is not too far-fetched) which seem to be falling into internal chaos or external vulnerability. Naturally EC resources are limited, and there is little prospect of major military actions or European Marshall Plans; but even the great powers these days have to face the limits of their capability in the Third World, and in certain respects the Europeans have instruments in Africa denied to both the US and USSR.

Elsewhere, the picture has been modified severely. The EC tried to head off extremism in Grenada by funding its tourist industry through a new airport (against American wishes). This stopped neither the murder of Maurice Bishop nor the overthrow of his successors by invasion from the United States. Still, the circumstances building up to the American action were unusual, and the European policy was not lacking in potential in the medium term. Similarly, in the Pacific, the multilateral relations built up through Lomé may prove to be an important counter-attraction for the micro-states currently being wooed with fishing agreements by the Soviet Union. This indirect, and multifaceted influence certainly seems to have rather more to be said for it, even in terms of efficacy, than the US policy of military bases and client dictators which has proved so disastrous (and undemocratic) over the years.

Other diplomatic groupings have shown great interest in being linked to the Community in recent years, which must denote the attraction of a power-center of some kind. The Association of South-East Asian Nations (ASEAN) has had a Cooperation Agreement with the EC since 198O, which has bred increasingly close political consultations, partly because of the ASEAN states' desire to counterbalance Vietnam in the region without resorting to the United States. As an Indonesian scholar recently observed: "There is almost unanimity of views among observers that ASEAN-EC relations are primarily political in nature."[3]

Similarly, the Contadora countries have welcomed the interest shown by the Community states in the problems of Central America, partly in the (admittedly) vain hope of extracting substantial financial assistance, but partly as a way of attempting to convince Washington that there were middle ways to be found in the conflict over Nicaragua. The journey by ten EC foreign ministers to meet with their Contadora counterparts in Costa Rica in September of 1984, was a blatant signal to the United States, and possibly, from the American viewpoint, it constituted an act of diplomatic intervention. It did not have a dramatic effect, but it was a definite input, a decision to exert independent pressure. Along the same lines may be the talks about setting up an inter-bloc agreement with the Gulf Cooperation Council, this time not to obstruct the United States, but to encourage without provocation those brittle, yet crucial states to resist the influence of Iran.

The interpretation, then, of the European Community as something of a power-bloc in international relations, if not overstated or measured by ideal standards, has quite a lot to be said for it. This is particularly so if we do not freeze the action in the present, but are willing to conceptualize a dynamic process. With its population bigger than either superpower, its great political traditons, experiences, and intellectual skills, its stability and trading power, the EC/Twelve have the capacity to be a superpower. That they are not, and are not likely to be in the foreseeable future, is well-known. The separate states are a long way from being

---

3 Hadi Soesastro, "The Political Dimensions of ASEAN-EC Ties," in R.H. Taylor and P.C. I. Ayre, eds., *ASEAN-EC Economic and Political Relations* (Great Britain: University of London, School of Oriental and African Studies 1986), p. 4O.

sufficiently congealed into each other, and there is little sign of any desire to attain such a goal. Nonetheless there has undoubtedly been disproportionate progress with respect to the Community as an external actor as compared to the internal development of the Community. The grafting on of EPC, the effective negotiating positions in the Tokyo round of the GATT, and the increased attractiveness to third states, are all testimony to that fact.

In the discussion of state interests versus global needs, those in favor of the EC being seen as a power bloc can claim that this would be consistant with the needs of the overall international system, but only by the usual sleight of hand that the powerful employ to justify their actions. It can be said, as it is often said in Moscow or Washington about their respective national policies, that a strong European Community is necessarily a force for peace, or that it would contribute to an effective balance of power system by ending bipolarity. But such talk is no more convincing than that coming from any other prejudiced source. If the Community is a power bloc above all, then it will naturally be furthering state interests (in the sense of the European state interests) and will behave like large states do, with regard for its own concerns before any other values come into play. This may be the case as long as it retains its separate identity and essentially protectionist economic nature.

EUROPE AS CIVILIAN MODEL

The second of our three ways of interpreting the inter-relations of the Community, its member states, and the global system, however, provides a very different perspective. This is the *Community as civilian power*. What does this notion mean, as we approach the 199Os? When coined by François Duchêne in 1972, it naturally reflected the dominant atmosphere of the time, although that has been forgotten in the attacks and caricatures of the idea which have become increasingly fashionable in the 198Os.

Duchêne did not argue that Europe would turn into a pacifist actor in international relations. When he said that "Western Europe could in a sense be the first of the world's civilian centres of power," he was referring primarily to internal developments, where Europe might be "the first major area of the Old World where the age-old process of war and indirect violence could be translated into something more in tune with the twentieth century's notion of civilised politics."[4] The Community could certainly be a model for other regions in the sense that its whole purpose was to set aside the use and threat of force *between* member states - a task in which, helped by other circumstances, it has gloriously succeeded. In its external orientation, Duchêne saw an actual development of Community defense arrangements, both to prepare for the possible withdrawal of American troops and to raise the nuclear threshold in the event of a Soviet attack. Then, "once West European defense arrangements were under way, it might rapidly become apparent that they were not only compatible with but even helpful to arms cuts and East-West relaxation. The often asserted incompatibility between West European integration and East-West cooperation would be likely to prove insubstantial." This analysis sounds remarkably fresh today, and it proves that the notion of civilian power is not simply a new version of pacifist utopianism.

It is true that in what are now called "out of area" affairs, Duchêne did not envisage that military force would be a desirable instrument of foreign policy. Armed forces were necessary for the time being, for the purposes of deterrence on the central front, but there would be no advantage in trying to defend more far-flung interests by force. He argued that "more and more, security policies today, even for the superpowers, consist in shaping the international *milieu* often in areas which at first sight have little to do with security" - or, one might add, everything to do with security in the wider sense than that of physical defense. Here partly because the Community was likely to settle down into what de Schoutheete has called *une structure confédérale*,[5] the emphasis would have to be on many different forms of collective activity and cross-cutting connections with other groupings. If Europe is to be active in the world, then it should take note, as Dahrendorf said in 1978, that "there may be people, and even governments, all over the world who feel the need for a non-military super-power along the line of

---

4 All the references to the ideas of François Duchêne are taken from his "Europe's Role in World Peace," in Richard Mayne, ed., *Europe Tomorrow: Sixteen Europeans Look Ahead* (London: Fontana/Collins for Chatham House/PEP 1972), especially pp. 42-47.

5 Philippe de Schoutheete, *La Cooperation Politique Européenne* (Brussels: Labor 1986), p. 221.

Europe's best possibilities."[6]

The idea of civilian power is, as Duchêne noted at the time, "soggy with good intentions," and it was not surprising, with sharpened East-West tensions toward the end of the 197Os, that it should run into severe scepticism. Hedley Bull attempted to demolish it in 1983, when he wrote that the influence exerted by the European Community was "conditional upon a strategic environment provided by the military power of states, which they did not control."[7] From this viewpoint, "Europe is not an actor," because those who do possess "real" power can simply ruin the best-laid plans of mere "civilian" toilers, by flexing their muscles - as Israel, incidentally, killed off EPC's initiative in the Middle East with its invasion of Lebanon in June 1982. This is part of a generalized hostility to the "interdependence paradigm" which came to the fore in the study of international relations in the 197Os, and seemed to some to be consigning military force prematurely to the scrap-heap of history.

Hedley Bull jumped too quickly to conclusions, in this instance. The concept of civilian power has more to be said for it than he allowed. Firstly, the international system is not constantly being moved onwards by military force alone, so that other kinds of activity are nullified. In fact the broad framework of diplomacy changes comparatively slowly, and it is arguable that the really important structural developments are created by long-term trends as much as by the traumas of defeat or victory in war. This means that precisely the kinds of attributes possessed by the European Community - the intellectual impact of a new model of interstate relations, the disposition of considerable economic influence over the management of the international economy, the possession of a vast network of contacts and agreements with every region of the international system - are those most capable of influencing the very environment which determines whether or not military strength will need to be used.

Secondly, the positive use of military force to intervene in third

---

6 Ralf Dahrendorf, "Europe: A Model?" in his *A New World Order? Problems and Prospects of International Relations in the 198Os* (Ghana: University of Ghana 1979), p. 46.

7 Hedley Bull, "Civilian Power Europe: A Contradiction in Terms?," in Loukas Tsoukalis, ed., *The European Community: Past, Present, and Future* (Oxford: Basil Blackwell 1983), p. 151.

countries has a dubious record so far as the world's major powers are concerned during the post-war period. Assuming that the European states would no longer wish to invade other states to enforce a sphere of influence as the Soviet Union has done as recently as 1979 (and Britain and France did in 1956), the most likely scenario of intervention is that of support for one side in a civil war, or against some prior source of external interference. No doubt this will continue to happen, and occasionally be desirable. But in general, the record of actions such as have occurred in Vietnam and Lebanon is not an encouraging one.

Thirdly, it can be argued that the record of civilian power in action is not insubstantial. This does not refer to the degree of successful influence exerted over third parties by non-military means; that would be a re-run of the analysis under the heading of "power-bloc." Rather, the reference is to three distinctive contributions: the emphasis on persuasion rather than coercion; the use of multiple avenues and forms of discussion rather than seeking exclusively to reinforce the European institutions; and the relative willingness to envisage open diplomacy and to encourage a more sophisticated public discussion of foreign policy matters.

So far as the emphasis on persuasion is concerned, some would say that the Community has simply made a virtue out of necessity in seeking to engineer negotiated solutions, without being able to bring to bear obvious pressures, in the Arab-Israel dispute, the Central American embroglio, and the Afghan war. But with the UN apparently becalmed, the need for initiatives, mediation, and imagination in international politics is even more pressing then before, and the *bona fides* of the Europeans are still probably as respected in all the different sections of the world community as any, with the possible exception of the neutral states and the Vatican, neither of which carry the same weight. Many problems are intractable - Olaf Palme made no headway with the Gulf War - and in others, the European position will be contaminated by self-interest. Yet, this is no reason for fatalism, for without the temptation of the capacity to make large-scale military interventions, "Europe is more likely to understand, and be appreciated, by other small nations than (are) the superpowers," to cite Dahrendorf again.[8]

---

8 Dahrendorf, "Europe: A Model?", op.cit., p. 45.

Even in the Middle East, Europe has not laboured wholly without effect. Its persistent and intelligently worked-out campaign to bring the main parties to the same table over the last few years has come as near to success as any other, and it has had some real influence over bringing the Palestinians nearer to the center of discussions over a settlement, despite all the obvious difficulties. Although such an approach can only succeed and be measured in the very long term, there can be little doubt but that it is consonant with a concern for global needs. If compromise, discussion, and negotiated outcomes are preferable ways of proceeding in international affairs, then the European Community is prominent among the forces of light. As we have seen, other groups of states have been sufficiently impressed by the model the Community provides for internal peace and collective diplomacy that they wish to emulate it. Apart from ASEAN and the Contadora countries, it should be noted that the Caribbean Community (CARICOM) made foreign policy coordination one of the major objectives in its founding treaty,[9] while the " front-line states" of Southern Africa have increasingly striven to harmonise their diplomacy on the major question confronting them, economically in the form of the Southern African Development Coordination Conference (SADCC).

If the emphasis on negotiation is one contribution which a civilian Europe makes to international relations, the concept of "Europe à la carte" is another. By this it is meant the now dominant view in the Community, that cooperation, which can only occur at the pace of the slowest, tends to promote a "Europe-first" approach of the kind more favored by the "power-bloc" school. This, in the end, might simply serve to heighten competition and parochialism in world politics, rather than adressing global problems at their proper level. In contrast, the actual practice of the member states has increasingly been, at least since enlargement began, to go ahead, were necessary, in smaller groups than the full membership and also at times to accept that certain members will wish to work in close association with certain outside states. This last is inevitable, given the existence of the Commonwealth and the Nordic Council *et.al.* But ties from the past have been augmented by such schemes as

---

9 See Pamela Beshoff, Foreign Policy Cooperation and Regional Integration in the Caribbean, in *Millennium: Journal of International Studies*, Vol. 15, No. 1 (Spring 1986), p. 83.

Eureka, the program to advance high technology which includes a number of non-EC European states, and the "Trevi" anti-terrorist mechanisms, which since 1986 have been opened up to all members of the now 24-strong Council of Europe.

Similarly, in defense, the seven (now nine) members of the Western European Union have chosen to revive that moribund institution for the purposes of strengthening the European pillar of NATO, rather than extending the discussion of "security" matters into defense within EPC. This obstructs any linear development toward a fully-fledged European power pursuing a "European interest" independent of both the US and the USSR, but it does accept realities and keeps provocative new developments to a minimum. In parallel, various industrial cooperation schemes like Airbus, Ariane, or Tornado, involving various inner groupings of the Community, and sometimes outside partners, help to reinforce the pattern of cross-cutting connections which is so frustrating to supporters of Community-building, but may be so important in strengthening the cobweb of international society. The activities of the EC in the world are less a validation of the theory of "complex interpenetration." With its numerous functional interests and ties across ideological and geographical divisions, the Community and its states are in a position indeed to transcend parochialism. The aftermath of the Chernobyl disaster, when the EC reacted swiftly and open-handedly, and the Soviet Union acknowledged the importance of the help it was getting, was an important indication of this fact. The world needed the technical expertise of Euratom, the Europeans' ability to focus on the problem rather than search instinctively for partisan advantage, and the sophisticated diplomatic framework which facilitated communication.

The last way in which the record of "European foreign policy" can be presented as a form of "civilian model," is by focusing on its contribution to the democratization of foreign policy. This over-worked phrase gives many hostages to fortune, but here it related to the necessarily open qualities of EPC. This would be contested by those who quite rightly point to the way that EPC has drained off foreign policy issues from national parliaments without providing proper mechanisms of accountability in the European Parliament. Despite its deficiencies, however, European Political Cooperation in this regard represents something of an advancement. Since it is the product of the Twelve working together, it is difficult to sustain any serious dissimulation or covert operations, of the kind that have recently brought the United States into disrepute. EPC is simply too leaky for that (although individual states may well be involved in both, the need to keep in line with the group should act as a constraint). Moreover EPC is very much a matter of grand diplomatic strategy, rather than fine-grained tactics, and as Harold Nicolson pointed out, it is much easier (and more sensible) to have the discussion of *policy* out in the public domain, than the details of negotiations. Lastly, EPC's deliberations are fairly transparent. Not only are the subjects of discussion announced after the meetings of foreign ministers, but the European Parliament keeps a close watch on events, and by the kind of questions it insistently asks, makes sure that most trends are noted. The Presidency makes a regular report to the Parliament, while the press is alert to the publicity-value in such headlines as "Howe promotes EEC as third superpower, or "EEC shows solidarity with Palestinians."[10] Representatives of organizations like the information service *Agence Europe* constantly talk to ministers and officials, and provide commentators with much of their ammunition.

So European foreign policy discussions are unusually open in world terms, perhaps in proportion to the lack of the conventional instruments of power. This may denote therefore colossal irrelevance, but it may equally be interpreted as a major contribution to the emergence of a wider, more knowledgeable, and ultimately more legitimatized debate about international relations among the peoples of the world. If the Europeans can continue to engage in calm, sustained, and reasonably open dialogue with the ACP states, with China and Japan, with India, with the CMEA, with the United States, and the Latin American countries (currently eager to extend their contacts), as they do at present, then this will be enormously time consuming, but it might also be of enormous benefit to political communications in the world. At present the main arteries of the international system are clogged, as the result of decades of hate-filled diplomacy. New channels are badly needed, and with the non-aligned movement as cumbersome as the UN, the EC at least has the potential to be a kind of *poste-restante* for third states or other actors

---

10 Respectively, in the *Financial Times*, 9 July 1986, and *The Independent*, 28 October 1986.

that might find direct communication difficult in the first instance.[11]

EUROPEAN FOREIGN POLICY AS FLOP

There is another way of interpreting the impact of EPC on the world which is altogether less positive than either of the two considered so far. Some oberservers are dismissive, not to say derisory, about Europe's foreign policy aspirations. They might regard it as "sound and fury signifying nothing," a massive diplomatic system producing verbiage but few substantive achievements. These views can even be found in the member states themselves, usually outside the foreign ministries amongst those professionally sceptical about the prospects for diplomacy, whether in defense circles or where specialists in particularly intractable regional conflicts gather together. Among non-Europeans, the superpowers have tended to downplay EPC's significance, with the Soviet Union's attitude revealed by UN Ambassador Malik's ironic reference to "the mighty Nine" in 1974, and Andrei Gromyko's scathing rejection of the EC's proposal for a peace conference on Afghanistan in July 1981. Recently, the Soviets have become more ambivalent about EPC, seeing what the US has recognized for years, that it could provide an alternative fount of Western policies. Yet, the Americans themselves have not worried unduly about EPC; they have become increasingly satirical about the European's inability to make progress on the path of integration.

There are six main grounds on which the critical observer might conclude, after nearly two decades of experience on which to judge, that *the effort to produce a European foreign policy is a resounding flop*. The first is the indubitable truth that EPC is an essentially voluntary system which cannot compel its members to observe discipline. Until 1986 Political Cooperation was parallel but separate from the Community proper, and had no legal basis. Even now, after the Single European Act and the Treaty on EPC, there is only an obligation to *consult* placed on member states, while the possiblity of failure to do so being adjudicated by the European

11 On the idea of bridge-building, see Christopher Layton, Europe and the Global Crisis: A European Contribution to World Order, in *The European*, Vol. 1, No. 1, pp. 24-27.

Court, let alone punished, has been carefully averted. In any case, formal obligations are only one aspect of the peer pressures which are EPC's only hope for the convergence of national policies. And there can be little doubt that these have often proved inadequate.

The Community is, after all, particularly heterogeneous in the attitudes which members take to the wider international system. Ireland is a neutral country, unwilling to join any ventures which appear to touch on defense matters. Greece continues to show sympathy for the USSR's position in East-West relations, and to give the benefit of the doubt to Colonel Gadhdhafi, in ways that few partners share. West Germany still carries the burden of its own past, and the problem of German unification lurks only just beneath the surface of its external relations. France and Britain show no signs of wishing to relinquish their extensive links with ex-colonies, or their independent nuclear forces. Such diversity, often overlooked by outsiders surprised at European bickering, is rooted in long-established national traditions and cannot be dissolved overnight. It makes systematic unity almost impossible, given the range of issues upon which EPC comments. Thus embarrassing unilateralism is commonplace, as when the new Mitterrand government in France blithely announced that there was no longer a "European initiative" on the Middle East, and appeared to renege on a long-agreed position of even-handedness toward Israel and the PLO. That this move in turn was backed away from, did not undo the damage. Once again the Europeans had apparently shown themselves as inconsistant and divided. The same seems to have happened in the UN, where the prized convergence in voting of the 197Os has fallen away since Greece's accession, while only recently, on a most serious issue of vital concern to one member state (the question of Syrian responsibility for the Hindawi bomb-plot against El-Al) most states ran for cover when asked to agree to joint sanctions. Not long before, during the last crisis of the Marcos regime in the Philipines, the Europeans had not even been able to agree on how to indicate sympathy for Mrs. Aquino and her supporters.

The second plank of "the Emperor has no clothes school" is the argument that the Community has no military capacity and therefore no teeth (echoing the Hedley Bull view discussed earlier). How can an actor with no divisions of its own hope to influence states possessing all the panoply of armed force? The concentration of military means in national hands within the EC must surely act as a powerful constraint on its future development, given that individual states will be unwilling to risk the transfer of power to the collective, and will be continually tempted to act alone, as France did in Shaba and Chad, or Britain in the Falklands. Moreover, dependence on the United States for help with defense, and almost all actions on behalf of Western interests ouside the NATO area, is a near-fatal weakness in a system which aspires to provide an alternative forum for Western diplomacy - indeed to some extent to modify US policy itself. Other powers are also unlikely to take notice of European appeals if they can see that EPC is incapable of military intervention to change the balance of power. Israel has easily shrugged off Europe's attempts at mediation, and no amount of high-level visits to Southern Africa are likely to persuade Pretoria from destabilizing Mozambique.

This leads us into the third accusation: that whatever the claims for the capacity of diplomacy and civilian instruments to shape events, their actual impact has been minimal. Certain cases are regularly cited in this regard. In Central America, it can be said, the fanare of multilateral diplomacy, aid packages, and declarations of support for the Contadora process, has not changed the basic situation at all. The wars in El Salvador and Nicaragua continue, without either the United States or the Sandinista government feeling the slightest constraint as a result of European intervention. If anything, moreover, the Contadora states' salience in the affair has gone down since EPC came to their assistance.

In Southern Africa, likewise, the Europeans have signally failed to act in the one way which might have had an impact on events, by imposing full-scale and water-tight sanctions. Instead, they have taken refuge in rather limp attempts to open up channels of communication between the various parties, and have been reduced to otiose "fact-finding" missions by the Presidency, which led in 1986 to Sir Geoffrey Howe being humiliated by his reception in South Africa and Zambia, neither the Botha regime nor the Kuanda government being impressed by his efforts or by what the Community had to offer.

The Middle East, above all, has been the site of EPC's biggest effort and its biggest failure. A great deal of effort and prestige was spent in the "initiative" of 198O-1982, and was invested in the Belgian and Danish Presidencies' attempts in 1987 to revive the idea of a Middle East peace conference. Yet when compared to President Carter's efforts during the Camp David process, the record looks poor. Israel hardly responded, except with contumely, and the Europeans dared not go far enough toward the PLO to stand any chance of giving the moderates in that organization anything for which they would risk their internal position. The shuttle diplomacy of Holland's Chris Van der Klaauw and Luxembourg's Gaston Thorn never attracted the attention that Henry Kissinger has been able to command. European impotence was finally exposed with a certain *Schadenfreude* by Menachem Begin, who forced certain member states to accept that their participation in the Sinai Oberserver Force was under the auspices of Camp David, and was not an EPC contribution to the peace process.

Connected to scepticism about their capacity for impact is the fourth reason for regarding European foreign policy as a flop - the view that it is based on a classical illusion of liberals in international relations, the belief that negotiation is always the best way. Indeed, it can be said that the EC has no choice but to insist on negotiations, having little serious leverage to offer. They are thus in danger of resuscitating appeasement as a philosophy of foreign policy. If this last accusation is not quite fair, since in EPC the Community tends to act in a mediatory role rather than bargain away its own security, it is still plausible to argue that on occasions the insistence on diplomatic intervention can not only fail to have a positive impact - it can make things worse. Israel may well have been marginally hardened in its resistance to change by resentment at the lead being offered by West European states, many of whom it still distrusts because of acts or commissions in the 194Os. South Africa, too, constantly stresses that it will not discuss internal change at the behest of outsiders whom it sees as willfully misinformed about conditions in the country. It may indeed, in such a case, be a form of panglossian self-delusion, to expect bitter adversaries to be able to sit down at the table of compromise, rather than resolve the issue by brutal but decisive force.

The fifth justification for a dismissive approach to EPC and its adjuncts is a direct extension of the fourth. It is sometimes said that EPC amounts only to "a seminar," with the implication that it represents the luxury of an academic, unrealistic, discussion of pressing problems. Furthermore it is "declaratory" rather than operational, and there is a penchant for high-minded moralizing about situations in which EPC barely has an interest. Certainly, communiqués issued after the meetings of foreign ministers harp with irritating regularity on the iniquities of the Chilean or South African regimes, the Vietnamese occupation of Kampuchea, or the horrors of terrorism. Yet, when more than rhetoric is required, the EC states are reticent. They were slow to take measures against Iran over the seizure of hostages in 1979-198O, with the result that American frustration built up, culminating in the disaster of the rescue mission. The same pattern was repeated in 1986 over Libya, when European reluctance to condemn Libya by name may have confirmed the US's view that force was necessary. The very idea of sanctions usually sets off a frisson of commercial fear in West Europe.

Lastly, the "flop" view of Europe's foreign policy can point to the way in which other institutions or groupings exert a centrifugal force on EPC solidarity. The WEU has already been mentioned, but NATO is far more important. Among the Twelve, only the peripheral states of Ireland, Greece, and Spain are not fully committed to the alliance; France, out of the military command structure, has in practice been moving back toward it, and was more enthusiastic about NATO's INF policy than some of the actual hosts of Cruise Missiles and Pershings. Fear of the effects on NATO is a formidable constraint to the further development of a Community security policy. In the area of foreign economic policy, the seven-nation summits, and the G5 (where monetary discussions like those of 1986 to bring the dollar down, take place) are at least as important as intra-EC deliberations. The magnetism of the United States, and the unwillingness of Britain to place Sterling in the exchange-rate mechanism of the European Monetary System (EMS), keep the Community hamstrung. The need for coordination with other developed states cannot simply be ignored in favor of exclusive EC consultations, and to the meetings of the OECD, or the IMF Board of Governors, inevitably reduce the possibilities of distinctive actions by the Twelve. In 1986-1987, over Britain's demand for a separate seat at the Conference on International Economic Cooperation in Paris, there have been embarrassing disputes over whether Italy should be kept out of the inner G5 group.[12] Such conflicts seriously damage the Community's credibility as an

12 See *Financial Times*, 13 March and 6 May 1986, and 23 February 1987.

international actor, even though they do not immediately touch upon foreign policy concerns.

CONCLUSIONS

The idea that European foreign policy amounts to nothing very much in international politics obviously implies that it serves neither state interests nor global needs. The most that this perspective will allow is that EPC is an irritant, occasionally fouling up more productive mechanisms. For the most part, however, EPC is seen as promising far more than it can deliver.

Whether this interpretation, or either of the other two outlined in this chapter, provides a convincing and comprehensive explanation of EPC's success and failures, is largely for the reader to judge. It must be re-emphasised that all of them are slightly over-stated to make the point. Even without caricature, however, all three are deficient, in the view of this writer. European foreign policy is not a flop: it serves functions which are undramatic but nonetheless real, such as the development of a coherent Western outlook on international relations which is not simply a pale echo of the United States, whose views are inevitably colored by its own interests as a superpower. It has helped to draw a disparate group of states together in a broadly common cause, and is thus able to reinforce the internal movement toward cooperation which was otherwise faltering. And, so long as it is judged by standards no higher than those which are applied to other actors in the international system (who also can be seen to have regularly failed in the quagmires of South Africa or the Middle East), it is fair to say that EPC has made a modest contribution to the process of calm, rational discussion of major conflict areas - particularly in its own backyard, with the CSCE. The Europeans have even, on occasions like that of the Siberian gas pipeline dispute with the US, shown the will to stick fast, and thereby force another protagonist to climb down. This is always more likely to happen where foreign policy and economic issues come together.

If it is not a complete flop, however, the Community clearly is not a true power-bloc in the sense that any political scientist or historian would recognize. True, the EC is not devoid of power in the external realm, but its strengths are patchy and inconsistently applied. Although third states show many signs of accepting that the Community is an important actor *in certain sectors* of international activity, there is a qualitative gap between the perceptions held of NATO or the Warsaw Pact, and those of the EC. The latter will almost certainly have to develop its nascent security policy and develop a defense identity, if it wants to leap up to the next level of power politics.

In my view, the civilian power analysis comes closest, despite its current unfashionability, to rendering the truth about the EC and its international possibilities. Clearly, the concept is inadequate in a number of important aspects, particularly in its strong element of wish-fulfilment, in the assumptions it makes about the changing nature of influence in international relations, and in the possibility that it is simply a contradiction in terms: as some would say, either seek to exercise proper power, in all its forms, or adopt a new paradigm altogether (say, "interdependence"); but don't expect to protect your interests or further your values simply by persuasion or example.

Yet it is worth attempting to rehabilitate the civilian power approach, because of its basic flexibility. It allows that the Community, and the kind of international relations which it conducts, is essentially *sui generis*, an unprecedented development in world history which must not be cramped by forcing it into inappropriate conceptual models derived from the study of nation-states. To some extent the EC and EPC provide a new model for a democratic foreign policy, leaning as they do on the twin assumptions that (1) democratic states eschew force in their mutual relations, and (2) their populations are increasingly reluctant to envisage the use of military force in all but the dire circumstances of defense against attack. They also make the by no means utopian assumption that major conflicts may be best alleviated by taking the long view, and by tackling fundamental questions of economics and perception. That the Europeans do not themselves have all the necessary resources to practice what they preach (and have not yet done what is needed inside the Community, in Northern Ireland), is not an invalidation of the argument. At least, the EC has been relatively positive and dynamic in the development of its "foreign policy" (still too ambitious a term). It has overcome set-backs, steadily moved on in terms of relationships between the Community and EPC, and not been afraid to take intiatives to improve the overall international milieu in which we have to live.

It is at this point, perhaps, that a normative concern for "global needs" somewhat understandably begins to color analytical judgement as to what exactly is the nature of Europe's capacity and achievements. There seems to me little doubt that the world would be better served if the European Community was to turn out neither a flop or a power-bloc, but was to move more along the line that François Duchêne optimistically (but not naively) predicted fifteen years ago. If it is a failure then there will be a vacuum into which others, perhaps less mellowed by the traumas of war, will move. Plus the great inheritance of Europe's experience and civilization will be degraded. Alternatively, if it becomes a power-bloc *en route* to superpower status, the reactions of the existing incumbents are likely to be nervous and hostile. Future candidates will learn that the old lessons about how to exert influence in the world were right all along. If, as a third option, Europe can demonstrate that civil relations between already friendly states can actually be extended into the realm of relations between the suspicious, the adversarial, or the merely different, then it will have performed a profound service for the community of mankind.

3

European Trade Policy at Mid-Decade: Coping with the Internal Menace and the External Challenge

Roy H. Ginsberg

INTRODUCTION

Rationale and Working Definitions

From the perspective of 1990, the mid-1980s was a time when the European Community (EC) faced the twin challenges of the removal of obstacles to internal trade to more fully unify the customs union - the "internal menace;" and responsibilities and demands placed on it by the international community - the "external challenge." The question of the relationship of state behavior to the international system has been studied by scholars for a long time.[1] Little thought, however, has been given to the behavior of groups of states, such as the EC, as they collectively pursue state interests.[2] Do state groupings behave differently from individual states in pursuing their objectives? Do state interests pursued in a collective

---

1 This question was the theme of the 27th annual convention of the International Studies Association (ISA) in Washington, D.C., 14-19 April 1987.

2 This chapter was one of three papers (see C. Hill, chapter 2, and R. Rummel, chapter 4) presented on a panel organized by the author for the ISA convention in Washington, D.C., 1987 dealing with the EC as an unorthodox actor in pursuit of state interests and global needs.

mode take into account global needs? And, if so, is this an indication for the assertiveness of such a collective actor.

The search for answers to these questions points to the case of EC trade policy since (A) this is a sector where the member governments have transferred authority to the EC to act on their behalf; and (B) the EC is the world's largest trader whose policies substantially influence, and are influenced by, the global trade order. This chapter identifies areas where EC members have pursued trade interests that have, and have not, been responsive to the needs of the global trade order. Definitions of state interests, global needs, and global responsibility are suggested.

With all the obstacles encountered in the pursuit of European integration, the Rome Treaty's trade powers are still unprecedented in the history of modern interstate relations. Discussion of Europe's global conscience in trade is timely. Trade policy - the waylaid centerpiece of EC integration - is again the driving force behind the quest to unify the customs union by 31 December 1992 (the so-called "1992 plan"). The Europeans are now trying to finish the job they had begun three decades earlier and to make headway in achieving a common market. Four questions about what drives EC trade policy help to organize this chapter:

- Is EC trade policy driven by state interests?
- Is EC trade policy driven by collective regional interests?
- Do the Europeans have a global conscience in trade?
- Do European collective trade interests intersect with global needs?

Two themes emerge from the discussion of these questions. One, the EC as a unit of states does amply show that it has a global conscience in trade. This is evidenced, for example, by modest but unprecedented nonreciprocal concessions to 76 nonmember beneficiaries of the Lomé Convention and of the Mediterranean Policy, by EC participation in the General Agreement on Tariffs and Trade (GATT) and adherence to GATT rules governing the liberal multilateral world trade order, by the relative openness of the EC market to imports of industrial products from nonmembers, and by financial and political support for other regional groups seeking cooperation in part based on the European model. Two, despite evidence of a global conscience in trade questions, the core *raison d'être* of the EC is to create an exclusive club - customs union - that tends to demarcate the EC from (rather than integrate it into) the global trade order in such sectors as textiles, agriculture, and steel. The export subsidies of the Common Agricultural Policy (CAP) have wrecked havoc in international trade in agriculture - a triumph of state interests, funnelled through the EC, over global needs. Finally, the murky world of non-tariff barriers (NTBs) that the member states have engaged in so as to restrict imports from fellow members (and nonmembers alike) marks the EC's record of receptivity to the needs of the global trade order and points to the triumph of state interest.

The paradox of the EC at mid-decade and beyond is that the EC makes contributions to the global trade order through responsible acts, but is fundamentally designed to be demarcated from the global trade order to derive many commercial benefits not generally available to outsiders in product areas for which the EC has gained self-sufficiency or wishes to achieve self-sufficiency. The 1992 plan is designed to provide opportunities for EC firms to garner larger shares of the European market and thus become more globally competitive (clearly showing, incidentally, how member interests are being pursued in a regional mode). The irony of the 1992 plan is that, to achieve this new competitive posture, the EC must still permit nonmember firms access to the enlarged European market. If the EC took a "Fortress Europe" approach and restricted imports, its exports would suffer as nonmembers - particularly nonmembers on whose markets the EC heavily depends for sales - would retaliate. As the EC, especially West Germany, is heavily dependent on export trade, it cannot afford to cordon off the customs union. Of course, this is not to say that there will be no specific problem areas for nonmembers' access to the EC market; indeed, there will be a number of disputes between the EC and its trading partners, but the broad flow of imports into and exports out of the EC should continue relatively unscathed by the 1992 plan. Thus almost inadvertently, the EC must be responsive to global needs given the existence of trade, capital, and technological interdependence among capitalist states and their multinational corporations. There is a large intersection between the EC's regional needs, on the one hand, and global needs, on the other, forcing the EC to act in ways more responsible than its members would perhaps like.

Before elaborating more extensively on the internal obstacles and the external challenges of West Europe's trade policy, several key analytical notions should be defined.

State Interests

The Rome Treaty precludes member governments from unilaterally executing foreign trade policy. Member governments must funnel their trade policy interests through the EC. In this context, state trade interests refer to the set of objectives pursued by the member governments through the EC in internal and external commerce. The EC pursues a universally criticized policy of export subsidies to enable its farmers to export certain surplus produce at prices which at times fall below world market levels, depressing world market prices. The EC views the CAP as an article of faith - a bedrock of the entire experiment in regional integration thus not negotiable even in the face of demand for change from the global community. Blind attachment to the CAP, although some of its programs distort the flow of world farm trade and sap EC resources from other more productive ventures, is a triumph of state interests over global needs.

Global Needs

Global needs refer to the maintenance requirements of the so-called liberal multilateral world trade order that has provided a framework for trade conflict resolution, trade liberalization, and most-favored-nation treatment (MFN) among capitalist states in the post-war period - a period of expanding world trade. The global trade order needs a set of constraints on state behavior lest states retreat into the mindset of beggar-thy-neighbor policies that plagued the interwar years when global trade ground to a halt and the seeds of discontent were sown. The GATT system, for all its inadequacies, still resolves more trade disputes than it leaves unresolved. The GATT is only as viable and effective as the contracting parties allow it to be since, unlike the EC, it has no supranational authority. Continued existence of the GATT system is a triumph of global needs over more narrowly-based state interests.

Global needs also refer to the economic development (and other emergency) needs of the less developed countries, needs that are addressed in multilateral fora, such as the specialized agencies of the

United Nations, in nongovernmental organizations, and in developed countries' bilateral aid programs.

Global responsibility

Responsibility for maintaining a semblance of order for the global capitalist trade system, embodied by the rules of the GATT, refers to the tempering of state interests with global needs. Global responsibility in trade (again with reference to capitalist states) includes a commitment to the multilateral world trade order and its rules and norms on trade methods, import relief, equal terms of trade, and trade conflict resolution. Global responsibility also refers to the need to maintain a balance of interests so that the existing framework continues to constrain runaway protectionist action or export credit/subsidy wars. Global responsibility commits the developed countries to assist the Less Developed Countries (LDCs) with tariff-cutting measures to increase their exports, e.g., the EC's Generalized System of Preferences (GSP), and thus ease their debt burden. The EC has innovative policies toward the Mediterranean and Lomé Convention countries which are recipients of nonreciprocal tariff cuts (known as preferences) for agricultural products, duty-free trade for most industrial products, economic development assistance, and financial aid. These forms of assistance help raise the standard of living in these countries and enable the EC to play a constructive role in their overall political, economic, and social development. The Lomé Convention and the Mediterranean Policy are triumphs of global over state interests because they point to responsible action by a group of prosperous states toward the well-being of two (far less prosperous) large regions of the world.

The Political Economy of the EC at Mid-Decade

The consensus which emerged by 1985 to reverse what had become known as "Eurosclerosis" had much to do with the stagnant economic situation in the EC during the early and mid-1980s. Unemployment in the EC averaged about 12 percent at mid-decade and economic growth was sluggish. It was not until 1986 that the EC registered a slight increase in the number of new jobs - the first time since the early 1970s! Still, by the late 1980s, unemployment in the EC states averaged 11 percent. The EC market was flooded with imports of high-tech products from Japan, the United States, and the newly industrialized countries (NICs) - the external challengers - while EC member firms were stymied by intra-community restrictions on crossnational R&D and business collaboration - the internal menace. Restrictions on Europeanwide access to public procurement markets of the twelve states - only 2 percent of public procurement markets in the member governments was (and is now) open to firms from other member states - contributed to the fragmentation of the European market and lost opportunities for economies of scale and cost savings for public sectors, including savings for many R&D projects that are duplicated needlessly on a scale of twelve. Twelve separate sets of production and other standards mean EC member firms (and nonmember firms) have to tailor production not to a unified market, such as Japan or the United States, but to a series of smaller ones.

The irony of the European dilemma of the 1980s is that the NTBs that member governments thought would protect their domestic economies from imported competition from other member-states, ended up depriving member firms of the benefits a customs union should offer - free flow of goods, services, capital, and labor. Indeed increased usage of NTBs - a practice that became more visible after the EC removed all internal tariffs in 1968 - points to the triumph of state over regional needs as well as over global needs. NTBs rob EC firms, foreign firms doing business in the EC, and foreign firms in pursuit of exports to the EC of the benefits a completed customs union should provide.

By mid-decade, a coalition of EC member governments and many of their large multinational corporations realized that a new approach - or rather an old approach in need of rediscovery - would be necessary to reverse Europe's economic fortunes. The approach - long proposed in parts by the EC Commission over the course of the previous decade but doomed to political impotency in the Council of Ministers - set out to progressively eliminate (or in certain cases substantially reduce) NTBs, from opening up public procurement markets to adopting common health and production standards to eliminating customs formalities, by 31 December 1992. Of course, the approach is nothing short of what the Europeans had set out to do in 1958 and thus in many respects highlights the failure rather than the success of the EC to date.

The blueprint to guide the EC from a fragmented to a fuller customs union is mapped out in the 1985 *White Paper on Completing the Internal Market*[3] and spelled out in legal form in the 1987 Single European Act which was the first amendment to the Treaty of Rome. The logic behind the 1992 plan is stunning. If the plan is implemented as conceived - considering the existence of some political opposition to it and unforeseen developments such as recession - it will, according to proponents, create a single continental size market of 323 million people so that businesses may exploit larger economies of scale and undertake crossnational business and R&D collaboration, resulting in more competitive European firms able to meet the foreign competition within Europe and competition on a worldwide scale as well. Loss of employment in the short-term would be a necessary evil as uncompetitive firms go out of business under the new market conditions. However, the plan's logic points to growth in the number of jobs in Europe in the medium-term as firms that do survive the new market conditions expand production for "exports" to the larger European market and exports to markets abroad.

TREATY PROVISIONS OF EC TRADE POLICY

The Rome Treaty transfers members' sovereignty in the areas of trade to the EC. On occasions, when conflicts over trade policy questions arise between the individual member states and the EC institutions, then the European Court of Justice - the EC's supreme court - has interpreted the Rome Treaty in favor of the EC's prerogatives. Some students of international relations have dismissed the supranational aspects of the EC as not very relevant to regional politics in Europe because the EC has not become a superpower or because it has not fulfilled expectations for political union of earlier observers. Premature assumptions about the EC tended to skip over the Rome Treaty's immense trade powers in an international system that, by the 1970s, put much more weight on the political and economic aspects of security - what was once called

---

3 *Completing the Internal Market: White Paper from the Commission to the European Council* (Brussels: Commission of the European Communities, June 1985).

low politics - and much less weight on the physical use of force - once called high politics. The fusion of high and low politics in the 1970s and 1980s made EC trade powers the legal substance on which its foreign relations and policy actions have come to rest.[4] Should the EC realize even some of the goals of the 1992 plan, the ability to exploit its supranational trade powers for economic and political purposes is of great moment to students and practitioners of international relations.

The Rome Treaty [5] (A) puts brakes on member states' trade and trade-related interests; (B) embodies member states' trade interests; (C) embodies collective trade interests that demarcate the EC from the global trade order; and (D) embodies needs of the global trade order.

The Rome Treaty Puts Brakes on Member States' Trade and Trade-Related Interests

Article 10 empowers the EC Commission to act in complete independence of the member governments in performing its Treaty duties. Articles 38-47, the legal bases for the CAP, subject members' farm economies to EC rules. Articles 85-86 are the legal bases for the EC's common competition policy. These articles prohibit business practices that prevent, distort, and restrict competition among the members. It falls to the EC Commission to enforce free movement of goods, services, capital, and labor throughout the membership. Firms found abusing a dominant position may face financial penalties. For example, in 1988, the EC fined Sabena Airlines 100,000 European Currency Unit (ECU) for refusing a British airline access to its computerized reservation system and fined British Dental Trade Association 100,000 ECU after an investigation revealed its rules for exhibition excluded foreign firms.[6] Articles 90-93 empower the EC Commission to regulate the granting of member government subsidies or other

---

4 Roy H. Ginsberg, *Foreign Policy Actions of the European Community: The Politics of Scale* (Boulder: Lynne Rienner 1989).

5 An abridged version of the Rome Treaty and the full text of the Single European Act appear in *Treaties establishing the European Communities.* (Luxembourg: Office for Official Publications of the European Communities 1987).

6 *General Report on the Activities of the European Community in 1988* (Brussels: Commission of the European Communities 1989) p. 200.

exclusive privileges to domestic industries. State subsidies and other exclusive grants that distort intra-Community trade are prohibited under most circumstances by the Treaty. In 1988, under Article 90, the Commission required that member governments liberalize rules on the supply of telecommunications terminal equipment (e.g., modems and telex terminals) to introduce greater competition into the European market.[7] Articles 113 and 116 empower the EC to conduct all facets of the members' internal and external trade policies. Article 164 empowers the European Court of Justice, the highest court in the EC, to interpret the Treaty, and thus all EC institutions and member governments, firms, and citizens are subject to its judicial decisions. Article 234 calls on members that have rights and obligations from accords with non-member states entered into before the Rome Treaty came into being to eliminate these accords to the extent that they are incompatible with the Treaty.

The Rome Treaty and the Single European Act Embody Member States' Trade Interests

The Rome Treaty preamble commits the EC to ensure the economic and social progress of the member countries by common act to eliminate the barriers which divide Europe. The CAP (Articles 38-47) benefits EC members (particularly major food producers) with price supports, export subsidies, and other farm support mechanisms. Article 115, the Treaty's safeguard clause, permits the EC Commission to restrict goods imported into a member state - from other member states - that originated in third countries - if it can be shown to the Commission's satisfaction that such safeguard action is needed to respond to extreme economic difficulty. Article 115 is used frequently by some of the members to restrict imports from Japan and some of the Pacific Rim countries. Articles 113 and 116 permit the EC to impose antidumping and countervailing duties against imports from non-member states that are found to be in violation of GATT code rules. For example, in 1987, the EC imposed antidumping duties on imports of electric motors from Yugoslavia and mercury from the Soviet Union under its Treaty powers. The New Community Instrument adopted into law in 1984 empowers the EC to deal with "unfair trade practices" used by foreign governments that prejudice EC trade inside Europe and

7 Ibid, p. 202.

abroad. Articles 129-130 empower the European Investment Bank to provide loans and grants to member states with economic development needs in depressed areas. Article 130c (as amended by the Single European Act) empowers the European Regional Development Fund to participate in the development and structural adjustment of backward regions of the EC in order to redress such imbalances. Articles 123-125 empower the European Social Fund to provide relocation and vocational retraining assistance to workers who have lost their jobs.

Lastly, Section II, Article 8A, of the Single European Act commits the EC to adopt measures with the aim of progressively establishing the internal market for a period to end on 31 December 1992. The Act defines the internal market as an area without internal frontiers in which the free movement of goods, persons, services, and capital is ensured in accordance with the provisions of the Rome Treaty. With the exceptions of labor movement and fiscal harmonization, the Council of Ministers, pursuant to Article 8B of the Single European Act, is empowered to pass directives to achieve the 1992 plan on the basis of a qualified majority - a large step away from the vote of unanimity that was a chief cause for the EC's earlier failures in achieving the goal of a free and completed internal market. Passage of the Single European Act symbolized the members' consensus that as individual markets they were too small, fragmented, and inefficient to compete on a global, much less European, scale. The Act embodies the members' acceptance that their interests are best served in a completed rather than a fragmented customs union. Passage took political will, but the bitter dose was sweetened by the prospect of economic revitalization and renewed competitiveness on a regional and global scale.

The Rome Treaty Embodies Collective Trade Interests that Demarcate the EC from the Global Trade Order

Articles 113-116 enable the members to protect their interests through joint EC action. These articles empower the EC to regulate, administer, and manage the customs union. This includes control of the Common External Tariff, adjustments of tariff rates, imposition of import quotas, minimum import prices, and negotiations with nonmembers for preferential trade, cooperation, association accords, and voluntary restraint accords. Article 113 specifically empowers the EC Commission to recommend to the Council when accords with third states are needed and directs the EC Council to authorize the Commission to open and conduct negotiations. Article 228 empowers the EC Commission to negotiate trade and tariff accords with nonmembers and international bodies. Article 229 empowers the EC Commission to ensure the maintenance of all appropriate relations with the United Nations, the GATT, and other international bodies. Members enjoy the privileges of being part of an exclusive club. Nonmembers try to find accommodation with the EC for market access. The chief objective of the EC is to increase internal trade which, for all intents and purposes, demarcates the EC from the outside world in such sectors as agriculture, steel, and coal.

The Rome Treaty Embodies Needs of the Global Trade Order

The EC has a keen sense of responsibility to global needs which is evidenced by its own Treaty provisions. The Preamble refers to the desire to contribute, by means of a common commercial policy, to the progressive abolition of restrictions on international trade. The Preamble also states the members of the EC confirm solidarity with "overseas countries" to ensure their development in accordance with the principles of the Charter of the United Nations. Article 110 directs the member states to contribute to the harmonious development of international trade through the progressive abolition of restrictions on international trade, and the lowering of customs barriers. Article 113 empowers the EC to enter into tariff and trade negotiations with nonmembers, which gives the EC a chance to respond to global needs. Article 131 permits the EC to associate with non-European countries and territories, thus enabling the EC to reach out to former colonies and overseas territories with trade-and-aid benefits. Article 228 empowers the EC to conclude accords with nonmember countries and has served as the legal basis for the Lomé Convention and the Mediterranean Policy. Article 229 empowers the EC to work with relevant international organizations and has served as the legal basis for the EC obtaining membership or observer status in nearly forty international organizations or agreements - a testimony to the EC's global commitments.[8] Membership in the EC is extended to other European countries under Article 237 (witness the doubling of EC membership between 1958 and 1986) and

8 Ginsberg, *Foreign Policy Actions, op.cit.,* pp. 62-63.

association with the EC is extended to any third country under Article 238 (witness the association of Turkey, Malta, and Cyprus).

Is EC Trade Policy Driven by State Interests?

The response is affirmative on two accounts. On the first account, the EC was set up to serve state interests by creating an exclusive internal market where the watchword is "Community preference," i.e., domestic producers are the preferred provider of goods and services. A large internal market free of tariffs, surrounded by a Common External Tariff to give the internal producer a competitive advantage, was designed to permit EC firms to exploit economies of scale. One might also add that for such states as the UK, "politics of scale" were also served by membership in the club, i.e., the collective unit would be larger and more powerful than its constituent parts in the effectiveness and weight of its foreign policy actions.[9] On the second account, the very same states that sought the benefits of membership have worked, ironically, to mock the internal market by devising NTBs that shield domestic markets from the flow of sensitive imports from other members. The NTBs were thought to address the needs of certain domestic constituents - particularly declining industries - but in effect superimposed a domestic problem onto other members of the EC.

The EC was created to serve members' common interests. The concept of a customs union is to ensure free internal trade between members to the exclusion of outsiders. Thus, in a sense, the customs union is hostile to the concept of a liberal global trade order defined by the GATT even though Article XXIV of the GATT Treaty permits its creation. However, when the GATT Treaty was ratified no one knew that the EC would develop the CAP and become one of the world's largest food producers and exporters. In the liberal multilateral world trade order, the premium is placed not on demarcating regions from the global order but on keeping them open.

However, as much as an outsider looks to the EC and sees a huge internal market where member firms enjoy the benefits of free

---

9 Ibid, p. 3.

access to a consumer market much bigger than the United States or Japan, the observation is an illusion. Use of NTBs by member governments to protect domestic markets from imported competition serves neither regional collective interests as defined by the Rome Treaty nor global needs as defined and managed by such international bodies as the GATT. If the EC's own members encounter difficulties in exporting to one another, then the effect of this behavior on nonmember exports to the EC is even more pronounced. NTBs are a triumph of state interests over regional and global needs.

The CAP is a triumph of state interests over global needs because of its negative impact on the world farm economy. The CAP is the EC's beauty and beast. For those member governments with large export-led farm economies, the CAP is a "beauty" because farmers, no matter how inefficient, have had access to nearly unlimited subsidization of various forms. Conversely, the CAP is a "beast" for a member such as the UK, which is not a major farm producing state, but which must still contribute to the costs. The nearly 70 percent of the EC budget swept up by CAP costs is the "beast" of the EC Commission, which has sought in vain for CAP reform, and of the European consumer, who ultimately foots the bill in high food prices and taxes. Indeed, it falls to the EC Commission to act with prudence as it attempts to balance the demands of the members with the demands of the global community. The CAP is a "beast" to the world's major food exporters who try, often without success, to match the competition of subsidized European farm produce in third country markets.

For many years, the EC Commission has proposed CAP reform measures that have been either diluted or dismissed by the Council of Agricultural Ministers whose farm lobbies wield significant political power back home. For example, the West German Government - historically the most pro-European - bowed to internal farm lobby pressure and tried to block an EC Commission proposal in June 1985 to slightly reduce certain cereal support prices, claiming that this would have reduced German farm income.

So long as the CAP encourages open-ended farm production through the lure of high prices supports, and dislodges surplus produce abroad, depressing world market prices, the EC shirks its responsibility to the global order. The global trade order depends on a balance of interests between trading nations to minimize extreme state actions that disrupt historical trade flows. In all fairness, though, CAP reform has been moving since 1984 - albeit at a snail's pace - with the EC Commission proposing legislation more quickly and radically than the Agricultural Ministers would prefer. However, to discourage overproduction, the EC has been trying to reduce price support levels, increase taxes on producers to hold down production, encourage farmers to leave the land, and encourage land set-aside. Yet EC Commission proposals to provide direct income support to farmers (rather than providing income support for farmers through high price support levels which then cause overproduction) have not been acted on by the Council (at least by 1988).

Finally, while the Single European Act provides for majority voting on most directives governing the elimination or reduction of NTBs, it still provides member governments with the right of veto power over such critical matters as free labor movement and fiscal harmonization, admittedly two areas that cut deep into national sovereignty, and thus points to the triumph of state over regional interests.

Is EC Trade Policy Driven by Collective Regional Interests?

The response is affirmative as the EC was set up to promote collective regional interests. This has entailed costs and benefits for the member states. The costs to members of submitting trade policy authority to the EC include loss of sovereignty and rise in competition from other members. The benefits for members include partnership with the world's largest, most powerful trading bloc which protects members' trade interests in the outside world and offers them opportunities to exploit economies of scale and politics of scale. Examples of how collective regional interests prevail over state interests follow.

European Law

The EC's legal authority to conduct internal and external trade policy is explicit in the Rome Treaty. EC law is binding on all twelve member states and their citizens and firms. The European Court of Justice interprets EC law and is the final arbiter of disputes between members, between member firms, between members and the EC institutions, and between member and nonmember firms. Court rulings have generally upheld EC law over national law in commercial policy. The Court has interpreted EC law in favor of expanding EC trade policy authority by ruling that any foreign trade policy issues that involve the functioning of the EC may be handled by the EC. In a 1971 ruling, the Court stated that each time the EC lays down any rules pertaining to EC foreign trade policy, members no longer have the right to contract obligations toward nonmembers affecting those rules.[10] In areas in which the EC has authority to negotiate and conclude treaties in pursuance of common EC policy, the possibility of a concurrent authority on the part of the individual members is excluded, as any action taken outside the framework of the common institutions would be incompatible with the unity of the common market and the uniform application of EC law. The Court recognized the principle that EC external competence flows from its internal competence and that the EC Commission may be involved in foreign affairs so long as the subject pertains to the internal functioning and rules of the common market. The Court in 1985 again upheld previous rulings that there can be no national competence in the field of commercial policy in the case of Bulk Oil v. Sun International.

Enlargement

Accession of Spain and Portugal to the EC in 1986 showed that the common European good prevailed over individual state interests. The common good was to bring the Iberian states into the European mainstream to stabilize their nascent democracies and develop their economies. Some member state interests were shown to be hostile to enlargement. Southern French, Italian, and Greek farmers feared the effect of accession on their Mediterranean-type exports to the EC since Spain is a large producer of these products. Although their concerns were in large part "bought off" by the EC's Integrated Mediterranean Program - which provides EC financial resources for industrial modernization - the fact remains that in the end European regional collective interests triumphed over state and sub-state interests in at least three of the member countries. The EC accepted costs and risks with the accession of the Iberian states, but these

10 Re: ERTA: EC Commission v. EC Council, Case 221/70 (1971).

were outweighed by the political and geostrategic bonanza that Spanish and Portuguese membership brought to European security in an area some refer to as the continent's "soft-underbelly."[11]

Regional and Social Development

The EC provides a wide array of support for regional and social programs in the member states. The European Investment Bank, the European Regional Development Fund, and the European Social Fund represent a triumph of collective regional interests as development of the EC's needier regions is aided by the EC's wealthier ones.

The Single European Act

The Single European Act is also a triumph of collective interests because it challenges the member states to realize the fuller achievement of the internal market by 1993. Despite years of constructing or perpetuating NTBs that skewed the internal market away from its orginal purpose, and abusing the rule of unanimity to protect state interests over common needs, the members agreed to make a fundamental change. First, the new law commits members to remove many of the NTBs to which they have clung so closely. Second, in most matters involving liberalization of the internal market, the Council must vote on the basis of a qualified majority rather than by unanimity. This has already helped to speed up the process of liberalization. The Act adds eleven new articles subject to qualified majority voting to the thirty-five existing articles already subject to qualified majority voting.

CAP Reform

The EC Commission Green Paper on the CAP[12] and subsequent reform proposals call for price support restraints, cut-backs in guarantees and interventions, production quotas, early retirements, land set-asides, and more co-responsibility (i.e., when the producer pays a tax to help defray the cost of supports). Some limited progress has been made. To curtail excess production, the EC has

---

11 Ginsberg, *Foreign Policy Actions*, op.cit., Chapter 7.

12 EC News Flash. *Green Europe: Perspectives for the CAP*. (Brussels: Directorate-General for Information, Agricultural Information Service, No.33, July 1985).

increased the producer's co-responsibility levy on milk production, reducing the quantities of milk subject to price support guarantees, has imposed production limits on oils and fats, olive oil, and soya with penalties for exceeding limits, has frozen or decreased support prices for most farm products subject to the CAP, and has introduced a voluntary scheme of special aids to compensate farmers who agree to limit output of cereals, wine, or beef by 20 percent over five years without any parallel increase in production capacity in other product sectors.

Although the EC Commission claims it is making "substantial progress" in reforming the CAP, this is not really the case. Farm spending continues to consume about 70 percent of the entire EC budget and surpluses continue to run up for butter, milk, beef and veal, and certain cereals. The EC Commission has proposed the introduction of direct income payments to farmers to support income and thus provide incentives to leave farming, for example, through early retirement. Ideally, such direct payments, while costly, would avoid the problem of supporting farm income through high price supports that continue to contribute to unwanted and even costlier surpluses. By early 1988, the Council of Agricultural Ministers, true to form, had not responded to the proposal in the affirmative. Lastly, usage of export subsidies to lodge unwanted and expensive surpluses onto the world market at low prices continues to drain EC resources and draw international criticism.

By pressing for CAP reform, the Commission is attempting to inject a dose of reason and balance in Europe's most politically-charged commercial issue. CAP reform will depend on the political will in each of the member governments, continued pressure on the Commission to make reform proposals to the Council, and continued global pressure on the EC to act with more prudence. The CAP was originally set up in 1962 to support farm income and achieve self-sufficiency; thus it is one of the clearest and earliest examples of how EC trade policy was driven by the collective interests of the members. Now, nearly thirty years later, CAP reform will be slowly and grudgingly accepted by the Council of Agricultural Ministers because runaway costs will become politically unacceptable to the nonagricultural sectors. The irony of EC farm policy is that it was once the feather on the "cap" of European integration but it is now a victim of its own success.

Davignon Plan

To shed excess capacity that has driven European prices down for steel products, the member states were subject to a "manifest crisis" under the terms of the Paris Treaty (the constitution which established the European Coal and Steel Community in 1952) in 1980. This meant that the EC assumed emergency powers to force the member states to shed capacity, set price controls and minimum import prices, and restrict nonmember imports through negotiated accords. The Plan has indeed resulted in reduced capacity and improved efficiency, even though some emergency measures are still in place, and is an example of the pursuit of collective over state interests for the benefit of the common good, at least as defined by the EC institutions.

European Monetary System

Many economists agree that the European Monetary System (EMS) has helped the EC members to achieve a modicum of monetary stability in recent years. While participation in EMS is not mandatory, its success to date shows the benefit of monetary collaboration over unilateral action. For example, in 1987, EMS had only one realignment of the central rates.

R&D in Science and Technology

Since 1984, the EC has pushed the notion that member states are not benefitting from economies of scale in the area of R&D in science and technology (S&T). Duplication of R&D projects at the various national levels wastes productive resources and contributes to slower technological development in the EC. Historically, member governments, research laboratories, and firms have been loathe to work on R&D projects on a crossnational basis.

To break with the past, the EC enacted a framework program (worth 5.4 billion ECU) for research and development for the period between 1987-1991. The Single European Act calls for the EC to develop such a program as part of the effort to create a more integrated and competitive internal market by the end of 1992. The EC uses its resources to fund R&D programs that bring together firms and labs from different member states. For example, the EC's Strategic Program for Research and Development in Information Technologies (ESPRIT), originally set up in 1984, is a prime example of how the EC has provided the financial incentive for member firms and research laboratories to work crossnationally. To qualify for an ESPRIT research grant, applicants must show that their proposed project involves collaboration between firms or research centers in (at least) two or more member states. The goal is to provide the incentive needed for Europeanwide research and business collaboration to enable the Europeans to more fully exploit economies of scale in research, development, and production.

Other EC R&D programs include the Joint Research Center to promote scientific research, the research program in advanced technologies (RACE), basic research in industrial technologies (BRITE), and the European Research Cooperation Agency (Eureka). The EC's R&D programs, while they still represent a fraction of what member governments themselves spend on R&D, nonetheless point to the triumph of collective interests over state interests and to the logic of collaboration over fragmentation as the Europeans together forge a closer economic union to meet the challenges of international trade in the 1990s.

Do the Europeans Have a Global Conscience in the Area of Trade?

The response is generally affirmative with two exceptions: CAP export subsidies and NTBs. The EC is keen on responding to global needs. This is amply evidenced by its

- program for Generalized System of Preferences (GSP) which gives the world's poorest countries reduced access or duty-free access to the EC market without expecting reciprocal treatment;
- program of food aid, emergency aid, and development aid for a vast majority of the world's LDCs;
- association and cooperation accords that reduce import levies and provide financial, scientific, and development assistance for nearly all former colonies; and
- support for other regional groupings from Central America (Contadora Group) to South America (Andean Pact) to southern Africa (Southern African Development Cooperation Council) to the Persian Gulf (Gulf Cooperation Council) to South-East Asia (Association of South-East Asian Nations).

Behavior at the GATT

The EC record of global responsibility is in part marred by its farm subsidies and this is no where more evident than in the GATT where the EC is the most frequent target of complaints by other contracting parties. The EC's record in GATT dispute settlement procedures is a measure of its responsibility toward the global trade order. According to the United States International Trade Commission's study of the GATT during the period between 1948 and 1985, the EC was involved in 62 GATT cases, accounting for about 74 percent of all GATT and code panels, most often as the target of complaints.[13] Complaints against EC members concerned subsidies more frequently than any other type of trade measure. More than one-half of the complaints against the EC members (23 out of 42 complaints) have concerned its measures affecting trade in farm products. In the 1975-1984 period, 14 of the 17 complaints against the EC concerned its measures affecting farm trade.[14]

The Australians have led a coalition of farm exporting nations, the Group of 14, to press the EC to cease usage of farm subsidies. During negotiations to launch the Uruguay Round in the Fall of 1984, the Group of 14 called for the phased elimination of farm export subsidies. However, the EC, under French, Irish, Greek, and Spanish pressure, argued against an explicit reference to export subsidies and their removal over a fixed period of time. The EC argued that it was unfair to single out export subsidies since they were but one aspect of a broader problem, including US farm price supports. The EC feared a clear commitment on export subsidies would ultimately aim at eliminating the CAP, whose fundamental existence was not up for negotiation.

The EC did agree - a ray of hope on an otherwise gloomy horizon - to extend areas of discussion in the Uruguay Round to all direct and indirect subsidies and other measures affecting farm trade, but with no time table set. While this does not appear to be too much of a compromise to members of the Group of 14, it was an

13 *Review of the Effectiveness of Trade Dispute Settlement Under the GATT and the Tokyo Round of Agreements* (Washington, D.C.: United States International Trade Commission, Publication Number 1793, December 1985), pp. viii-ix.
14 Ibid.

unprecedented move on the EC's part and shows a rather grudging acceptance of global responsibility.

Despite the data on the EC as most frequent target of GATT disputes, the EC's role in the GATT has been indispensable for the GATT's continued existence. The EC was instrumental in contributing to the substantial reductions of industrial tariffs that have been achieved in previous GATT rounds.

Dairy from New Zealand and Sugar from the Lomé States

Two examples of the EC's global conscience concern benefits granted to New Zealand and the Lomé Convention states - at significant risks to the EC's own interests. Dairy products make a significant contribution to New Zealand's export earnings. The EC continued to permit certain New Zealand dairy imports into the British market on a preferential basis at reduced tariff rates after the UK acceded to the EC in 1973. This was done despite the EC's own excess dairy capacity and the high CAP costs associated with it. Surely, Britain was acting in its own interests to some degree, but the net effect of the EC action showed a capacity to address the needs of a nonmember. Another example of the EC's global conscience concerns sugar imports from the Lomé Convention states. The EC imports guaranteed amounts of sugar from the Lomé countries because of the importance of that export product to their economies. However, the EC does so at its own risk because it already has its own sugar mountain and must grapple with the high costs associated with it. Responsible actions such as these point to the triumph of global needs over more narrow state or regional interests.

Lomé Convention

The Lomé Convention's provisions for the stabilization of export earnings (STABEX) of 66 African, Caribbean, and Pacific (ACP) states, while still modest in monetary value, are the closest response of any of the developed states in addressing some of the basic needs of the Group-77 for more secure markets and guaranteed prices. In 1988, under the STABEX program, the EC processed 43 claims from the ACP states costing 803 million ECU, up from the cost of 255 million ECU in 1987. The real test of the EC's global commitment through the Lomé Convention came when the EC no longer insisted on reciprocal trade benefits for the CAP countries in the 1970s. The EC's commitment to guaranteed markets and prices, if only on a limited scale, is a testimony to its responsiveness to global needs and continues to be an unprecedented act of economic assistance in the capitalist world.

Enlargement

The decision to incorporate Spain and Portugal into the EC at high internal economic, social, institutional, and political costs was a triumph of global needs (at least those of the wider Atlantic Alliance) over state interests. Incorporating the Iberian states helped solidify political and economic stability in those countries and helped secure Europe's exposed southern flank. Enlargement strengthened the Western Alliance and contributed to the maintenance of a balance of power between East and West in the Mediterranean Basin. Enlargement was a method the EC could use as a civilian power to contribute to peaceful change in countries where political violence and nondemocratic procedures were more the rule than the exception.[15]

Mediterranean Policy

The EC's Mediterranean Policy, its premier foreign policy, shows the EC's commitment to playing a civilian role in an unstable area of the world.[16] Through tariff preferences, industrial free trade incentives, technical assistance, and other development aid the EC helps to stabilize a region that in the past has been prone to armed conflict.

EC Development Policy

The EC's foreign development policy is not limited to aiding the Mediterranean and the ACP states. The EC grants GSP benefits (tariff cuts) to all developing countries, which points to the EC's sense of responsibility in meeting global needs, although critics claim the benefits could be more generous for agriculture. The European Investment Bank offers loans to nonmembers for

---

15 Roy H. Ginsberg, "The European Community and the Mediterranean," in Juliet Lodge, ed., *Institutions and Policies of the European Community* (London: Pinter Publishers 1983), pp. 154-168.
16 Ibid.

development purposes. Food aid and transportation aid to carry that food to its destination form part of the EC's ongoing efforts to assist the neediest countries as well as efforts to meet emergency situations. The EC is the world's third largest food contributor to the World Food Program.

Regional Integration Outside Europe

The EC lends financial and political support to other regional groups in the world as it sees itself as a model for what can be achieved by cooperation on a regional basis.

Do the Europeans' Collective Interests Intersect with Global Needs?

The response is affirmative in some areas. For example, the Mediterranean Policy serves the EC's own commercial and geopolitical interests (the Basin states are major customers for EC exports and the vast bulk of EC imports travel through Mediterranean sea routes) as much as it serves the developmental needs of the Basin countries (the Basin states are heavily dependent on the EC market for trade and aid). The Lomé Convention serves the EC's interests in expanding markets in these countries and in maintaining influence in former colonial areas as much as it benefits the recipients in their quest for market shares and more secure prices in Europe. Working in the GATT rounds of Multilateral Tariff Negotiations (MTNs) to reduce industrial tariffs is as much in the EC's interest as it is in the interest of the global (capitalist) trade order. The EC has the most to gain from trade liberalization and the most to lose from trade protectionism given its virtual domination of world trade.

The goals of the Single European Act to achieve a fuller customs union free of internal barriers to trade can be said to intersect with global needs. Should the EC achieve its goals, nonmembers exporting to the EC will be able to base their production on a uniform set of standards rather than on those of twelve separate states, thus cutting their costs. A customs union free of many of the border controls that raise costs of doing business in Europe should also help nonmember firms. With a higher rate of growth fueled by the 1992 plan, the EC market should expand in size, opening up opportunities for nonmember trade and investment in the EC. A more economically prosperous Europe might be in a stronger financial position to aid developing countries, in a stronger financial position to provide for more of its own security needs and thus increase its independence from both the United States and the Soviet Union, and in a stronger political position to assume more global responsibilites in managing international relations in general.

Finally, the EC Commission appears to have a two-pronged strategy for realizing a freer and larger internal market that intersects with global needs. When a new round of MTNs was proposed by the United States in 1982, Japan quickly welcomed it, but the EC appeared reticent until 1984. This reticence was due in part to French fear of having to cope with more nonmember imports of high-tech products that had already come to dominate the European market. How could the EC enter a new round of MTNs when its own trading house was not yet in order? When the EC Commission confirmed its support for launching a new round, it did so to diffuse global criticism of its farm policy, soothe protectionist pressure in the US Congress and elsewhere, and act responsibly toward the world trade community. However, the EC Commission also supported the new round as (A) an external stimulus to hasten internal market reform by pressuring member governments with the prospect of more import competition that would result after the conclusion of a new GATT round; and (B) an attempt to buy time in the long-drawn out GATT negotiations to reform and thus strengthen the internal market to cope with new foreign competition. If the new round was not to end until the early 1990s, its effects would not be felt in Europe until after the turn of the century, thus buying the EC more time to reform while it appeared to the outside world to be committed to trade liberalization.

SUMMARY

This chapter discussed the EC's internal menace, state-sponsored NTBs that mock the Treaty's spirit and letter, stifle growth, and demarcate the EC from the outside world. The internal menace is a political problem that will change in piecemeal rather than radical fashion. The EC goal of eliminating NTBs by 31 December 1992 - while deadlines are politically imperative for recalcitrant actors - is much too ambitious. Surely the process of political change cannot occur so quickly given the nature of democratic governments, which come and go and whose priorities and perceptions shift, and the development of unforeseen exogenous events, such as recession or military conflict. The key to understanding the dynamic behind the 1992 plan is to realize that the deadline of 31 December 1992 is not very meaningful. The achievement of a fully unified customs union is a process that predated and will post-date 1992 so long as the political will remains sufficiently strong to suppress or accommodate individual interests that seek refuge behind the barriers that represent the politics of the past.

The chapter also touched on the EC's other primary occupation: the external challenge posed by the US, Japan, and the NICs who dominate the EC market for many high-tech products. There are twelve member governments wasting state resources for R&D geared toward the national rather than the European market. The member governments are duplicating each other's efforts. Their own markets are too small to cope with technological change and the threat of import competition. ESPRIT is one step in the right direction, but its limited endowment still pales in comparison to the ongoing efforts of the individual member governments to promote their own R&D. The EC market will continue to be dominated by high-tech industries from nonmembers if members do not rally around the spirit and letter of the Single European Act and its goal of achieving a freer internal market.

Yet another external challenge has been discussed in this chapter, that of the demands the global order places on the EC for market access, development assistance, and participation in the management and resolution of international problems. Between 1958-85, the EC took 480 foreign policy actions, responding to the needs of the world community and pursuing its own self-styled interests.[17] There is no reason to believe that the EC will not build on this record of international activity in the years ahead as the reinvigorated internal market will play an even larger role in the world economy. EC foreign policy activity will likely expand exponentially with the growth of the internal market.

---

17 Ibid.

One of the ironies of the EC is that although it promises a free internal market, the individual states will continue to compete with one another for shares in that market. EC states both cooperate and compete with one another with such mixed results as NTBs that mock cooperation and ESPRIT that encourages cooperation.

The EC pursues not just member interests but collective and global interests as well. Outside the CAP and the NTBs, the EC has attempted to respond to the needs of the global order in general and of specific trading partners in particular. The EC's responsible actions in this regard are unprecedented in the history of international cooperation. The paradox of the EC today is that it makes contributions to the global trade order through responsible acts, but is fundamentally designed to be demarcated from the global trade order to derive benefits not available to most outsiders. Yet the EC's record also shows the potential of a group of states to rise above the individual interests of its members to achieve broader purposes, either at the collective regional level (enlargement) or at the international level (Lomé Convention).

Finally, this chapter attempted to show that by the mid-1980s two developments came together that changed the direction of European integration: (A) political acceptance of failed internal trade policies and the political commitment to reverse them; and (B) global pressures on the EC to act as a unified actor to meet the demands of international competition and to meet international needs for access to European resources and to the European market. The confluence of the internal menace and the external challenge produced in large part the Single European Act and the quest to finish what the Europeans had begun in the 1950s.

4

West European Security Policy: Between Assertiveness and Dependence

Reinhardt Rummel

INTRODUCTION

Since the late 1940s, the fundamental reason for the quest to achieve European unity has been to help establish a better system of peaceful worldwide interaction between states. "La communauté elle-même n'est qu'une étappe vers les formes d'organisation du monde de demain." This is the last line of the Mémoires of Jean Monnet, regarded by many to be the "father" of West European integration. The post-World War II generation in West Europe has worked for the goal of peaceful cooperation. The record is both rich and modest.

The outcome of European integration is rich in two respects. First, it transcended the intra-European war, which had produced enmity as well as distrust, while gradually shaping an economic and a foreign policy as well as a security consensus among former enemies. Certainly, West Europe continues to be a heterogeneous collection of states with conflicting interests and policies, but, nowadays, disputes among them tend to be defused by peaceful rather than violent means - the perennial Irish/British and Turkish/Greek conflicts notwithstanding.

Secondly, the European integration effort has improved the capability of West Europe to identify common interests and to realize them through the process of international bargaining. National interests have been "Europeanized" in order to strengthen West

Europe in world affairs and achieve the maximum outcome for each member state. This has been largely the case via the European Community (EC) in the field of trade[1] and, less extensively, via the European Political Cooperation (EPC) in foreign policy matters[2]. Military security has been assured in the wider framework of the Atlantic Alliance; contributions by the European member states within NATO have helped guarantee far-reaching Western security.

The record of West European integration seems to be mediocre, however, when it comes to evaluating Europe's ability to shoulder those worldwide responsibilities which go beyond more narrowly defined regional or local interests. What does West Europe contribute to meet and overcome global socio-economic imbalances, such as ecological disasters, poverty, belligerent conflict, and political coercion via military means? West Europe has cautiously and indirectly assumed worldwide responsibilities, but, given its material resources, the EC obviously could achieve more.[3]

Certainly, there are enough reasons for a mainly introverted European Community: enlargement from six to twelve members, institutional and financial problems, alarming unemployment rates, the project of the Single Market by the end of 1992, etc. Yet, internal problems aside, the Community has done fairly well in international relations. The EC might not have squarely met "global needs," but it can claim to have worked toward that end, directly and indirectly. Doesn't the process of the Conference on Security and Cooperation in Europe (CSCE), which the Europeans have actively kept alive during trying times of the Cold War, help balance the still dangerously antagonistic character of East-West relations? Wasn't the Lomé Convention founded with global needs in mind? Doesn't the European plea for an international peace conference to resolve the Palestinian-Israeli-Arab conflict have as a goal to provide more stability to a region in unrest?

---

1 For a detailed assessment of the Community's trade policy see Roy H. Ginsberg's chapter in this volume.

2 For a detailed assessment of the EPC's foreign policy see Christopher Hill's chapter in this volume and A. Pijpers, E. Regelsberger and W.Wessels, eds., *European Political Cooperation in the 1980s* (Dordrecht: Martinus Nijhoff 1987).

3 Christopher Layton, *A Step Beyond Fear* (Great Britain: Federal Trust for Education and Research 1989).

Granted, these activities are not prompted by European altruism. Rather they follow an enlightened definition of European self-interest. This, of course, is the key to the methodological question what are "global needs?" Furthermore, by whom are such needs defined or claimed? In the sector of security, the question of "global needs versus national self-interest" raises a particular difficulty. Controversy has always existed between East and West as well as between North and South over the definition of objective needs to guarantee a balanced and stable security system. For example, the acquisition of a specific arms system could be as destabilizing as the decision to dismantle it. To assign more ships to the Persian-Arabian Gulf could be interpreted by some as a stabilizing measure. Yet, by others it would be regarded as pouring oil on the fire. These examples show that rules and norms have to be commonly agreed upon before one can discuss whether global security needs are met by a country or a group of countries.

The following reflections consider whether the group of West European states has demonstrated a new level of assertiveness by successfully reconciling national security interests and global security needs within an effort of regional cooperation.

BURDEN-SHARING IN THE ALLIANCE: A "GLOBAL NEED?"

NATO has guaranteed the peace in Europe. Under American leadership the Atlantic Alliance has maintained military strength, to counter any antagonistic forces, and political flexibility, so as to take advantage of opportunities for cooperation with potential adversaries. Have the West European NATO members contributed their fair share to this achievement or have they taken the path of acquiring "cheap security?" The United States Congress has long reproached the West European allies for an insufficient contribution to the collective Western defense. Yet, the West European governments have always felt that they actually meet their obligations. In fact, it is very complicated and dubious to make clearcut assessments or even numerical calculations.[4] Rather it would seem appropriate to tackle the question by looking at some of the overall political trends, behaviors and policies of the Alliance partners and thus try to answer the question of how West Europe responds to needs within NATO and whether these actions meet global demands.

While it was appropriate forty years ago for Atlantic nations to join together to collectively defend the West against the Soviet threat, joint defense does not necessarily mean that the United States should always carry the largest share of the burden within the alliance. Thus far, Americans and Europeans have profited equally from the transatlantic security structure, although lately this assumption is subject to some dispute.[5] Furthermore, there are some signs of change which might lead to a gradual restructuring of NATO.[6] Europeans feel that they will have to take on more of the common defense burden in order to gain more influence in assuring their own security. Will this mean a contribution to meet "global needs?"

One set of reasons for the new attitude in West Europe derives from changes within the United States. Secular shifts of American preoccupation from the Atlantic Basin to the Pacific Rim have been evident since Ronald Reagan entered and left the White House. Transatlantic trade disputes, coupled with huge US trade and budget deficits and the relatively low percentage of budgetary spending earmarked for defense in most European countries, set the stage for demands from Washington, and especially from the United States Congress, that the allies should increase their share of the common burden. The popular argument is that 24O million Americans do not understand why they should defend more than 32O million Europeans against 28O million Russians. Congressmen have tried to warn the Europeans by proposing the withdrawal of substantial numbers of American troops currently stationed in West Europe. Europeans can rely on the maintenance of American forces at

---

4 Lawrence Korb, "Measuring U.S. Contribution to NATO Defense," in Stanley R. Sloan, ed., *NATO in the 1990s* (Washington: Pergamon-Brassey's 1989), pp. 193 - 208.

5 See the writings of Earl Ravenal and Melvyn Krauss.

6 The school of devolutionist thinkers in the US who want to reshape NATO by transfering more responsibility and leadership to European allies is growing ever since Henry Kissinger made his proposals in the mid-eighties.

existing levels for a while longer. It is in America's self-interest to keep substantial US forces in West Europe as long as the Soviets continue to maintain massive forces in East Europe. However, Europeans can already feel the longterm pressure for change.[7]

The other set of reasons for this new attitude in West Europe is due to widespread dissatisfaction and impatience among the Europeans themselves. People in Europe demand more influence in decision-making on security matters; they increasingly dislike their dependence on American guidance. The popular version of this impression was demonstrated by the peace movements of this decade. The message is clear: Europe must not become a (nuclear) battlefield! But European governments, especially political conservatives, also questioned Washington's wisdom on strategic concepts such as the SDI fantasy, America's interventionist answers to state-backed terrorism, or President Reagan's arms control policy at Reykjavik in 1986. In each of these cases Europeans were frustrated because, while American (and Soviet) policies have tangible repercussions on West Europe, the governments and peoples of the region have only limited ways and means available by which to influence such policies.

Both sets of reasons, American and European, express a large responsibility which can be seen as going beyond self-centered interests. In fact, Washington may overexert itself by single-handedly policing all the critical regions of the world and by guaranteeing the global balance vis-à-vis the Soviets. But who else can check Soviet agressions or interregional conflict escalation? The Europeans can show their degree of willingness to play an international role and discharge the Americans, in at least one region, namely Europe. Moreover, West European nations can bring more of their own capabilities and talents to bear in East-West relations. America may be strong on the superpower level, but West Europe maintains a special relationship with East European countries. The regional and neighborly role exerted in a global spirit, and the tacit or openly developed concept of a division of labor within the Western alliance, is as important as any worldwide task.

---

7 This change is a complex mixture of developments in the United States, Western Europe and, most recently, also in the Soviet bloc. For an extensive analysis see Stanley R. Sloan, ed., *NATO in the 1990s*, op.cit.

The conclusion is that West European nations may use the vehicle of cooperation and integration to work for a Western security concept which will become more balanced. Such a concept will therefore serve national as well as global needs; stability in East-West relations will foster peaceful change and economic as well as political reform in Eastern countries. Pessimists and critics of this concept, while granting the ubiquitous desire within West Europe for more assertiveness, do not believe that Europeans will give up the relatively convenient situation of "cheap security," provided for them by Washington's extended nuclear deterrence, in exchange for more political risks and financial burdens. These skeptical analysts claim to be the better realists. They paint a frightful picture of European nations, in a half-hearted attempt to Europeanize NATO, which produces more talk than substance and destroys the texture of the Alliance.

WHO PROFITS FROM THE EUROPEANIZATION OF DEFENSE?

In more or less periodic intervals, European governments have tried to organize their own defense through security cooperation. This process began with the Western European Union (WEU) and the European Defense Community (EDC) in the early fifties. It continued with the Fouchet Plans in the sixties and the establishment of EPC in the seventies. In the 1980s, attempts to reactivate moribund institutions, such as the WEU, are noteworthy as are the following measures: an intensification of Franco-German military cooperation, a security component to EPC, new tasks for Eurogroup, more use of the Independent European Program Group (IEPG). These actions foster the impression of a multifaceted, desperate struggle for more European identity and input in dealing with security issues.[8] Yet, are Europeans "producing" more defense today than they did twenty or even forty years ago?

In historical perspective, the challenge to effectively cope with the Soviet threat has increased in scope and complexity. Europe has

---

8 The momentum which exists to define a West European security identity is impressively illustrated by the activity of the European Parliament. See Thomas Grunert's chapter in this volume.

managed to adapt to these tasks. Together with the American allies, Europeans have successfully worked to deter war on the continent and to escape from Moscow's political pressure via military means. It is hard to judge whether (institutionalized) European cooperation has had a considerable share in this success and, if so, to what extent. But even if the share is insignificant, this result would not automatically determine future developments.

Franco-German military cooperation[9] is certainly a step toward a more cohesive defense posture in West Europe, and, in the Alliance at large, but the need for this effort derives from early Gaullism in France. Thus, it is more a repentance for past sins than an overt step toward a common European identity in the field of defense. Since the beginning of the 1980s, Paris is particularly worried about the Federal Republic which is perceived as susceptible to Soviet initiatives. France wants to anchor Germany in the West via closer security cooperation. Moreover, limited financial means and priorities for nuclear, as well as space oriented military systems, have forced French strategists to compromise on maximum independence and individual defense strategies. The new degree of flexibility in Paris is not substantial enough to speak of it as progressing toward *de facto* reintegration of France into NATO. Nor has a concept been devised which would include France in a military union in West Europe which, in turn, would integrate into the Atlantic Alliance. Yet, France and Germany have become actively aware of intra-European heterogeneity, and are now prepared to debate internal differences in order to find solutions which transcend them.[10]

Franco-German understanding is a major precondition for any further attempt to intensify intra-European security cooperation. Since 1970, the EC countries have established EPC, an intergovernmental concertation on foreign policy. The Single European Act of 1987, a treaty among the Twelve which provides the framework for cooperation in both internal economics and external political affairs, does not allow for joint defense. Instead, it

---

9 For a full account of the developments and implications of Franco-German military cooperation, see the chapters of David Garnham and Peter Schmidt in this volume.

10 See David Yost, La France et la sécurité europénne: un point de vue américain, in *Défense nationale*, October 1989, pp. 39-56.

encourages activities on "the economic and political aspects of security." The member countries have used EPC extensively in East-West relations, especially during the sensitive periods of the CSCE in Helsinki, Madrid and Vienna, but also for more specialized all-European dialogues such as those concerning human rights in Berne and confidence building measures in Stockholm. Both the Berne and Stockholm meetings finished with mixed results in 1986. The EPC contributed, together with the group of the neutral and non-aligned (NNA) European states, to the further development of cooperative elements within East-West relations. These states' initial assumption is that they can best live in an atmosphere of East-West détente.

To a greater extent than the United States, West European countries believed, and still believe, that to concentrate on the military dimension of the East-West conflict is a dangerous impasse which does not provide enough room for policy and compromise. This philosophy led West Europeans to stress the more comprehensive approach to East-West relations as elaborated in the 1967 Harmel Report. In the early eighties, their attitude caused major transatlantic divergencies, when a number of sensitive subjects appeared on the international security agenda: the buildup of Soviet SS-2Os; the Soviet invasion and occupation of Afghanistan; the (perceived) implication of Soviet presence in critical regions like the Persian-Arabian Gulf and Central America; the crackdown on the Polish reform movement; and the issue of Western sanctions against the Soviet Union.

By stressing their particular point of view, and risking divergencies within the Atlantic Alliance, did the Europeans act in a selfish and Euro-centric manner? Or did they keep the wider transregional interests in mind? Were Europeans right in following through with their position despite the partial, and temporary, nature of the adverse American view? Were they, by doing so, inviting the Soviets to drive wedges in the unity of the Alliance and thus destabilize the security framework of the West? It is not easy to find objective answers to these questions. The Europeans felt that during the first half of the eighties East-West relations needed a moderating voice to avoid further escalation. At one point during the superpower confrontation over Afghanistan, then German Chancellor Helmut Schmidt expressed the West European view when he referred to the pre-war constellation of 1914. Others -

mainly in the United States - evoked Munich of 1938 to express their attitude vis-à-vis Soviet behavior.

The crux of the matter seems to be that both approaches have their validity. History shows that a lack of escalation control can be as dangerous as an appeasement policy. A decision as to which of the two, escalation control or deterrence, is the more urgent task depends on a particular situation, but it is a wise and good practice to have both at the West's disposal in an "institutionalized" fashion.

The same methodological approach applies to the question which was debated in the second half of the eighties; namely, how should the West cope with the Gorbachev challenge? The problem here was, and still is, to make a meaningful distinction between the intentions for change in the Soviet Union and the reality of change. Most of the projections in the field of arms control have not yet materialized. The new doctrinal orientation toward a concept of defensive defense remains basically an intellectual construct in the Soviet military, while the military superiority of the USSR in numbers of weapons and soldiers, resupply and recruit possibilities remain almost unchanged. Most West European countries, especially the Federal Republic of Germany, have taken surface and peripheral changes too seriously, believing them to be more substantial than they are. In contrast, the United States has been inclined to underestimate the amount of change which has occured in the Soviet Union and in East Europe. Therefore, the task for Americans, and Europeans alike, is to define the appropriate conditions under which advantage can be taken of opportunities for change in East-West relations.[11]

Although EPC shares in the cooperative part of East-West relations, the responsibilities for the military balance (and the military forces) remain largely relegated to NATO. Despite growing British and French nuclear forces, it continues to be the United States which guarantees extended nuclear protection for West Europe. Even in the conventional component of the Western defense inventory, the US forces are indispensable for the defense of West Europe. Yet, a slight change has to be mentioned in this context because it might have some implications on the "global needs" question. In the mid-1980s, the Western European Union, founded

---

11 Christoph Royen, *Osteuropa: Reformen und Wandel* (Baden-Baden: Nomos Verlagsgesellschaft 1988)

in 1954 as a first step toward integrating the Federal Republic into the Western defense system, was reactivated. Given the limited competence of EPC in defense affairs, France and Germany, the main proponents of the WEU initiative, wanted to use the forum of the Seven (in 1988, with the accession of Spain and Portugal, the Nine) to discuss all aspects of security: the military balance; détente; arms control; the assessment of the Soviet threat; and Moscow's behavior in the Third World. WEU suited Paris' desire for a Europeanization of security policy without the price of reintegration into the military command structure of NATO. Bonn aimed to increase public support for Europe's role in Western security policy. Public debate in some of the European NATO member countries about the dependence on US military guarantees caused the German federal government to make better use of European institutions. More European-related concerns were introduced into the Alliance in order to oppose those anti-American attitudes present in some West European publics.

Until present, WEU has been a forum for discussion rather than a decision-making body. By producing elaborate reports on long-term security issues and discussing all major defense and arms control items on the current agenda, WEU is gradually becoming a clearing-house for strategic thinking among the West Europeans parallel to NATO. Atlantic-oriented members like Great Britain and West Germany try to ease confrontation with Washington. Paris, in contrast, is inclined to use the forum to underline differences between West Europe and the United States. Intra-European differences have weakened the consensus of the Seven/Nine on such demanding challenges as President Reagan's SDI concept, the assessment of the Reykjavik summit, the Western negotiating position for the Conventional Forces in Europe (CFE) talks in Vienna or the decision on the Follow-On To Lance (FOTL) systems.

WEU, like the EPC and Franco-German military cooperation, is trying to bring about a security consensus on a level above the mere national self-interest. From a West European perspective, these platforms are useful instruments to strengthen the Western Alliance via more assertiveness. The view from the Alliance "periphery" may be less positive. Countries on NATO's Northern and Southern flank often feel excluded from the "club" in the Center. Norway, Denmark, Greece and Turkey are not members of the WEU. As previously mentioned, Portugal and Spain have only recently joined the organization. Norway and Turkey do not even belong to the EPC. They not only feel that their particular security problems are not considered, but they also claim that the scope and quality of security cooperation among the core group of European NATO allies is substantially diminished because of the narrow geographical and strategic perspective of this group. They detect mainly destabilizing effects which flow from a two-tiered West European security community. WEU is, in their view, discriminating against them and not meeting "global needs."[12]

Many Americans perceive these Europeanization efforts as a danger rather than a support to the cohesiveness of the Alliance. Despite some successful efforts in security cooperation, such as the mine-sweeping operation in the Persian Gulf in 1987 which was organized with the help of WEU, West Europe is not regarded to be a distinct military actor.[13] When it comes to using military force as an instrument to counter a particular threat, most West European nations are extremely reluctant.[14] Many West Europeans want to be influential in world politics but they deny any ambition to become a superpower by implying that this would inevitably lead to the collective build-up and (mis)use of a huge military power potential.[15] Most Americans appreciate only "real action" on the part of West Europeans (such as the Gulf mine-sweeping operation) as opposed to "just talk."

To the extent that the West Europeans have achieved some security cooperation, it is either neglected or overestimated on the American side. Overestimation occurs particularly when West Europeans meet, consult on a security issue and come up with a position which is not shared by Washington. In these cases, many Americans perceive the Europeans to be "ganging-up" against the United States. They regard the activities of EPC and WEU as being

---

12 For an account of the diversity of views which exists within Western Europe see Robert Rudney and Luc Reychler, eds., *European Security Beyond the Year 2 000* (New York: Praeger Publishers 1988).

13 Alfred Pijpers, The Twelve Out-of-area: A Civil Power in an Uncivil World? in A. Pijpers, E. Regelsberger and W.Wessels, eds., *European Political Cooperation in the 1980s,* (Dordrecht: Martinus Nijhoff 1987), pp. 143 -165.

14 Reinhardt Rummel, "Political Perceptions and Military Responses to Out-of-Area Challenges," in J. Coffey and G. Bonvicini, eds., *The Atlantic Alliance and the Middle East* (London: Macmillan Press 1989), pp. 193-226.

15 Ibid.

anti-Americanism in disguise or as an easy way to circumvent the harsh realities and burdens of NATO. In their eyes, Europeanization is a sign of weakness rather than of strength, an element which introduces undue complication and irritation among the allies. Furthermore, it undermines the stability of the Western defense and transmits misleading signals to the Soviets. In brief, Americans reproach the Europeans with inviting the Soviets to exploit institutionalized diversities in the West.

Such impressions and evaluations cannot be altogether brushed aside. Right or wrong, they are part of the American perception of West European dynamics and, therefore, an important factor in the struggle for the most efficient structure of the Western defense institutions. This involves comparing the traditional hegemonic structure of NATO to a future twin pillar concept. Which of the two models produces the best result in terms of security and East-West stability? This question cannot be answered in the abstract; nor can it be answered appropriately in the context of this chapter. But it is at the heart of the issue of who defines "global needs" for NATO.[16]

The organization of Western security has to respond to the type of challenge which comes from the East. If the Eastern bloc is dominated by Soviet centralism, does NATO have to be organized likewise to successfully compete? Or should the West profit from its systemic advantages and make use of pluralism and equal partnership to deal with the Soviet empire? Which of the following two models guarantees more East-West stability and enables more peaceful change: a bipolar hegemonic superpower system or a mixed pluralistic/hegemonistic system? The Europeans know that for the time being they simply do not have the means or the influence to be able to choose between these alternatives, but they can work to broaden their options and, thus, to ameliorate the present system.

---

16 Paul Cook, *Toward a "European Pillar?" Enhanced European Security Cooperation and Implications for U.S. Policy* (Washington: Center for Strategic and International Studies 1988).

BEYOND CONTAINMENT: A NEW GLOBAL NEED FOR WEST EUROPEAN SECURITY COOPERATION

The post-Reykjavik constellation, in which both superpowers embarked on a substantially cooperative course, provides the West Europeans with challenge as well as opportunity. The present situation is unique in that the pillars of postwar stability are shaking. Some West Europeans are looking for a shelter, others try to restructure the Western Alliance as well as the East-West system of security. For four decades European stability has rested on four conditions:

- nuclear deterrence
- the United States' guarantee over West Europe
- the orthodoxy of the Communist rule in the Soviet Union
- the equation made between Europe's division and its stability

Today, all of these conditions are in flux. Mikhail Gorbachev's declarations and actions have evoked hopes, and fears, of a thaw within the Soviet system, with all its consequences for a stable European order. If the Soviet Union were really to change, would the Eastern satellites follow as well as the world's other socialist countries? Could all of this transcend Yalta or revitalize a superpower condominium?

A few years ago, people in Europe voiced the slogan "Let Europe be Europe!" Today, Europe needs more than slogans. The structure of the European order will continue to be dominated by the US and the USSR. But in a new East-West environment this dominance is becoming less and less axiomatic. In the on-going process of economic, political and military change in Europe, the European countries, East and West, acquire more room to influence the nature of intra-European relations. West European security cooperation will have to adapt to this new challenge. It has to focus more intensively on the cooperative side of East-West relations. While maintaining the present military balance, and gradually reducing it to accomodate a lower level of military forces, West European nations have to go beyond containment. It is necessary to initiate a wider range of confidence building measures, proposals for doctrinal change and arms control negotiations. These are the new

new global needs of security and defense in Europe which West Europe must fulfill.

Reflecting on the last forty years of stability and peace in Europe, it seems hazardous to renounce or alter the successful security structure already in place. On the other hand, the price for this long period of peace is the suppression and lack of self-determination in East Europe. Moreover, the question can be raised whether the mutual East-West nuclear deterrence displaced the East-West conflict to other areas in the world. From this perspective, regional stability becomes a major component of the global needs of security. Consequently, West European security cooperation must be improved to meet these demands.

To remove totalitarianism and suppression and to foster peaceful change in East Europe requires a new type of economic and political investment and cooperation among the group of West European countries in their collective foreign policy. Some of the experience which West Europe has had with its Mediterranean policy in the last fifteen years may be applicable in this regard. The Mediterranean policy, although largely built on economic and political development, was certainly designed as a longterm security measure. Military dictatorships have been turned into liberal democracies. Countries such as Spain, Portugal and Greece have become members or associates of the core group of the West European community system. Turkey, Cyprus and Malta are associated with the EC. What should a West European *Ostpolitik* look like? The Heads of State and Government of the Twelve have developed a plan during their European Council meeting in Rhodes, Greece, in December 1989.[17] Will they follow suit?

One of the obstacles to the implemention of a West European *Ostpolitik* is the divergent national interests among the Twelve concerning practical measures. Most EC member states are still reluctant to transfer a wider range of external economic relations to the Community in order to deal with the need in East Europe and the Soviet Union. With the joint declaration of June 1988[18] on the establishment of official relations between the European Economic Community and the Council for Mutual Economic Assistance (CMEA), Brussels has paved the way for substantial trade

---

17 See the declaration of the European Council in the Annex.
18 See the Joint Declaration of EC and CMEA in the Annex.

agreements with individual East European countries. But the EC member states continue to regard economic cooperation - an important instrument of East-West relations at this juncture of the reform process in East Europe - to be part of their national prerogatives. This attitude may well be characterized as driven by self-interest, but it may also serve the needs of East European countries. It remains an open question, whether a Community-based instrument for economic cooperation with East Europe and the Soviet Union would achieve better results.

To respond to the "Gorbachev revolution," West Europe must show prudence, firmness and imagination. Only then can it contemplate the inevitable end of the postwar order with serenity and participate in establishing a new one. The more the Europeans are able to assure their own security via meeting East-West and, subsequently, global needs, the stronger they will become.

CONCLUSIONS

Despite current impressive efforts to reduce military arsenals and manpower in East and West, Washington and Moscow will continue to be the leading powers in any future strategic stalemate situation. West Europe's dependence on the United States for strategic protection may be redefined, but it will not be fundamentally changed. Such dependence is not without its comforts for West Europe. It may even be tempting for some of the European NATO members to rely too much on the leader in the Alliance and to neglect their own fair share in the political, military and financial costs of collective defense.

On the other hand, West European countries want to increase their influence on security decisions in Europe as well as in other critical regions of the world. This struggle for asssertiveness has to be evaluated, however, on the basis of Europe's strategic dependence on the United States.

Nevertheless, the West Europeans have brought some of their particular power potential to bear on international relations. They have not only contributed to the maintainance of the military balance, but also to managing East-West interdependence and to enhedging ideological and military polarization. Some of the structural stability measures undertaken by the EC in the Mediterranean may even be regarded as a model for shaping East-West relations. West Europe has explored ways to reconcile national with regional cooperation while responding to global security needs. The policy of economic and political stabilization in the Mediterranean has been partly successful. In the 1990s this model of security building has to be adapted to the task of developing organic relations with East Europe. West Europe must be an active partner in the team designing the new architecture of security on the European continent.

PART II: West Europe's Particular Contribution to Western Defense

The appropriate means to establish a West European identity in the sphere of security is the focus of Part II. Institutional and bilateral links which influence the formulation of West European security policy are explored. The need for West Europeans to jointly define their security perceptions vis-à-vis the superpowers, as well as actors in other regions of the world such as the Middle East, is analyzed within the context of the overall contribution of West Europe to the Atlantic Alliance. The Europeanization of security policy is considered in various fora.

In the framework of the European Community, *Thomas Grunert* details the work of the European Parliament's (EP) Sub-Committee on Security and Disarmament in order to illustrate a willingness to incorporate the security dimension into the West European integration process. Franco-German bilateral initiatives are analyzed from an American viewpoint by *David Garnham*, who maintains that Franco-German security relations could be at the center of an eventual European Defense Community which encompasses the other members of the Western European Union (WEU). *Peter Schmidt* views the Franco-German relationship from a European perspective and concludes that, while progress has been achieved since the 1960s, the Soviet foreign policy of Mikhail Gorbachev may hinder further Franco-German initiatives. *Reinhardt Rummel* views the establishment of a West European challenge assessment unit in the light of provoking a more realistic transatlantic debate about issues of East-West security since the West Europeans would draw conclusions about the Soviet threat based on their own data sources.

Given the many West European initiatives in the security field, which include bilateral and intergovernmental (Franco-German) cooperation as well as multilateral (WEU) and supranational (EP) efforts, unity of political action is difficult to achieve. A proliferation of institutions slows down the decision-making process and makes coordination of procedures and goals less likely in the short term. Although Part II focuses on the aims of West European defense and arms control cooperation, there are factors of East-West cooperation, such as between the West German SPD and the East German SED, or the development of a West European Ostpolitik, which also have a significant impact on the "Europeanization" of defense issues.

5

Establishing Security Policy in the European Community*

Thomas Grunert

HISTORY

After the failure of the Pleven Plan for a European Defense Community (EDC) in 1954 and the rejection of the Fouchet Plans in 1962, which envisaged a joint defense policy in the context of political union,[1] there was little effort to introduce a security aspect into the institutional structure of the European Community.

It was not until the 1970s that there were once again tentative attempts to revive the idea of the European Community as the vehicle of a future joint foreign and security policy. With this idea in mind, European Political Cooperation (EPC) was created in 1970 as an instrument to coordinate some aspects of foreign policy. This has since done a great deal to stimulate the fusion of the Community member states into a political community. From the start, Political Cooperation was taken to include security elements. This view was clearly reflected in the report on European Union written in 1975 by the Belgian Prime Minister, Leo Tindemans, for the European

---

* This chapter reflects the personal view of the author and not necessarily the official opinion of the European Parliament.

1 Cf. K. Kaiser and P. Lellouche, eds., *Deutsch-Französische Sicherheitspolitik* (Bonn: Europa Union Verlag 1986), pp. 6 f.

Council.[2] The report observes that security policy must fall within the purview of the European Union. Consequently, the Tindemans Report urges the Community member states to conduct a regular exchange of views about West Europe's particular security problems.

This call was not ignored in the years that followed as the London Report on European Political Cooperation testifies. This report, adopted in October 1981 by the Foreign Ministers of the (then) ten member states, clearly states that the flexible and pragmatic procedure which had previously made it possible to consider the political aspects of security within the framework of EPC should be retained in the future.

The Heads of State and Government of the member states confirmed the Community's security mandate by signing the Solemn Declaration on the European Union on 19 June 1983. The document on which this declaration is based, known as the Genscher-Colombo Initiative, is an expression of the desire to take steps, within the framework of EPC, to coordinate the positions of the member states on the political and economic aspects of security.

With the entry into force of the Single European Act (SEA), designed to reform the treaties establishing the European Communities, in July 1987, the twelve member states of the European Community are now formally committed to giving their attention to cooperation in the sphere of security policy. Thus, it is stressed in the preamble of the SEA that the signatories undertake to act with consistency and solidarity in order to more effectively protect their common interests and make their own contribution to the preservation of international peace and security.

In order to achieve this self-imposed goal, the contracting parties declare their readiness to coordinate their positions more closely on the political and economic aspects of security and to jointly ensure that the technological and industrial conditions necessary for the security of the Twelve are maintained. The importance of close cooperation on security matters for the process of European integration itself is openly acknowledged by the contracting parties when they emphasize that this cooperation is most likely to promote the development of a European identity in foreign policy.

---

2 *EC Bulletin*, Annex 1/76 (Doc. 481/75).

THE EUROPEAN PARLIAMENT: A DRIVING FORCE FOR EUROPEAN DEFENSE COOPERATION

As early as April 1973, the European Parliament (EP) adopted a resolution on political cooperation and the political unification of Europe, on the basis of a report drawn up on behalf of the Political Affairs Committee.[3] The core of this resolution is the declaration that "in practice cooperation in the field of foreign policy can hardly ever be separated from defense and security policy."[4]

In 1975 the European Parliament took fresh steps to promote cooperation in matters of security policy. On the basis of the report on European Union, Parliament adopted a resolution clearly expressing the intention to stregthen cooperation in the field of security and to include security policy in the powers of a future European Union.[5]

Moreover, in a resolution on the effects of a European foreign policy on defense questions, adopted in late 1975, it was observed with regret that no progress had hitherto been made toward the harmonization of the defense policies of the member states; at the same time the members of the Community were urged to strengthen the North Atlantic Alliance by specific European efforts and to rationalize the production of defensive armaments.[6]

The latter proposal was included and defined more precisely in the resolution on European armaments procurement cooperation adopted in June 1978. This resolution called upon the Commission to submit a European action program for the development and

---

3 *Official Journal* , No. C 26 (30 April 1973).

4 *European Parliament, Session Documents 1973/74*, Doc. 12/73, 3. See the April 1973 Report on behalf of the Political Affairs Committee on political cooperation and the political unification of Europe. Rapporteur: Mr. J. A. Mommersteeg.

5 *Official Journal* , No. C 179 (6 August 1975).

6 *Official Journal* , No. C 7 (12 January 1976). The resolution was based on a report by Lord Gladwyn on behalf of the Political Affairs Committee (Doc. 429/74).

production of conventional armaments within the framework of the common industrial policy of the EC.[7]

Another milestone on the road to cooperation among the Community member states on security policy was reached with the adoption of the EP resolution of July 1981 on "European political cooperation and the role of the European Parliament." This resolution emphasizes the significance of the inclusion of European security in matters covered by European political cooperation which had been promised by the Foreign Ministers in May of that year. In addition, the resolution called for cooperation on security policy to be continued and extended.[8]

In December 1981 another resolution was adopted dealing with the surveillance and protection of shipping routes for supplies of energy and strategic materials to the countries of the European Community.[9]

In January 1983 a large majority of the members of the EP adopted a resolution that was directly concerned with the link between European security and European Political Cooperation. This resolution, which is central to the subsequent development of security cooperation, called upon the Community member states, on the basis of an analysis of their common security concerns, to give substance to a true concept of European peace and security, founded on the priciples of détente policy, arms limitation and peaceful co-existence between all states and all peoples.[10]

The adoption of the resolution on arms procurement within a common industrial policy and on arms exports was regarded as

---

7 *Official Journal* , No. C 163 (10 July 1978). The resolution was based on a report by Mr. Klepsch on behalf of the Political Affairs Committee on European armaments procurement cooperation (Doc. 83/78).

8 *Official Journal* , No. C 234 (14 September 1981). The resolution was based on a report by Lady Elles on behalf of the Political Affairs Committee on European political cooperation and the role of the European Parliament (Doc. 1/335/81).

9 *Official Journal* , No. C 327 (14 December 1981). The resolution was based on a report drawn up by Mr. Diligent on behalf of the Political Affairs Committee on the surveillance and protection of shipping routes for supplies of energy and strategic materials to countries of the European Community.

10 *Official Journal* , No. C 42 (14 February 1983). The resolution was based on a report drawn up by Mr. Haagerup on behalf of the Political Affairs Committee on European security and European political cooperation (Doc. 1-946/82).

another important step in promoting cooperation between Community member states in the sphere of security policy.[11]

Demands for a common position on security issues and for the development of a European security concept were again at the center of a resolution on the "shared European interests, risks and requirements in the security field." This resolution, based on a report by Mr. Klepsch on behalf of the Political Affairs Committee, was adopted by the European Parliament on 11 April 1984 by 136 votes to 67 with 8 abstentions.[12] The Klepsch Report, and the subsequent resolution, were regarded as indicators of possible future developments with regard to cooperation on security policy. Both documents dealt with a wide range of matters effecting security policy as well as relations between the Community and the Atlantic Alliance. Furthermore, these documents instruct the Political Affairs Committee "to establish a permanent subcommittee on political and economic aspects of security." When a subcommittee of this kind was actually set up after the direct elections to the European Parliament in June 1984, it marked something of a breakthrough for security policy in the work of the European Parliament.

With the organization of the Subcommittee on Security and Disarmament in September 1984, the European Parliament began to view security policy as genuine part of its field of activity. This is also clearly demonstrated by the way in which the EP, in the second half of the 1980s, has attracted attention with an impressive number of its own reports, questions and emergency resolutions relating to security policy. In this process the Subcommittee of the European Parliament's Political Affairs Committee, has served as the architect, forum and driving force for Parliament's initiatives in the sphere of security policy.

The Subcommittee on Security and Disarmament has 21 members. This membership corresponds to the relative political strength of the parties in the European Parliament: the Socialist

---

11 *Official Journal*, No. C 322 (28 November 1983). The resolution was based on a report drawn up by Mr. Fergusson on behalf of the Political Affairs Committee on arms procurement within a common industrial policy and arms sales (Doc. 1-455/83).

12 *Official Journal* , No. C 127 (14 May 1984). The resolution was based on a report drawn up by Mr. Klepsch on behalf of the Political Affairs Committee on the shared European interests, risks and requirements in the security field (Doc. 1-80/84).

Group has six representatives; the European People's Party has four; and the European Democratic Group has three; the Communist Group, the Liberal and Democratic Reformist Group and the Group of the European Democratic Alliance are represented by two members each; the Rainbow Group and the Group of the European Right each have one representative. As a rule the Subcommittee meets once a month. Its reports deal with topics and problems such as disarmament and arms control, the security of West Europe, checks on arms sales and arms policy cooperation.

Apart from its work in preparing parliamentary reports and resolutions, the Subcommittee has also attracted attention in other ways. A number of oral questions on cooperation in the sphere of security policy have been put to the Foreign Ministers meeting in EPC[13] and a series of hearings have been staged. The public hearing organized in December 1985 on the position and prospects of security policy in Europe attracted particular attention.[14] The main point which emerged from the papers and discussions at that hearing was that the European Parliament must continue to press for a European security policy to ensure that European Political Cooperation gives security questions greater priority in future.

The future of the European arms industry and ways to improve its efficiency and competitiveness through cooperation and coordination between individual industries in the Community countries has long been a focal point of expert discussions in the Subcommittee. Among those who have addressed the subcommittee on these problems in recent years were the chairman of the Independent European Program Group (IEPG) Study Group on Improving the Competitiveness of the European Arms Industry, Mr. Vredeling, and the EC Commissioner responsible for trade and industry, Mr. K.-H. Narjes.

To summarize, the Subcommittee on Security and Disarmament has rapidly developed into a major center for initiatives and discussions. This applies both to its efforts to attract the interest of the European Parliament and the other European Community institutions in matters of security policy, and to its many externally

---

13 See for example Doc. B2/953/88, Doc. B2-1415/87 and Doc. B2-976/86.

14 See H. G. Pöttering, ed., *Perspektiven europäischer Sicherheitspolitik* (Bonn: Europa Union Verlag 1986). H. G. Pöttering was chairman of the Subcommittee until June 1989.

oriented activities, which are effective in influencing outside opinion.

In recent times, the activities of the European Parliament concerning defense and security issues have increased. This is partly due to the INF agreement. The US-Soviet decision to dismantle and scrap their entire stockpile of intermediate range nuclear missiles is considered by many experts to be the start of a new era in security policy. The agreement calls for a rethinking of strategic doctrines, a review of the way in which tasks and burdens are distributed within the Western Alliance, and new ideas about arms policy. The necessity for further steps in conventional disarmament and the elimination of biological and chemical weapons are additional considerations. Moreover, there is a call for the partial redefinition of relations between all the European countries; this is accompanied by the demand that the member states of the European Community accept their joint responsibility, and should now finally make their own contribution toward the preservation of world peace and international security.

These considerations were apparent in the resolution passed at the January 1988 partial-session on security policy cooperation within the framework of European Political Cooperation.[15] In this resolution Parliament asserts that the basic preconditions for a security policy are that existing arms control agreements should be scrupulously honoured and that both Alliances should abandon the goal of military superiority. It also observes that the political, economic and military aspects of security are interrelated, thus placing a broad interpretation on the provisions of the Single European Act with regard to security policy cooperation.[16] A similar tendency is manifest in the statement that, after the conclusion of the INF Treaty, the European Community has a greater duty than ever before to develop its own identity in security policy within the Western Alliance. Consequently, the Community should draw up a comprehensive target list of security policy measures which takes into account the specific security interests of West Europe. Security

---

15 European Parliament 120.085. *Minutes of proceedings of the sitting of January 22, 1988*, Part II, p. 4.

16 See *European Community Bulletin*, Supplement 2/86, p. 18 (Title III, Article 30(6)). The security-related part of this document is reprinted in the Annex.

policy is viewed not in terms of confrontation but in a spirit of openness toward détente, cooperation and give-and-take between East and West.

In order to translate this basic position into action, the resolution calls for the CSCE process to be used as an instrument of a comprehensive European security policy and as a means to guarantee respect for human rights in accordance with the provisions of the Helsinki Final Act.

This was also the spirit of the speech by Mr. Genscher, the West German Foreign Minister, to the European Parliament at the beginning of the German Presidency on 20 January 1988 in Strasbourg. He said that, apart from defense aspects, arms control, disarmament and efforts to achieve a dialogue and wide-ranging cooperation between East and West are integral parts of a comprehensive security policy which aims to create a just and lasting peace throughout Europe.[17] The European Community as a whole, and the European Parliament as one of the main Community institutions, has a vital role to play in this process. This now ubiquitous view was also taken by the German Presidency so as to strengthen cooperation in the field of security policy within the framework of EPC.[18] The President-in-Office of the Council stated that it is primarily the task of the European states themselves to work for a lasting peace in Europe.[19] On the role of the European Parliament he said: "I can imagine that it is possible for the Presidency to draw attention to Parliament's opinion ... on any aspect of security policy discussed within the framework of EPC. I should like to see the European Parliament have an in-depth debate on all aspects of European security because it is unsatisfactory that European security policy should be discussed only in the national parliaments ... and that it should be only on this basis that we form our opinions in the Council. So I should like to see the European Parliament decide to have an in-depth debate."[20]

In view of these statements, there is a place for the institutions of the Community as they develop common positions in defense

17 *Report of the proceedings of the European Parliament*, Strasbourg, 19-20 January 1988, p. 128.

18 Doc. B2-1415-87 (16 December 1987).

19 See *Report of the proceedings of the European Parliament, op.cit.*, 1988, p. 128.

20 Ibid., p. 175.

policy. In any event, it may prove impossible for questions like arms procurement to be completely excluded from any future agreements. The European Parliament has already achieved a high level of competence in this field; a number of reports from the early 1970s to the present, which deal with many aspects of defense and security, illustrate this fact. Although the Parliament remains a relatively weak body, the new consultative powers gained through the Single European Act enhance the catalystic role which it has successfully played in the past.

THE EEC TREATY AND THE SINGLE ACT

The provisions of the EEC Treaty concerning internal market regulations (competition rules, economic policy, public procurement regulations, etc.) do not entirely apply to the armament industries of the member states. In the "General and Final Provisions" of the EEC Treaty, it is established that "no member state shall be obliged to supply information the disclosure of which it considers contrary to the essential interests of its security" (Article 223a).

Moreover, any member state is allowed to take measures "as it considers necessary for the protection of the essential interests of its security which are connected with the production of or trade in arms, munitions and war material; such measures shall not adversely affect the conditions of competition in the common market regarding products which are not intended for specifically military purposes" (Article 223b). To this end, the EC Council, acting unanimously, draws up a list of products to which these provisions apply. The Commission has the right to propose changes to this list. The Council must agree unanimously in order for these changes to be adopted.

The Single European Act[21] implements no new regulations limiting the validity of the provisions of Article 223 of the EEC Treaty. Hence there is no legally binding impact of the SEA on the arms procurement policy of the individual member states. The preamble of the Single European Act and a number of regulations in

21 See the text of the Single European Act in *Bulletin of the European Communities* (Supplement 2/86). For the articles relating to this chapter, see the Annex.

Title II and Title III, however, aim directly or indirectly at a greater liberalization and harmonization in the sphere of arms procurement. In the preamble of the SEA, the Heads of State and Government express their determination to make their own contribution to the preservation of international peace and security, and their willingness to improve the economic situation by extending common policies and pursuing new objectives.

In the provisions relating to the foundations and the policy of the Community (subsection internal market), it is clearly stated that the internal market shall comprise an area without internal frontiers in which the free movement of goods, persons, services and capital is ensured in accordance with the provisions of this Treaty.

Subsection V of the provisions relating to the foundations and the policy of the Community deals with research and technological development. This section gives a new legal basis to the Community's endeavour to strengthen the scientific and technological basis of European industry and to encourage it to become more internally competitive. In order to achieve this, the Community shall in particular enable undertakings to exploit the Community's internal market potential to the full, specifically through the opening up of national public contracts, the definition of common standards and the removal of legal and fiscal barriers to that cooperation.

Particular account shall be taken of the connection between the common research and technological development effort, the establishment of the internal market and the implementation of common policies, particularly as regards competition and trade. Furthermore, Article 130 enables the Community to carry out activities such as

- implementation of research, technological development and demonstration programs, by promoting cooperation with enterprises, research centres and universities;
- dissemination and optimization of the results of activities in community research, technological development, and demonstration.

Policies in the field of research and technological development shall be coordinated between the member states in liaison with the Commission. In this context, the Commission is encouraged to take any useful initiative to promote such coordination (Article 130H).

Article 130M calls on the Commission to make provisions for the implementation of a multi-annual framework program for participation in research and development programs undertaken by several member states, including participation in the structures created for the execution of those programs.

In sum, the provisions of Title II of the Single European Act theoretically provide an enlarged basis for Community-wide arms procurement programs within the framework of an industrial policy of the EC.

Title III of the SEA deals with the provisions on European cooperation in the sphere of foreign policy. In this title, there are two key paragraphs which explicitly refer to European cooperation in the field of security. In Article 30(6), as previously mentioned, the contracting parties consider that closer cooperation on questions of European security would contribute in an essential way to the development of a European identity in external policy matters. They are ready to coordinate their positions more closely on the political and economic aspects of security. In the same article, the contracting parties express their determination to maintain the technological and industrial conditions necessary for their security. They shall work to that end both at national level and, where appropriate, within the framework of competent institutions and bodies.

One may argue that these provisions remain vague and do not necessarily serve as a legally binding basis for enhanced European arms procurement cooperation. On the other hand, if one combines the general commitment expressed by the Heads of State and Government in the preamble, the provisions of Title II, notably those concerning the internal market and cooperation in the field of technology and research, and the distinctly security-related provisions of Title III, Article 30(6), one may conclude that the Single European Act may well prepare the ground-work for enhanced European arms procurement cooperation despite the provisions of Article 223 of the EEC Treaty.

However, member state reactions to recent initatives, aimed to enhance European armaments cooperation, prove how difficult it is to get the Council's unanimous agreement on a common armaments policy, and notably a revision or "reinterpretation" of Article 223. This became evident when the Commission proposed an amendment to Directive 77/62 related to the "coordination of procedures on the award of public supply contracts." In this context the Commission maintained, with the support of the European Parliament, that the scope of the new directive should in principle include defense contracts and insisted that, if any exemptions were to be made, the member states should only be allowed to exempt arms, munitions and war materials intended for specifically military purposes from the Directive. Hence, the list referred to in paragraph 2 of Article 223 had to be applied within the limits of paragraph 1(6). However, some national delegations maintained their principal opposition to the inclusion of the armament sector into the scope of the new directive. The final text, adopted on 23 March 1988, does not take the point of view of the Commission and the Parliament into account.

Similiar problems seem to occur with regard to the Commission's proposal for a Council regulation "temporarily suspending import duties on certain weapons and military equipment" (COM(88) 502 final). This proposal aims to enable the member states to procure for the use of their armed forces the most technologically advanced military equipment. Accordingly, European Community manufacturers should be able to meet the greater part of these needs. In order to ensure implementation, the Commission asks the member states for greater transparency concerning their arms imports and suggests agreement on the suspension of import duties during a given period of time on a list of military equipment. In other words, import regulations in the armaments sector would be harmonized, monitored by the Commission, and a common external tariff on military equipment not covered by the list might be established. Once again the discussion of the proposal within the Committee of Permanent Representatives to the European Communities (COREPER) has shown substantial reservations on the part of some member states regarding the proposal. A decision by the Council has not yet been taken.

In addition to EC initiatives for enhancing European armaments cooperation based on the provisions of the Single European Act, it is worth mentioning similar initiatives taken in the framework of IEPG. The Luxembourg meeting on 9 November 1988 of the defense ministers of the 13 IEPG member countries could give new impetus to the construction of a European Armaments Market. This is particularly true with regard to the IEPG "Action Plan on a stepwise development of a European Armaments Market," based on the European Defense Industry Study team report titled "Towards a Stronger Europe," which has been approved by the IEPG-Ministers at the Luxembourg meeting.

A NEW START FOR DEFENSE COOPERATION?

Although it would be unrealistic to suggest that Article 30 of the SEA is a watershed in West European relations, it seems that the 12 EC member nations have finally admitted that it is unrealistic to engage in serious foreign policy coordination without considering its security implications. The following pages provide an analysis of some of the major security problems West European governments are facing in the late 1980s as well as some potential solutions offered by the Single European Act and the further development of EPC.

Article 30 is in many respects a compromise between the growing aspirations of certain members of the community to cooperate more closely in the area of security and the unwillingness of a few to see their traditional defense postures undermined. In hindsight, probably the best and only solution has been found in that the SEA incorporates the area of security into the Treaty of Rome, and hence EPC, while respecting the independent position of each nation state.

The defense of West Europe has been in "crisis" for much of the post-war period. Some have even suggested that the very existence of such crises has ensured the cohesion of the Western Alliance. Crises have occurred for a number of reasons; many have been transitory but a few have reoccurred with fatal persistency. There is no doubt that a widening gap exists in NATO between European and American perceptions of the military threat facing the West. This gap seems to have widened in recent years with the ascendency of a younger and more liberal approach in the Kremlin and what Europeans perceive as the extremes of American foreign policy. US priorities are no longer Euro-centric, but concentrate instead on communist penetration in Central America, the growing economic importance of the Pacific Basin, the security of Western oil supplies from the Gulf and the dramatic growth in the Soviet capacity for global application of military power. Such developments have combined to divert the attention of American planners from the European theatre. As Lord Chalfont has stated:

> "It is not too extreme to suggest that we can no longer take for granted the permanent presence of 300,000 American troops in Europe. What we are faced with is the fading credibility of the US nuclear guarantee, the possiblitity of a substantial reduction in the US military presence, and now the proposed withdrawal from Europe of intermediate and shorter range nuclear weapons".[22]

In effect, the strong links that were established across the Atlantic in the early post-war years have been seriously eroded in a series of misunderstandings and disagreements. Such matters as the "neutron bomb," American pressures for "burden-sharing", the Soviet gas pipeline, US support for the Contras and heavy handed tactics against Libya have prompted increasing, yet insufficient, attempts by European Heads of State and Government to find a united and independent stance appropriate to their economic and political power. One can only conclude that the current political and military distribution of responsibilities within the Atlantic Alliance is no longer appropriate to deal with many of the security problems Europeans face. And yet very little has been accomplished to compensate for NATO's deficiencies. These unresolved problems pose a considerable challenge for West Europe. Likewise, the European reaction to SDI and to the maintaining of the European military industrial base are other major difficulties.

In 1986 the European members of the Atlantic alliance sold the US a record $2.9 billion worth of weapons which helped to bring the chronic US surplus in the transatlantic arms trade to its lowest point since 1945.[23] This figure shows the growing sophistication of the European defense industry in tackling the demands set by the present US administration and the increased willingness of the US to sell West Europe on average 10 times more than it is willing to buy. There is good reason to believe that this situation will continue. In all the major industrial sectors, and especially in defense, the total research expenditure of the European countries as separate entities is

---

22 *International Herald Tribune*, 23 July 1987.

23 *Financial Times*, 15 July 1987.

greater than that of the United States and Japan combined, yet their return is considerably less. The level of duplication and hence waste is enormous; in West Europe in 1986 there were:

- 11 firms in 7 different countries working on anti-tank weapons,
- 18 firms in 7 countries manufacturing ground to air missiles,
- 8 firms in 6 countries working on air to air missiles.[24]

In itself duplication poses two serious military problems for West Europe and the Atlantic Alliance. The resources wasted on duplication have added to a phenomenon known as "structural disarmament," a term used to decribe the recent effects of rising real unit costs and falling numbers of equipment. While procurement costs rise every year, governments have less to spend on research and development. This means they have to spend an increasing proportion of their defense budgets simply to maintain existing stocks.

The major military problem resulting from the fragmented defense base is lack of "standardization" or "interoperability" whereby national governments deploy completely different defense systems. This problem is especially severe in the vital area of communications. In December 1974 during NATO exercises in the North Atlantic, Alliance forces "shot down" half of their own aircraft due to lack of interoperability.[25] By the early 1980s this problem had worsened. Due to the almost complete exclusion of French forces from NATO planning, seven allied nations deployed six new tactical communication systems; none of these could communicate with NATO's integrated communications system (NICS).

The European defense industry plays a crucial role not only in security but also in the general economy in terms of jobs and technology, "spin-offs" and the balance of payments. The continuing fragmentation of the industry in the face of an enormous US investment program (SDI) and growing global competition poses a serious threat to what Tugendhat described as "our ability to

---

24 *Europäische Wehrkunde, WWR*, 3/1987.
25 David Abshire, Arms co-operation in NATO , in *Armed Forces Journal International* (December 1985), p. 3.

afford all the equipment we feel we need or to maintain the industrial capacity to provide it."[26] By the early 1980s some reasons for optimism had arisen.

Possibly the most important development in the post-war years has been the growing willingness of West European governments to cooperate on a number of issues. Until the 1980s defense and security had largely been avoided by the European Community and European Political Cooperation. Governments attempted to exclude both while discussing foreign and industrial policy. This situation has led to the revitalization of certain institutions outside the political framework of the Community and the growing tendency for government and industry to cooperate on an ad hoc basis.

Attempts to secure greater cooperation between the European members of NATO and yet include France have not been very successful. The Independent European Program Group and the Eurogroup have both been operational for some time. Both have attempted to coordinate a European position in posture and procurement. Although these two bodies have done much good work, they are either too specific in purpose or lack the right membership. These shortcomings led to the revitalization and enlargement of the Western European Union (WEU).

The WEU defense commitment is much more binding than that of NATO in that its members undertake to afford each other "all the military and other aid and assistance in their power." France is therefore legally obliged to defend West Germany with all its forces including the "force de frappe." For many years the WEU lay dormant but in the early 1980s, after requests made by President Mitterrand, it became the focus of increased attention. Thus, WEU could be the first step toward a more concerted European defense policy.

Although various initiatives have been taken at European level to defend and promote the European technological base (notably ESPRIT and Eureka) many of the real success stories have been within a framework of what David Greenwood describes as " à la carte" cooperation. There have been various suggestions to incorporate a defense procurement provision into a future European industrial policy. Some have even gone as far to suggest that the

---

26 Christopher Tugendhat, *Making Sense of Europe* (Great Britain: Penguin Books 1986).

Community should be responsible for defense procurement. There may be some advantages to such action; however, bearing in mind the experience of the Common Agricultural Policy any future *overall* common industrial policy implies serious risks. On the other hand, the success of cooperative projects such as Ariane, Tornado and Airbus are perfect examples of European governments and industries working together to create an economically viable product which preserves the fundamental interests of all the participants.

Some aspects of the Single European Act have created greater potential within the Community framework for increased participation, discussion and cooperation of defense issues at all levels. The intention to complete the internal market by 1992 combined with increased foreign policy cooperation is bound to draw the EC countries closer in the field of security and disarmament. In the meantime, Europeans would do well to resolve some of the outstanding problems we face including the role of the independent nuclear forces and the position of West Germany which have been too ambiguous for too long. In the short term the European Institutions could play a major role in achieving 3 crucial objectives which could provide a major impetus to cooperation in the European defense industry:

- forging closer European links which encourage less dependence on US protection and greater French participation;
- helping to build more comprehensive industry to industry and industry to government links within Europe;
- assisting in establishing procurement policies which will ensure European competitiveness in world markets.

INSTITUTIONAL DILEMMA AND CONCLUSIONS

The 1980s have witnessed a growing awareness of the need for a greater West European identity in defense and security matters. As an example which illustrates the commitment to move toward a West European Security Community one may quote the "Platform on European Security Interests," adopted by the WEU member states on 27 October 1987. Paragraph 2 of the Platform recalls "our committment to build a European Union in accordance with the

Single European Act, which we all signed as members of the European Community. We are convinced that the construction of an integrated Europe will remain incomplete as long as it does not include security and defense."[27]

Moreover, the WEU member states express their conviction that a more united Europe will make a stronger contribution to the Alliance, will ensure the basis for a balanced partnership across the Atlantic and strengthen the European pillar of the Alliance. They also express the European determination "to carry our share of the common defense in both the conventional and the nuclear field, in accordance with the principles of risk- and burden-sharing, which are fundamental to allied cohesion."[28]

In other words, the basic premises are largely accepted by the political elites of West Europe: Europe needs a common security policy, including defense, and this policy has to be, to a certain extent, compatible with that of the Atlantic Alliance. However, such a vague common denominator is not sufficient to develop a common European security policy because too many aspects are still controversial and far from being generally agreed upon. Among the fundamental questions which still have to be answered are the following:

- how is Europe defined when we talk about a common security policy?; therefore, which countries will participate?
- what are the appropriate institutional arrangements for a common security policy?
- what are the fundamentals of a European security and defense strategy?
- what will be the form of the "European Pillar" of the Atlantic Alliance?
- what are the common denominators of a comprehensive West European security concept in terms of threat assessment, response to the "Gorbachev challenge", arms control and disarmament negotiations, and a common armaments market?

---

27 Western European Union, *Platform on European Security Interests*, 27 October 1987, p. 1. For the text of the Platform, see the Annex (Documents).
28 Ibid.

This list of questions could easily be extended and the items mentioned above are obviously interrelated. One explanation why no answers have been given to these questions so far lies in the fact that a large range of political actors, parties, governments and states call for a common European security policy but have completely different conceptions of this notion which range from a largely demilitarized Europe, equidistant from the superpowers, to a third military superpower called West Europe.

Different suggestions have been made concerning the questions raised above. With regard to the first two questions, many believe that the European Community should be the framework for European defense; others suggest considering the revitalized WEU, based on a revised Brussels Treaty, as the most appropriate institutional framework; others still would prefer to have a European Defense Community formed by the member states of the IEPG; and finally there are those who would like a European Security Community to develop well beyond the limits of EC member countries in the Atlantic Alliance.

The mainstream of ideas regarding the institutionalization of security and defense cooperation, however, concentrates on WEU, the European Community including European Political Cooperation, IEPG and Eurogroup[29]. Unfortunately, none of these institutional frameworks seems to be ideal: The EC and EPC framework excludes European members of the Atlantic Alliance but includes the problem of Irish neutrality; WEU excludes even more members of the West European "value community" but has no problem of neutrality; the Eurogroup or other NATO military bodies exclude France; the IEPG, which, at a first glance, seems to offer an ideal framework for European armaments cooperation includes members from outside the EC and, therefore, can not have the dynamic of a Community which is moving toward an internal market.

Against the background of this dilemma, it can be argued that before an institutional strategy can be developed, the scope and the limits of European security cooperation have to be defined as well as its aims and its relations with NATO. On the other hand, there are valid reasons to believe that scope, limits and aims of a transnational

---

29 For a brief explanation of the nature and functions of the existing institutions for European security cooperation, see the Annex.

or supranational security policy have to be developed on the basis of clear institutional provisions.

In order to escape from this vicious circle, various approaches are currently under discussion. One is to establish an appropriate division of tasks between the institutions previously mentioned. One such model could be envisaged as follows:

- to put armaments cooperation and the development of a common European armaments market under the authority of the EEC, and to "closely" associate those IEPG members who are not members of the EC
- to deal with the political aspects of security and defense within EPC
- to develop common positions with regard to the military-strategic aspects of security within WEU, in close coordination with corresponding NATO bodies such as the Nuclear Planning Group (NPG) and the Eurogroup and in close cooperation with EPC.

This multilateral set of interinstitutional links, including supranational as well as intergovernmental elements, is complemented by special cooperative links within a network of bilateral security relations. The Franco-German Defense Council and the Common Brigade, enhanced Franco-British cooperation regarding nuclear deterrence, and special cooperative measures envisaged between Spain and Italy may serve as examples.

If one considers all these initiatives, multilateral and bilateral relations as well as intergovernmental and supranational arrangements, it must be recognized that a pattern of "variable geometry" has developed in the field of European security cooperation, which impedes to a large extent unity of political action.

On the other hand, as was previously mentioned, European governments have shown in recent years considerable determination to develop a common security policy. Moreover, it is a matter of fact that the transatlantic consensus concerning common security is fragile and, hence, provides incentives for greater European defense cooperation. Whereas it is still generally acknowledged that Western security is indivisible, awareness is growing that in the long run, the United States may move away from Europe and that West Europe therefore has to be prepared to be responsible for its own defense. Consequently, leading politicians call for closer cooperation in a wide range of areas, notably defense procurement, military research, role specialization and joint training.[30] Others plead strongly in favour of a European conventional defense force with France extending its nuclear umbrella over continental Europe[31], and others still go further and advocate the establishment of a European Defense Union which would emerge among the EC member states and thus be an integral part of a European Union.[32]

For the time being, it can be said that measures such as the adoption of the Platform on European Security Interests, the enlargement of WEU, enhanced coordination between the 12 with regard to the new disarmament negotiations in Vienna (CFE), and increased acceptance to deal with the military aspects of security within EPC are signs of progress in European security cooperation. Certain initiatives of the EC Commission to move toward a common armaments market, signs of a military and strategic "rapprochement" of France toward the Western Alliance, proposals which envisage a ministerial council for defense ministers within the European Community, suggestions to establish a "European Nuclear Planning Group", a "European Agency for Arms Control"[33] and a "European Institute for Higher Security Studies"[34] indicate similar forward motion. Finally, the growing awareness that there is a certain contradiction between the economic power of West Europe and its obvious dependency in defense matters[35] proves that West Europeans would like to realize their goals in the field of security and defense. How to do so remains an open question.

---

30 Sir Geoffrey Howe in the *Financial Times*, 17 March 1987.

31 For example Helmut Schmidt. See *The Guardian*, 25 February 1987.

32 For example H.G. Pöttering, former chairman of the European Parliament's Subcommittee on Security and Disarmament. See:*VWD-Europa* (6 October 1988).

33 See S. Silvestri in *Moves towards a European Defence and Security Policy*, Draft for Action Committee Altiero Spinelli (November 1987), pp. 2 f.

34 This idea was put forward by Michel Rocard. See *Financial Times*, 16 December 1988.

35 This idea was expressed by W.F. van Ekelen, present Secretary-General of WEU.

6

Franco-German Defense Cooperation: A Basis for the Europeanization of NATO?

David Garnham

INTRODUCTION

François Mauriac's epigram, "I love Germany so much that I am happy there are two of them,"[1] precisely expressed French attitudes toward Germany in the 1940s and 1950s. In the debate preceding the French Parliament's rejection of the European Defense Community (EDC) in August 1954, one deputy recalled that Germany had invaded France in 1792, 1814, 1815, 1870, 1914 and 1940.[2] Earlier, in December 1944, de Gaulle had signed in Moscow a twenty year treaty of alliance and mutual assistance directed against

1 Quoted in Phillipe Moreau Defarges, "La France et l'Europe: le rêve ambigu ou la mesure du rang," in *Politique étrangère*, Vol. 51, No. 1 (Spring 1986) p. 203.

2 Alfred Grosser, "Germany and France: A Confrontation," in Daniel Lerner and Raymond Aron, eds., *France Defeats EDC* (New York: Frederick A. Praeger, 1957), p. 67. For analyses of the EDC, see Maurice Delarue, "1954, vie et mort d'une armée européenne," in *Le Monde*, 24 September 1987, p. 2; Edward Fursdon, *The European Defense Community: A History* (London: The Macmillian Press, 1980); Alfred Grosser, *Affaires Extérieures: La politique de la France 1944-1984* (Paris: Flammarion, 1984), pp. 106-112; F. Roy Willis, *France, Germany and the New Europe: 1945-1967*, revised and expanded edition (Stanford: Stanford University Press, 1968), pp. 130-184.

Germany.[3] And an October 1950 survey of French attitudes toward nine countries ranked Britain and the United States first and second, and Germany ranked last.[4]

Most Americans retain this now outmoded image of Franco-German relations tinged by *Erbfeindschaft* (hereditary enmity),[5] but since 1945 these ancestral enemies have successfully forged the closest relationship among the principal nations of West Europe. Their postwar security relationship has evolved through four stages: deep distrust from 1945 through the French rejection of the EDC, an initial period of cooperation in the late 1950s and early 1960s (especially under the leadership of Adenauer and de Gaulle), stagnation during the late 1960s and through the 1970s, and renewed progress during the 1980s.

Although further progress is impeded by traditional sticking points - especially France's quest for autonomy and West Germany's dependance upon the US defense commitment - events in recent years, including President Reagan's bargaining stance at the 1986 Reykjavik summit and the ongoing removal of intermediate range nuclear forces (INF) from Europe, have heightened the interest of Bonn and Paris (and also London) in European security cooperation. Former Chancellor Helmut Schmidt has repeatedly advocated a Franco-German defense community which would unite the two militaries (including the French nuclear deterrent force) under the French president.[6] Although this remains a distant goal, the evolving relationship renders it conceivable in the next century.

---

3 See Adalbert Korff, *Le revirement de la politique française à l'égard de l'Allemagne entre 1945-1950* (Ambilly-Annemasse: Imprimerie Franco-Suisse, 1965), p. 40.

4 See Jean Stoetzel, "The Evolution of French Opinion," in Daniel Lerner and Raymond Aron, eds., *France Defeats EDC* (New York: Frederick A. Praeger, 1957), p. 74.

5 For example, an editorial in the *New York Times* (9 September 1987, p. 22) discussed the idea of German reunification in terms of "the same German bellicosity, in war after war, that has frightened the French..."

6 See Helmut Schmidt, "Europa muß sich selbst behaupten," in *Die Zeit*, No. 48, 21 November 1986, p. 3. (translated in *The German Tribune*, No. 1253, 30 November 1986, p. 5 and No. 1254, 7 December 1986, pp. 6-7; "L'Equation Allemande: Entretien avec Helmut Schmidt," in *Politique Internationale*, No. 27 (Spring 1985), pp. 147-159; Helmut Schmidt, "La France, l'Allemagne et la Défense européenne," in *Commentaire*, No. 27 (1984), pp. 411-417.

WEST GERMANY

Geography makes West Germany the keystone of West European defense and the most vulnerable member of NATO. Among the NATO countries that border the Eastern Bloc (Norway, Greece, and Turkey), only the FRG has 30 percent of its population and 25 percent of its industrial capacity located within sixty miles of the East-West frontier. This proximity, and the absence of a national nuclear deterrent capability, makes the Federal Republic the most exposed member of the Atlantic Alliance.

The Federal Republic is also the most populous West European country (sixty-one million inhabitants in an area the size of Oregon), the largest West European economy, and the fourth largest global economy. In 1986, the FRG overtook the United States to become the world's principal exporting country.

Two devastating twentieth century wars left Germany defeated and divided. This experience, combined with feelings of guilt for Nazi atrocities, convinced many Germans that warfare was immoral, ineffective, and dangerous.[7] Article 26 of Bonn's constitution prohibits "Activities tending and undertaken with the intent to disturb peaceful relations between nations, especially to prepare for aggressive war..." This dovish inclination is reinforced by Germany's precarious position as the likely battleground for any European war, while France - and especially Britain and the United States - enjoy more favorable geopolitical positions. Furthermore, only diplomacy - not force of arms - can advance the goals of *Deutschlandpolitik*; the Soviet Union can effectively block improved inter-German relations as General Secretary Chernenko demon-

---

7 This contrasts with the American lesson that it is dangerous to "appease" aggressors. As Gerhard Wettig wrote:

> There is an elementary mood of "Never again!" Never again should the German people and the territory of Germany originate a threat to peace. Never again should militaristic attitudes and armament activities be prevalent in Germany. Never again should feelings of enmity be allowed to spoil German minds and hearts. The idea, therefore, that there is a potential adversary who poses a challenge may not be admitted. Instead one has to be unconditionally friendly toward anyone who is supposedly antagonistic.

Gerhard Wettig, "Europe and the Idea of Common Security," in *The Washington Quarterly*, Vol 8, No. 2 (Spring 1985), p. 94.

strated by preventing East German leader Erich Honecker from visiting the Federal Republic in 1984.[8]

Following World War II, West Germans renounced aspirations to great power status and became skeptical of strategic concepts based on Realpolitik and Vegetius' maxim, "Let him who desires peace, prepare for war."[9] German thinking is influenced more by notions of "common security," which Egon Bahr, a leading member of the Social Democratic Party (SPD), defined as an awareness that "the security of the potential enemy is my own, and vice versa. Both sides will survive together, or be destroyed together."[10] Or, as one Bonn foreign policy specialist expressed it, "We cannot sleep very well if our Eastern neighbor is afraid of us."

The philosophy of common security prevails on the Left, but its influence extends across the political spectrum. There is a broad consensus among German elites that ultimate security cannot come from military preparedness; it must be based on arms control and other diplomatic approaches which recognize the East's legitimate security concerns. Therefore, a retired Bundeswehr officer exaggerated only slightly in stating, "I do not think there are any hawks in this country."

FRANCE

Compared to the Federal Republic, France enjoys a preferable security situation in two major respects: the West German buffer shields French territory from direct exposure to Warsaw Pact aggression, and France possesses its own nuclear deterrent force.

---

8 Honecker said in a *Die Zeit* interview that he lacked "unlimited scope" for normalizing inter-German relations. Quoted by Hermann Dexheimer, "Tragic reality of the two German states," in *The German Tribune*, No. 1216, 2 March 1986, p. 3. (translated from *Allgemeine Zeitung*, Mainz, 15 February 1986).

9 See Hans-Peter Schwarz, *Die gezähmten Deutschen: Von der Machtbesessenheit zur Machtvergessenheit* (Stuttgart: Deutsche Verlags-Anstalt, 1985), pp. 107-151.

10 Egon Bahr, "Observations on the principle of common security," in R. Väyrynen, et al., eds., *Policies for Common Security* (London and Philadelphia: Taylor & Francis, 1985), p. 34. This volume also contains an article by the late Alois Mertes, a foreign ministry official in the Kohl government, "Common security and defensive security," pp. 187-191.

France's policy of "deterrence by the weak of the strong" (la dissuasion du faible au fort) presumes that the Soviets will be deterred if the damage that France can credibly threaten to inflict on Soviet territory exceeds Soviet benefits from defeating France.[11] French military forces consist of strategic nuclear forces, tactical nuclear weapons, conventional forces, and the more recently created Force d'action rapide (FAR) which is a highly mobile intervention force of 47,000 soldiers intended for use in Europe or the Third World. Except for the FAR, all of these forces have deterrence rather than war-fighting as their principal or sole mission.

French military thought differentiates three strategic circles: the first circle (French national territory, often called the Hexagon), the second circle (Europe), and the third circle (the rest of the world).[12] Strategic nuclear policy pertains to the first circle, but since the mid-1970s when President Giscard d'Estaing and General Méry introduced the concept of "enlarged sanctuary," the consensus has progressively embraced a more expansive definition of French interests to include some portion of the second circle.[13] At least rhetorically, this concept is now endorsed by the three principal political groupings: Parti Socialiste (PS), Rassemblement pour la République (RPR), and Union pour la Démocratie Française (UDF).[14] However, specifications of French vital interests remain

---

11 See David S. Yost, *France's Deterrent Posture and Security in Europe, Part I: Capabilities and Doctrine*, Adelphi Paper Number 194 (London: International Institute for Strategic Studies, Winter 1984-85), pp. 14-15.

12 See Charles Hernu, *Défendre la paix* (Paris: Editions J.-C. Lattès, 1985), pp. 26-27 and Lucien Poirier, "Le deuxième cercle: La défense égoïste de la citadelle et la grande aventure au-delà de la contrescarpe," in Lucien Poirier, ed., *Essais de stratégie théorique* (Paris: Fondation pour les études de Défense nationale, *Collection les septs épées*, No. 22, premier trimestre 1982), p. 293.

13 See General Guy Méry, "French Defense Policy," in *Survival*, Vol. 18 (September-October 1976), pp. 226-228 and Charles Hargrove, "Valéry Giscard d'Estaing," in *Politique étrangère*, Vol. 51, No. 1 (Spring 1986), p. 121. However, General Lucien Poirier is correct that it is actually "enlarged deterrence" rather than an "enlarged sanctuary" as there is no intention to use strategic weapons to defend interests in the second circle. See Lucien Poirier, "La Greffe," in *Défense nationale*, Vol. 39 (April 1983), p. 21.

14 See Paul Marie de La Gorce, "Dissuasion française et défense européenne," *Le Monde diplomatique*, No. 378 (September 1985), pp. 1, 22-23; Le Parti Socialiste, *La Sécurité de l'Europe* (Paris: PS, 1985); Rassemblement pour la République, *La défense de la France: 4 ans de gestion socialiste, Propositions*

enigmatic and are left ultimately for the president to interpret in extremis. According to French specialists, nuclear weapons "would be employed for the defense of the 'vital interests' of the country and ... it is for the president of the republic to define them when the moment comes."[15]

In addition, although West Germany's defense consensus unraveled in recent years, the Gaullist doctrine for autonomous defense of French territory with nuclear weapons is embraced with various nuances by all major political parties.[16] The consensus runs so deeply that French defense policy is insulated from electoral shifts such as those from Giscard to Mitterrand in 1981 and to cohabitation (with the right of controlling the parliament and the Socialists the presidency) between March 1986 and June 1988. It is notable that the Socialists abstained (rather than opposing) when the 1987 and 1988 defense budget passed the National Assembly, and they supported the new five year military plan (loi de programme militaire 1987-1991) drafted by the Chirac government (albeit with a substantial input from President Mitterrand) when it passed in April 1987.[17]

---

pour le renouveau (Paris: June 1985); Union pour la Démocratie Française, *Redresser la défense de la France* (Paris: November 1985).

15 Paul-Marie de La Gorce, "Dissuasion française et défense européenne," in *Le Monde Diplomatique*, No. 378 (September 1985), pp. 1, 22-23. Also see writings by two former Socialist defense ministers: Paul Quilès wrote that "the implication of French vital interests cannot be defined a priori: the assessment of that comes back, on a case by case basis, to the chief of state, the only one empowered to trigger the nuclear fire." ("Au-delà des fausses querelles," in *Le Monde*, 7 March 1986, p. 23) and Charles Hernu wrote that, "The President of the Republic, and he alone, is charged to appreciate if these interests are threatened and to take the measures demanded by the circumstances." (*Défendre la paix* (Paris: Editions J.-C. Lattès, 1985), pp. 28-29).

16 The Communists accepted nuclear deterrence in 1977 and the Socialists followed in 1978; see Michel Dobry, "Le jeu du consensus," in *Pouvoirs*, No. 38 (September 1986), p. 48.

17 See Paul Lewis, "France Approves Arms Plan Linked to European Allies," in *The New York Times*, 11 April 1987, p. 3.

GERMAN ALLIANCE VERSUS FRENCH INTERDEPENDENCE

To protect its exposed position, Germany has formulated a defense policy based upon three principles: alliance, forward defense, and nuclear deterrence. In addition to the 495,000 men of the Bundeswehr, more than 400,000 troops from six allied armies (US, UK, France, Netherlands, Belgium, Canada) are based in the Federal Republic. The key foreign contribution is American: the United States contributes approximately one-quarter of the NATO forces on the Central Front and also extends a nuclear guarantee. According to the Defense Ministry's 1985 White Paper, "The close integration of West Europe with the United States is indispensable for the preservation and shaping of peace on the European continent... Without the military protection of the United States, West European security cannot be guaranteed."[18]

In contrast to Germany's alliance strategy, France withdrew from NATO's integrated military structure in 1966 to pursue a policy of independent nuclear deterrence. French strategists recognize that an aggressor might disguise his true objective to avoid provocations which could justify use of France's nuclear weapons. Therefore, the principal purpose of French conventional forces (which absorb eighty percent of the defense budget) is to test the adversary's intentions to determine if vital interests are threatened. According to the ultraorthodox position of influential strategist General Lucien Poirier, "This operation being only the means to inform the chief of state, it has nothing to do with a defensive battle delivered with the hope of stopping the assailant ... these forces pertain to deterrence: it is their only purpose..."[19]

If the president concluded that vital French interests were threatened which would vindicate use of strategic nuclear arms, the French intend to signal their resolve by firing tactical nuclear weapons. In 1983, the Socialist government rechristened French

---

18 Federal Minister of Defense, *White Paper 1985: The Situation and the Development of the Federal Armed Forces* (Bonn: The Federal Minister of Defense, 1985), p. 8 and p. 17.

19 Lucien Poirier, "Le deuxième cercle: La défense égoïste de la citadelle et la grande aventure de la contrescarpe," in Lucien Poirier, *Essais de stratégie théorique* , op.cit., p. 308. Also see Lucien Poirier, "La Greffe," in *Défense nationale*, Vol 39 (April 1983), p. 12.

tactical nuclear weapons "prestrategic" to emphasize that they were not battlefield weapons but the *ultime avertissement* (final warning) prior to the use of strategic forces. The principal prestrategic weapon, Pluton, is a groundbased missile with a maximum range of 120 kilometers.[20] Beginning in 1992, Pluton is scheduled to be replaced by forty-five launchers capable of firing 180 Hadès missiles with a range from 80 to 480 kilometers. It will then be possible to strike targets in East Germany and Czechoslovakia from French territory thus reducing the likelihood that French use of prestrategic nuclear weapons would inevitably occur on West German territory.

Forward Defense versus Nonbelligerency

The second principle of orthodox German thinking, forward defense, stipulates that the Federal Republic must be defended at the border. Domestic opinion precludes any plan to wage modern warfare on densely populated German territory. But Bonn justifies this policy in alliance terms by arguing that, "Forward defense close to the border ... is also in the interests of our allies. Vigorous defense from the very beginning will offer a reliable guarantee for the protection of their territories as well."[21] The SPD, while embracing the principle of forward defense, rejects the overall policy of Bonn's center-right ruling coalition. The Social Democrats seek an alternative defense which is non-nuclear, "non-provocative," and less costly.[22] However, the task of defining a plausible forward defense which fulfills these contradictory goals is sisyphean, and many SPD loyalists would be satisfied by a policy which was merely less nuclear and less provocative.

Deep and unresolved contradictions remain between France's autonomous nuclear defense of the Hexagon and the multilateral

---

20 There is disagreement concerning the number of Plutons, but apparently it exceeds one hundred. See David S. Yost, *France's Deterrent Posture and Security in Europe, Part I: Capabilities and Doctrine*, op.cit., p. 49.

21 Federal Minister of Defense, *White Paper 1985: The Situation and the Development of the Federal Armed Forces*, op.cit., p. 35; also see p. 76 and Geoffrey Manners, "Forward defense 'indispensable' CINCENT tells Allies," in *Jane's Defense Weekly*, Vol. 3, No. 18 (4 May 1986), pp. 746-747.

22 Specifically, the party supports a reduction in military spending to the level of the last SPD defense budget in 1982.

conventional defense of the Federal Republic. West German territory is extremely narrow, equal to only two stages of the Tour de France as de Gaulle said, and French leaders acknowledge that any aggression against Germany would immediately threaten their security. Furthermore, France has deployed troops in the Federal Republic since the FRG became sovereign in 1955: there are 50,000 troops in three armored divisions plus nearly 30,000 dependents and 10,000 civilian employees.

Contingency plans exist for French participation in the conventional defense of the Federal Republic, and since 1980 France and Germany have staged joint exercises to test these plans. In 1986, 3600 French troops participated in the first French military exercise east of the Main. In September 1987 the much larger "Bold Sparrow" exercise near Augsburg in Bavaria demonstrated that 20,000 FAR troops equipped with 240 helicopters and 500 armored vehicles could intervene quickly to help defend the Federal Republic. Despite the achievements of this exercise, including the profound symbolism of French troops serving under a German commander, "Bold Sparrow" exposed Franco-German incompatibilities. These arose from language problems and the French army's lack of familiarity with NATO procedures.

According to the West German *White Paper*, "The stationing of the II French Corps with its three tank divisions and about 50,000 men clearly indicates that France will participate in the defense against an attack in Central Europe."[23] Bonn believes that although France refuses to rejoin NATO's integrated military structure, she will participate in the common defense. As the German Defense Ministry official Lothar Rühl wrote:

> France's allies count, in truth, on the efficacious support of French forces which have the mission of operational reserves; they suppose that these forces would be available in case of need and are convinced that France will act in a realistic manner during

---

23 Federal Minister of Defense, *White Paper 1985: The Situation and the Development of the Federal Armed Forces* , op.cit., p. 120.

an acute crisis in Europe, seeking its security with its allies without too much waiting for the evolution of the conflict.[24]

In the mid-1980s, Germans believed that French interests demanded rapid French intervention because any aggression against the Federal Republic had dire implications for French security, because French forces in Germany were hostages,[25] and because French forces were too weak to mount a credible defense at the Rhine. Therefore, German military officers privately asserted that they had "no doubt that France will participate as an operational reserve in the event of war" and called French involvement "definite."

Nonetheless, this view contrasted sharply with official French policy statements. As former defense minister Hernu had written, France's "engagement in Europe would not be automatic since it is not a question of reintegrating in the NATO military structure nor of occupying a sector in the 'forward battle'...France, and France alone, will decide the moment when she will join her forces to those of her allies."[26] General Poirier pointed out that de Gaulle withdrew France from the integrated alliance structure precisely to avoid being "automatically involved in the struggle even though she had not wished it."[27] Even the 1987 *loi de programme militaire* asserted that:

---

24 Lothar Rühl, "1982: La relance de la coopération franco-allemande," in Karl Kaiser and Pierre Lellouche, eds., *Le couple franco-allemand et la défense de l'Europe* (Paris: Economica, 1986), p. 42.

25 This opinion is sometimes echoed in France. Ambassador François Puaux has written that, "Their presence ... is a physical and human token infinitely superior to all the guarantees that we could give." ("La France, l'Allemagne et l'atome: Discorde improbable, accord impossible," in *Défense nationale*, Vol. 41 (December 1985), p. 14).

26 Charles Hernu, *Défendre la paix* (Paris: Editions J.-C. Lattès, 1985), p. 59. François Gorand (pseud.) of the Foreign Ministry wrote that, "There is nevertheless one point on which the German consensus is not in doubt: it is the hostility to non-automatic intervention by France in case of conflict. Now it is a point which, in principle at least, is not negotiable for us." ("La politique de sécurité européenne de la France de 1981 à 1985 et après," in *Commentaire*, No. 33 (Spring 1986), p. 14.)

27 Charles de Gaulle, Declaration of 21 February 1966; quoted in Lucien Poirier, "Le deuxième cercle: La défense égoïste de la citadelle et la grande aventure au-delà de la contrescarpe," in Lucien Poirier, *Essais de stratégie théorique*, op.cit., p. 297. Ambassador François de Rose presented a contrasting

> ... France will honor her commitments according to modalities that, as in the past, she will freely determine. Her independent position does not permit her to integrate her means in advance within a mechanism over which she could not exercise her sovereign decision when the time comes. This preoccupation in no way affects France's determination to intervene in Europe along side her allies. If the survival of the nation comes into play at the borders of the country, her security can come into play at her neighbors' borders with the president judging in light of the circumstances whether the country's vital interests are threatened.[28]

Therefore, even as the French became increasingly convinced that French and West German security interests were inseparable,[29] the option of nonbelligerency remained a central element of France's official policy. Of course, this did not prove that Bonn's expectation of French assistance was mistaken. Perhaps French politicians were privately committed to forward defense but unwilling to publicly

---

view. He wrote of the NATO withdrawal, "Its goal was never to permit us to shirk these commitments from the moment one of our allies was the victim of aggression." (François de Rose, "Lettre ouverte au future Président de la République," in *L'Express*, 11 December 1987, p. 22.)

28 Assemblée Nationale, *Projet de loi de programme relatif à l'équipement militaire pour les années 1987-1991* (Paris: Huitième session ordinaire de 1986-87), No. 432, pp. 9-10. Poirier saw "nothing contradictory or ambiguous in this position...[France] retains the possibility of choosing the moment, the place, and the means of our military engagement according to the attitude of the allies and also according to our interests involved in the crisis." (Lucien Poirier, "Le deuxième cercle: La défense égoïste de la citadelle et la grande aventure au-delà de la contrescarpe, " in Lucien Poirier, *Essais de stratégie théorique*, op.cit., p. 298).

29 For example, Pierre Lellouche argued that "The only way to transmit this signal is to redeploy the whole of our system no longer on the Rhine but precisely on the Elbe." (Pierre Lellouche, *L'Avenir de la Guerre* (Paris: Editions Mazarine, 1985), p. 281). François Heisbourg called for "the political affirmation at the highest level of the automaticity of the engagement of our forces in case of aggression in Europe." (François Heisbourg, "Défense Française: L'impossible statu quo," in *Politique internationale*, No. 36 (Summer 1987), p. 150) Also see Henri Froment-Meurice, "L'Allemagne n'est pas notre glacis," in *Le Monde*, 30 April 1985, p. 2 and Christian Megrelis, "Pour une confédération franco-allemande," in *Le Monde*, 5 February 1986, p. 2.

disavow autonomy which was seen as a cornerstone of the French consensus. In fact, President Mitterrand raised the following rhetorical question in a 1986 book:

> What is the "forward battle" when less than two hundred kilometers separate the Rhine from the Thuringian salient which is three-quarters hour by air for an airmobile division and six minutes for a formation of planes? A theoretical dispute... I have difficulty conceiving our troops encamped in the Federal Republic as they are today and, at the first alert, executing a half turn to return home.[30]

French strategists also justified their ambiguity by arguing that deterrence is actually strengthened by uncertainty. But the Germans were not convinced. General Franz-Joseph Schulze, former commander of NATO's Central European forces, forcefully critiqued the French contention that "uncertainty on the part of the adversary concerning the moment and extent of French intervention would constitute an essential element of deterrence..." He argued that:

> In reality, not responding to the question of if, when, and with what forces one wishes to react to aggression does not increase the adversary's uncertainty but that of one's own allies ... The most important and effective deterrent element is the potential aggressor's conviction that an absolute solidarity exists among all the allies ... what is necessary for us is the demonstration of the French wish to participate as soon as possible in the common defense. It is this clear signal, and not an imprecise announcement of the type 'it is practically sure,' that the partner needs and that the potential enemy will not ignore.[31]

---

30 François Mitterrand, *Réflexions sur la politique extérieure de la France: Introduction à vingt-cinq discours (1981-1985)* (Paris: Fayard, 1986), pp. 98-99. During the Bold Sparrow maneuvers, Mitterrand said that "in a conflict, when there was an immediate peril, the duty of France would be to come to the aide of those who are her allies and to Germany." (Jacques Isnard, "M. Mitterrand a lancé le projet d'un conseil de défense commun," in *Le Monde*, 27-28 September 1987, p. 3).

31 Franz-Joseph Schulze, "La nécessité d'une réaction de défense immédiate et commune," in Karl Kaiser and Pierre Lellouche, eds., *Le couple franco-allemand et la défense de l'Europe*, op.cit., p. 161 and p. 168.

French conventional forces have two roles: to defend the FRG conventionally alongside the allies if the president makes that determination but also to conduct the national deterrent maneuver (to test the enemy's intentions) prior to the use of prestrategic (*l'ultime avertissement)* weapons. Pierre Lellouche is among those who criticize "this ambiguous situation where the 1st Army sees itself entrusted with two missions which are difficult to reconcile..."[32]

During 1987 this major obstacle to improved Franco-German security cooperation was largely resolved. On 26 March, former French prime minister Raymond Barre presented a significant speech in London before the International Institute of Strategic Studies and asserted that, "all must be made aware that for France, the battle begins the very moment West Europe, and primarily West Germany, suffers aggression."[33] In the words of *L'Express*, "For the first time a French politician broke openly with the ambiguity of an unquestioned Gaullist tradition."[34]

Then in June 1987 Chancellor Kohl proposed creating a mixed Franco-German brigade. Kohl's proposal responded to American nuclear policies and CDU parliamentary leader Alfred Dregger's more far-reaching proposal that France should lead a future European security community and extend its nuclear guarantee to the Federal Republic.[35] France's political elite responded quickly and positively to Kohl's suggestion, and a survey indicated that 60

---

32 Pierre Lellouche, *L'Avenir de la Guerre* (Paris: Editions Mazarine, 1985), p. 269.

33 Raymond Barre, "1987 Alastair Buchan Memorial Lecture: Foundations for European Security and Cooperation," in *Survival*, Vol. 29, No. 4 (July/August 1987), p. 298. Also see Barre's 4 July 1987 speech at La Rochelle on France's world role, in *Le Monde*, 7 July 1987, p. 9.

34 Jérôme Dumoulin, "Les nouvelles armes de Barre," in *L'Express*, 3 April 1987, p. 23.

35 Alfred Dregger was a longtime supporter of close German-American ties, but press reports indicated that, "In his party's private councils, Mr. Dregger has been bitterly saying that the United States betrayed and abandoned West Germany." (James M. Markham, "Paris and Bonn Start to Think of a Special Alliance," in *The New York Times*, 24 June 1987, p. 3.) Also see, Henri de Bresson, "Le chancelier Kohl propose de créer une brigade franco-allemande," in *Le Monde*, 21-22 June 1987, p. 4.

percent of the French public supported the concept.[36] Dissent was limited to the Communists and dogmatic Gaullists such as Michel Debré who feared it would lead indirectly toward French reintegration into NATO.

Although both countries wanted the brigade to be more than a-symbolic gesture, difficulties arose from Bonn's reluctance to remove forces from NATO's integrated command and Paris' refusal to place its forces within NATO. The solution was to draw the two German battalions from the 55th Brigade of the Territorial Army which is under national rather than NATO command. By October 1990, the brigade will consist of 4,200 men in two infantry battalions, one armored battalion, and one battalion of artillery based at Böblingen, south of Stuttgart. A German speaking French officer was the first to fill the rotating command.

In the event of war, the two governments will exercise joint control over the brigade which could be assigned to defend the rear of the battle area or used to reinforce a French or NATO unit. German officers point out that the brigade could then come under the orders of SACEUR. The brigade was further evidence of France's willingness to defend West Germany. As one French officer said, "In case of conflict, how could France not be automatically pulled in when a part of her forces would be organically joined to German forces?"[37]

On 12 December, 1987, Prime Minister Chirac finally committed France unambiguously to automatic participation in the FRG's defense. According to Chirac's speech before the *Institut des hautes Etudes de défense nationale* (IHEDN):

> France now possesses means which permit the affirmation of the European dimension of her security. The maturation of our prestrategic nuclear forces allows us more flexibility in using our

---

36 See "M. Chirac: tout ce qui renforce les liens entre les deux pays va dans le bon sens," in *Le Monde*, 25 June 1987, p. 3; Jacques Isnard, "Paris est favorable à l'idée d'une brigade franco-allemande," in *Le Monde*, 23 June 1987, p. 1 and p. 3; Daniel Vernet, "Paradoxes franco-allemands," in *Le Monde*, 25 June 1987, p. 1 and p. 3; and Thankmar von Münchhausen, "Schmidt idea about joint Franco-German force gathers rapid momentum," in *The German Tribune*, No. 1280, 5 July 1987, p. 3 (translated from *Frankfurter Allgemeine Zeitung*, 25 June 1987).

37 See Jérôme Dumoulin and Dominique de Montvalon, "Europe: la brigade du Rhin," in *L'Express*, 3 July 1987, p. 6.

> air and ground forces. During the period when Pluton was the principal instrument of the nuclear warning, its use was the priority mission of our forces, and this situation impelled us to withhold these forces for a deterrent maneuver conducted as close as possible to our border.The deployment of air-to-surface missiles frees us from this constraint. Pluton's replacement in 1991 by much longer-range Hadès missiles will perfect this evolution.
>
> Were West Germany to be the victim of an aggression, who can now doubt that France's commitment would be immediate and wholehearted? There cannot be a battle of Germany and a battle of France.[38]

President Mitterrand echoed these views in a well-publicized interview in the *Nouvel Observateur* and, less explicitly, in his own IHEDN speech in 1988.[39]

The most significant recent accomplishment of Franco-German relations may prove to be the bilateral Defense and Security Council. President Mitterrand proposed the Defense Council in September 1987, and its first meeting was held in April 1989. The Council includes the German chancellor, the president and prime minister of France, the foreign and defense ministers, and the army chiefs-of-staff. Mitterrand modeled his proposal on the French defense council, chaired by the president, which determines French military policy. It is intended to harmonize all aspects of defense policy including organization of the brigade, joint maneuvers, arms control, interoperability of weapons, and armament cooperation. The council has its secretariat in Paris and must meet at least semi-annually.

---

38 "<<L'engagement de la France serait immédiat et sans réserve dans l'hypothèse d'une agression contre l'Allemagne fédérale>>," in *Le Monde*, 13-14 December 1987, p. 3.

39 See François Mitterrand, "La stratégie de la France," in *Le Nouvel Observateur*, 18-24 December 1987, pp. 22-26 and François Mitterrand, "Allocution de M. Mitterrand Président de la République devant les auditeurs de l'institut des hautes études de défense nationale le 11 octobre 1988," in *Défense nationale*, Vol. 44 (November 1988), pp. 13-27.

The third principle of German defense policy is the assumption that nuclear deterrence is indispensable to European security and that, "Dependence of West European defense on the nuclear capabilities of the United States could be reduced, but not eliminated."[40] This is a complex issue for Germany as the "double-zero" imbroglio illustrated. Between 1959 and 1983, a defense consensus prevailed in the Federal Republic which the SPD shattered by opposing the Pershing-II and Cruise Missile deployments.[41] In 1987, the prospect of removing all short- and longrange (500 to 5500 kilometers) superpower missiles from Europe caused disarray within West Germany's ruling coalition.

Nuclear threats are controversial because they are two-edged: they reinforce deterrence but risk potentially catastrophic outcomes if deterrence fails. Throughout the postwar era, German governments have emphasized the positive effects of deterrence. For example, in January 1987 Manfred Wörner (then German defense minister and now NATO's secretary general) argued that:

> There is no substitute for the nuclear strategy which has helped preserve the peace of America and Europe; and it makes no sense to take nuclear weapons, for instance, out of the compound system of the military instruments of that strategy in order to subject them, in isolation, to arms control, while the conventional forces would remain free from control and could again be used for war as a means of an aggressive policy.[42]

---

40 Federal Minister of Defense, *White Paper 1985: The Situation and the Development of the Federal Armed Forces*, op.cit., p. 36.

41 See Karl Kaiser, "L'IDS et la politique allemande," in Karl Kaiser and Pierre Lellouche, eds., *Le couple franco-allemand et la défense de l'Europe*, op.cit., p. 282; Catherine McArdle Kelleher, *Germany and the Politics of Nuclear Weapons* (New York: Columbia University Press, 1975), pp. 115-116; and Philip Windsor, "The Role of Germany," in *Avoiding Nuclear War: Common Security as a Strategy for the Defense of the West* (London: Brassey's Defense Publishers, 1985), pp. 87-98.

42 Manfred Wörner, "Security Policy Perspectives and Tasks of the North Atlantic Alliance in the Light of Changing East-West Relations," Munich, 24th *Wehrkunde* Meeting, 31 January 1987 (Bonn: Defense Ministry mimeo), p. 12.

By comparison, the Greens and large parts of the SPD have feared that the nature of politics among the great powers, and arms race dynamics, make the eventual use of nuclear weapons, and the concomitant annihilation of Germany, nearly inevitable. Believing that potential aggressors cannot be deterred by suicidal nuclear threats, the German Left has devised numerous proposals for non-nuclear defense.[43]

This profound German ambivalence toward nuclear weapons is not unique; as Richard Betts has argued, "For European populations as much as the American, the logic of extended deterrence is acceptable only when it is out of mind."[44] Even in France, a 1987 survey found that only 41 percent of the public (compared to 48 percent opposed) favored using France's nuclear weapons "if the USSR invaded French territory."[45] But German *Angst* is intensified by the knowledge that the country's fate rests so completely in foreign hands. At the 1986 SPD party congress, Bundestag member Andreas von Bülow revealed that a secret defense ministry study found that despite NATO's first-use policy, thirty-five percent of commissioned officers and sixty-five percent of non-commissioned officers thought there were no circumstances which could justify using nuclear weapons.[46] And when asked in September 1985, "Should NATO fall back upon the use of nuclear weapons if it is being threatened by a defeat in a conventional war?", only 11 percent

---

43 See Horst Afheldt, *Pour une défense non suicidaire en Europe* (Paris: Editions La Découverte, 1985). (German title: *Defensive Verteidigung*, Reinbeck bei Hamburg: Rowohlt Taschenbuch Verlag, 1983); Andreas von Bülow, "Vorschlag für eine strukturelle Nichtangriffsfähigkeit," in *Europäische Wehrkunde*, Vol. 35, No. 11 (1986), pp. 636-646; Hans Günter Brauch, "West German Approaches to Alternative Defense," Paper presented at International Studies Association Convention, Washington, D.C., 14-18 April 1987; and David Gates, "Area defense concepts: The West German debate," in *Survival*, Vol. 29, No. 4 (July/August 1987), pp. 301-317.

44 Richard K. Betts, "Nuclear Weapons," in Joseph S. Nye, Jr., ed., *The Making of America's Soviet Policy*, (New Haven: Yale University Press, 1984), p. 108.

45 Source: Sofres survey conducted 21-25 November 1987; N=1000. Michel Colomès, Sommet Reagan-Gorbatchev: l'esprit de défense des Français," in *Le Point*, 7 December 1987, p. 42. Earlier but similar findings are cited by Pierre Lellouche, *L'Avenir de la Guerre* (Paris: Editions Mazarine, 1985), p. 20.

46 Jonathan Steele, "SPD plans direct talks with Moscow," in *Manchester Guardian Weekly*, 7 September 1986, p. 7.

of the German public agreed and 80 percent disagreed.[47] According to French Defense Minister Jean-Pierre Chevènement, an unidentified German politician told him that, "If a single atomic rocket happened to explode on German territory, we would not be more courageous than the Japanese in 1945: the white flag would go up immediately."[48]

Furthermore, although Germans frequently assert that it is allied (and Soviet) opposition which precludes the possibility of a West German nuclear deterrent force, the repudiation of German nuclear weapons is actually stronger within the Federal Republic than elsewhere in West Europe. In a 1984 poll, only 10 percent of Germans agreed that "it would be a good thing ... to authorize the Federal Republic of Germany to have its own nuclear weapons?" This compared to 30 percent of the French and 25 percent of the British respondents.[49]

The German perception of nuclear weapons is schizophrenic. Although the majority believes that nuclear deterrence has maintained the peace since 1945, there is substantial questioning of NATO policy, and a sizeable minority condemns all nuclear capabilities. This is understandable considering Germany's location at the center of East-West tension, residual feelings of guilt for Nazi policies, and

---

47 *Newsweek* (German edition),7 October 1985. This compared to 29% and 27% who answered yes in France and the United Kingdom (negative 62% and 66%). The poll was conducted by Gallup between 18-23 September 1985. The sample size exceeded 500 in each country.

48 Jacques Amalric and Jean-Louis Andréani, "M. Chevènement: il faut une volonté politique franco-allemande," in *Le Monde*, 24 September 1987, p. 3.

49 Opinion surveys under the general supervision of SOFRES: France (N=1000) 13-18 April 1984; FRG (Infas, N=1219) 19 March-8 April 1984; UK (Gallup, N= 779) 4-9 April 1984. Jacques Fontaine, "A quoi rêvent les européens," in *L'Expansion*, No. 239 (25 May-7 June 1984), p. 86. The results were:

	Bad	Good
France	52%	30%
UK	56%	25%
FRG	74%	10%

In 1985, a French survey indicated that a majority of the French public approved a German nuclear deterrent (32%) or had no opinion (26%). See Claire Tréan, "Un sondage IFOP pour <<Le Monde>> et RTL: La France doit garantir la sécurité de la RFA estime une majorité des Français," in *Le Monde*, 28 June 1985, p. 2.

dependence upon capricious foreign leaders for the very survival of the state.

Given this ambivalence, Gorbachev's acceptance of the global zero option confronted the Bonn coalition with a thorny dilemma. During the heated 1983 domestic debate on Pershin-II and Cruise Missile deployments, the German government justified the INFs as necessary responses to the Soviet SS-20s. And in 1987, the Reagan administration used this argument to justify the double-zero treaty; for example, Richard Perle argued that NATO's INF deployments were "largely conceived to counter the Soviet SS-20s ..."[50]

From Europe's perspective, this was not an accurate description of INF's purpose. The INFs were intended to reinforce deterrence by increasing the probability that any European war would quickly escalate and engulf Soviet and American territory. As Ambassador François de Rose argued:

> The truth is that from the moment when the anti-aircraft defense of the Warsaw Pact rendered the penetration of manned planes too onerous and hazardous, it was necessary, even in the total absence of SS-20s, to have in Europe some American weapons capable of reaching at least the western regions of Russia. This threat of involvement of its territory would obligate the Kremlin to respond against American territory which would assure the "coupling" between the defense of Europe and the American strategic system.[51]

---

50 Richard Perle, "N'abusez pas du parapluie américain," in *L'Express*, 2 October 1987, p. 19.

51 François de Rose, "L'option zéro une erreur grave," in *Le Figaro*, 9 March 1987, p. 3; As former French Prime Minister Raymond Barre stated, "The Pershing II missiles are not solely a response to the SS-20s, as was claimed some years ago. They are an indispensable link in the chain of deterrence that should continue to bind Europe and the United States, since they can reach Soviet territory directly from Western Europe." (Raymond Barre, "1987 Alastair Buchan Memorial Lecture: Foundations for European Security and Cooperation," in *Survival*, Vol. 29, No. 4 (July/August 1987), p. 295). Also see Richard M. Nixon and Henry A. Kissinger, "To Withdraw Missiles We Must Add Conditions," in *Los Angeles Times*, 26 April 1987, Part IV, p. 1 and p. 3 and François Puaux, "<<Découplage>> et bon sens," in *Le Monde*, 14 March 1987, p. 2.

This perceived need for strengthened "coupling" did not arise from Soviet deployments of long or short range intermediate nuclear forces. It was a function of the Warsaw Pact's conventional superiority and American vulnerability to Soviet strategic attack.

When forced to choose between accepting the zero option to honor the public commitment made in 1983, or retaining INFs to avoid decoupling, the German coalition splintered. Foreign Minister Hans-Dietrich Genscher of the Free Democrats was an enthusiastic proponent of the zero option, but the late Franz Josef Strauss, leader of the Christian Social Union, argued for rejection despite NATO's 1979 dual-track decision and the rhetoric of 1983. Chancellor Helmut Kohl of the Christian Democrats perched on the fence. Like many in the CDU, he hoped the US would replace a small number of Pershing-II missiles with Pershing-IBs (a shorter-range version) to minimize "decoupling." But May 1987 state elections in Hamburg and the Rhineland-Palatinate served as quasi-referendums on this issue and demonstrated strong public support for the FDP's position. Thus domestic politics, and strong American pressure, eventually caused Chancellor Kohl to go even further and scrap Germany's 72 Pershing-IA missiles whose warheads were under US control.[52]

The French reaction to double-zero was less ambiguous but not without confusion. Most politicians criticized the possible "denuclearization" of West Europe - especially Defense Minister André Giraud who compared it to the 1938 Munich Conference. The skeptics included both past Socialist defense ministers (Charles Hernu and Paul Quilès) and prominent conservatives such as former prime minister Raymond Barre and former president Valéry Giscard d'Estaing. President Mitterrand was the significant exception, but he was constrained by his past advocacy of "Neither Pershing nor SS-20." Like the Bonn government, Mitterrand faced a credibility problem if he refused to take yes for an answer. Mitterrand was also reluctant to widen the gap between France and her European allies - especially the Federal Republic - on this crucial issue. Because Prime Minister Chirac wished to minimize dissension between the

---

52 Henry Kissinger described, "enormous pressure put on the Federal Republic of Germany to accept the withdrawal not only of the American medium-range missiles on its soil but also of Pershing 1As ..." Henry A. Kissinger, "A New Era for NATO," in *Newsweek*, 12 October 1987, p. 579.

Matignon and the Elysée on defense policy issues during the period of cohabitation, he was swayed by Mitterrand, and Paris muted its opposition.[53]

Contradictions arise in French nuclear doctrine if her vital security interests are defined to encompass territory beyond the Hexagon - particularly if France plans to fight alongside NATO allies. When French policy focused on deterring attacks on the "national sanctuary," there was a consistent nuclear doctrine. Contradictions arose when France redefined her vital security interests to encompass territory beyond the Hexagon, for the "national deterrent maneuver" and the "final warning" could take place on West German territory, that is within the territory of France's vital interests. Would France destroy Germany in order to save it?

French decision-makers tried to resolve this contradiction between nuclear autonomy and Franco-German cohesion. There were two approaches, and both involved dividing French conventional, tactical nuclear, and strategic nuclear forces into two categories. President Mitterrand's approach differentiated conventional forces from both tactical and strategic nuclear forces. Jacques Chirac, Valéry Giscard d'Estaing, and André Giraud (Chirac's defense minister) packaged tactical nuclear forces and conventional forces together and treated strategic nuclear forces as a separate category.

Giscard argued that France must "put in place two distinct deterrent levels: the strategic level and the tactical level intended to destroy the invader's forces ..."[54] Tactical nuclear weapons could then be used to support conventional forces permitting what Chirac has called a coupling between the "maneuver of conventional forces and the threat of recourse to nuclear weapons."[55] On this point, the

---

53 On the general French reaction, see D. Bruce Marshall, "France and the INF Negotiations: An 'American Munich'?," in *Strategic Review*, Vol. 15, No. 3 (Summer 1987), pp. 23-26.

54 Quoted in Frédéric Tiberghien, "Puissance et rôle de l'armement préstratégique français," in *Le Monde Diplomatique*, Vol. 34, No. 395 (February 1987), p. 14.

55 Jacques Chirac, "La politique de défense de la France: Allocution du premier ministre le 12 septembre 1986, lors de la séance d'ouverture de la 39e session de l'Institut des hautes études de défense nationale," in *Défense nationale*, Vol. 42 (November 1986), p. 12.

Socialist Mitterrand is more Gaullist than the General's political heirs, for he rejects any notion of flexible response and insists that prestrategic weapons are inseparable from the overall strategy and not "a simple extension of the conventional battle."[56] According to Mitterrand, it is not possible "to carve up the nuclear warning into small pieces."[57] His alternative envisions a conventional battle for Germany (using the FAR and the First Army) and a separate nuclear battle for France.

The approach of Chirac, Giscard, and Giraud is weakened by its refusal to extend a strategic nuclear guarantee to the Federal Republic while contemplating a limited nuclear war on German territory; this feeds German anxieties rather than quelling them.[58] Mitterrand's position is flawed because it permits the Soviets to attack the Federal Republic with less fear of French nuclear reprisals.[59]

An essential step toward Franco-German agreement on nuclear issues was taken during the summit of 28 February 1986 when President Mitterrand pledged to Chancellor Kohl that, "In the limits imposed by the extreme rapidity of such decisions ..." he would "consult the chancellor of the FRG on the eventual use of French prestrategic weapons on German territory."[60] But for Bonn genuine consultation involves more than a telephone link so that, time permitting, the French president can announce his decision. Bonn wishes to know whether the First Army will be committed, if it will be equipped with Pluton, what targets have been selected, and how the ultimate decision will be made.

These subjects are under discussion, but apparently President Mitterrand rejected the proposal of François Fillon (the conservative

---

56 Quoted in Pierre Lellouche, "Défense: division française," in *Le Point*, 3 November 1986, pp. 24-25.

57 Claire Tréan, "M. Genscher salue <<un puissant encouragement à l'Europe>>," in *Le Monde*, 24 October 1987, p. 3.

58 See Frédéric Tiberghien, "Puissance et rôle de l'armement préstratégique français," in *Le Monde Diplomatique*, Vol. 34, No. 395 (February 1987), p. 14.

59 This assumes added significance in the context of double-zero. See Pierre Lellouche, "Défense: division française," in *Le Point*, 3 November 1986, pp. 24-25 and David S. Yost, *France and Conventional Defense in Central Europe* (Boulder: Westview Press, 1985), p. 95.

60 Mitterrand also stated that he and Kohl had agreed to establish technical means for immediate consultation during crises. (*Le Monde*, 2-3 March 1986, p. 4).

former chairman of the National Assembly's defense committee) and others that France's nuclear war plans be shared with Bonn.[61] Moreover, the director of France's Cours supérieur interarmées (CSI), which includes Bundeswehr officers, said that "You will easily understand that you do not discuss together the nuclear attack plans!"[62]

During his state visit to the Federal Republic in October 1987, Mitterrand attempted a further clarification of French policy. In a well-publicized declaration Mitterrand affirmed that, "Nothing allows one to say that France's final warning against the attacker would be delivered on German territory."[63] Apparently, the final warning prior to strategic nuclear attacks could take various forms. It could be nonnuclear and possibly even nonmilitary.[64] Alternatively, France could adopt François Heisbourg's suggestion and offer the Federal Republic the option of deploying Hadès missiles in Germany, "if the Bonn government expressed the desire for it," which "would permit them to fire beyond East German territory."[65] However, Chancellor Kohl told *Le Monde* that, "It is completely out of the question that we would demand a second key to use these [French nuclear] arms."[66] Mitterrand agreed; he told *Die Welt,* "it is not conceivable that the Federal Republic, or any other country including the United

---

61 See Claire Tréan, "L'Affaire du Président," in *Le Monde*, 23 January 1988, p. 3.

62 Quoted in Elie Marcuse, "Défense: Paris va de l'avant," in *L'Express*, 22 January 1988, p. 44.

63 See Claire Tréan and Luc Rosenzweig, "<<La stratégie nucléaire de la France s'adresse à l'agresseur et à lui seul>>, affirme le Président de la République," in *Le Monde*, 21 October 1987, p. 3.

64 See Kosta Christitch, "Mitterrand en RFA: ambiguïté stratégique," in *Le Point*, 26 October 1987, p. 41.

65 François Heisbourg, "Défense Française: L'impossible statu quo," in *Politique Internationale*, No. 36 (Summer 1987), p. 147. A similar proposal was made by Charles Hernu, who later retracted it, and Pierre Messmer. See François Schlosser, "Paris-Bonn: le malentendu nucléaire," in *Le Nouvel Observateur*, 16-22 October 1987, p. 41.

66 Luc Rosenzweig and Daniel Vernet, "Le chancelier Kohl expose au <<Monde>> sa conception de la sécurité européenne," in *Le Monde*, 20 January 1988, p. 6.

States, could take part in the decision to use French nuclear weapons."[67]

A final possibility is to eliminate short range tactical nuclear forces and transfer the final warning to longer-range delivery vehicles, such as the Mirage 2000 and Super-Etendard aircraft equipped with air-to-surface missiles. Mitterrand has always considered Pluton and Hadès mistakes, and their purpose has remained ambiguous: are they battlefield nuclear weapons intended to offset the Warsaw Treaty Organization's conventional superiority or logically inseparable from the strategic forces? Increasingly, French opinion conceives the final warning as a limited counter-force attack against the adversary's home territory, but even Hadès' longer range will be inadequate for that. Hadès could also fall victim to a "triple zero" option which would eliminate all groundbased missiles from Europe. And, as Charles Hernu observed, even equipped with "neutron" warheads Hadès' use would entail nuclear warfighting. Therefore, Hernu proposed that Franco-German agreement on basic issues of European security could be facilitated by "sacrificing" Hadès and fulfilling the prestrategic mission with air-to-surface missiles.[68]

Unlike Pluton or Hadès, a major advantage of longer-range airborne systems is a continued ability to threaten Soviet territory when the American INFs are withdrawn. Disadvantages include greater vulnerability to adverse weather conditions and enemy defenses. Reliance on attacks against Soviet territory also contradicts France's traditional strategy by blurring the distinction between prestrategic and strategic strikes and ignores the view that landbased tactical nuclear weapons are needed to compensate for the Eastern Bloc's conventional superiority.

The taboo of nonbelligerency was shattered, but France still confronts the issue of extended nuclear deterrence. Former Socialist Prime Minister Laurent Fabius said that, "It is now necessary to consider the extension of our strategic nuclear guarantee to German security."[69] Former US ambassador to Paris Evan Galbraith echoed

---

67 "<< Même alliance, même Europe et, je l'espère, même avenir>>," in *Le Monde*, 19 January 1988, p. 3.

68 Jacques Isnard, "M. Hernu propose de sacrifier le missile Hadès au nom de la coopération franco-allemande," in *Le Monde*, 24 December 1987, p. 20.

69 "M. Fabius propose d'étendre à la RFA la <<garantie nucléaire>> de la France," *Le Monde*, 17 June 1987, p. 8. A similar but less explicit proposal is

this possibility by urging France, "to become the nuclear guarantor of Germany to compensate for the loss of the Pershings which were the only missiles in Europe capable of attacking the USSR."[70] At the 1988 *Wehrkunde* conference, Defense Minister Giraud obliquely implied a similar view by observing that France's deterrent was intended to protect vital interests and these are partially based upon France's political, economic, and cultural ties with her neighbors. "Thus, a threat can intervene in front of our borders, and likewise our own nuclear deterrent can be concerned in these same circumstances."[71] Moreover, 50 percent of the French public favors using French nuclear weapons to defend the Federal Republic.[72] So far, however, official French thinking rejects this option. President Mitterrand refuses to share the nuclear decision with Bonn and dismisses extended deterrence as a NATO rather than a French responsibility.[73]

German reactions to this issue are also somewhat Delphic. Although Chancellor Kohl described the existence of France's deterrent force as reassuring to Germany, he added that, "it is obvious that she cannot assume the weight of the defense of the Federal Republic and West Europe."[74] Willy Brandt cautioned the FRG not to be too demanding: "It is for France to determine its own interests."[75]

---

contained in Laurent Fabius, "La défense de la France à l'aube du XXIe siècle," in *Défense nationale*, Vol. 43 (November 1987), p. 22.

70 Quoted in Jean Schmitt, "Chaban met la Défense en avant," in *L'Express*, 17 January 1988, p. 30.

71 Quoted in "Washington met en garde l'Europe contre une dénucléarisation totale," in *Le Monde*, 9 February 1988, p. 3.

72 See "Un Français sur deux est partisan d'une garantie nucléaire à l'Allemagne fédérale," in *Le Monde*, 9 February 1988, p. 15. The survey (N=1000) was conducted 11-20 January 1988 by IPSOS for *Le Journal du Dimanche*.

73 See "Allocution de M. François Mitterrand Président de la République devant les auditeurs de l'institut des hautes études de défense nationale le 11 octobre 1988," in *Défense nationale*, Vol. 44 (November 1988), p. 26.

74 Luc Rosenzweig and Daniel Vernet, "Le chancelier Kohl expose au <<Monde>> sa conception de la sécurité européenne," in *Le Monde*, 20 January 1988, p. 6.

75 Quoted in "Willy Brandt: ni pacifistes ni neutralistes," in *L'Express*, 29 January 1988, p. 22.

FRANCO-GERMAN RELATIONS

Following World War II, many French and German citizens vowed to end the cycles of violence between their countries,[76] and efforts to erase historical animosities became increasingly successful following the EDC debacle.[77] The first of fourteen meetings between President Charles de Gaulle and Chancellor Konrad Adenauer was held in September 1958. In January 1963, they signed the Elysée Treaty whose preamble proclaims the conviction:

> that the reconciliation of the German people and the French people, ending a centuries-old rivalry, constitutes a historic event which profoundly transforms the relations between the two peoples... [and recognizes] that increased co-operation between the two countries constitutes an indispensable stage on the way to a united Europe, which is the aim of the two peoples ...

After the signing, the small existing network of Franco-German "sister cities" grew rapidly, and there are now approximately 1,200 relationships between French and German cities and more than 2,500 similar affiliations between schools.[78] There are also regularly scheduled meetings of the defense and foreign ministers every three months and semiannual summits. *L'Express* reported that

---

76 Indeed, the Bureau International de Liaison et de Documentation (BILD) was formed in 1945; it was followed by the Comité Français d'Echanges avec l'Allemagne Nouvelle as well as the Deutsch-Französisches Institut in 1948. See F. Roy Willis, *France, Germany and the New Europe: 1945-1967*, revised and expanded edition (Stanford: Stanford University Press, 1968); John E. Farquharson and Stephen C. Holt, *Europe from Below: An Assessment of Franco-German Popular Contacts* (London: George Allen & Unwin, 1975); and Caroline Bray, "Cultural and Information Policy: Bilateral Relations," in Roger Morgan and Caroline Bray, eds., *Partnership and Rivals in Western Europe: Britain, France and Germany* , (Brookfield, VT: Gower Publishing Company, 1986), pp. 93-96.

77 See Nicole Gnesotto, "Le dialogue franco-allemand depuis 1954: patience et longueur de temps," in Karl Kaiser and Pierre Lellouche, eds., *Le couple franco-allemand et la défense de l'Europe*, op.cit., pp. 11-30.

78 See "Intérêt de l'un pour l'autre," in *Le Monde*, 21 January 1988, p. 5 and *The Franco-German Youth Office* (Paris and Bad Honnef: Office franco-allemand pour la Jeunesse and Deutsch-Französisches Jugendwerk, n.d.), p. 30.

Chancellor Kohl and President Mitterrand met some fifty times through October 1987. There were eleven meetings during 1985, and during 1986 Kohl met Mitterrand six times and Prime Minister Chirac five times.[79] Lower level meetings are generally more frequent depending upon personal relationships. For example, German Foreign Minister Genscher is much closer to French Foreign Minister Roland Dumas than to Jean-Bernard Raimond who led the Quai d'Orsay during cohabitation.[80]

Bonn and Paris agreed in 1986 to exchange diplomatic personnel for extended periods, and subsequently a French diplomat worked for nearly a year within the German foreign ministry and even represented the FRG officially at a CSCE meeting in Vienna.[81] There are also modest exchanges of military officers. In 1988, four German officers participated in the CSI at the Ecole militaire, with the number expected to triple by 1990, while three French officers attended the *Führungsakademie* in Hamburg.[82]

Other efforts were less fruitful. For nearly twenty years, the Elysée treaty failed to harmonize Franco-German defense cooperation. De Gaulle sought to construct a European consensus independent from the superpowers, but in ratifying the treaty the Bundestag appended a preamble which confirmed the priority of the Federal Republic's American connection. This preamble referred not only to European unity but also to "a close partnership between Europe and the United States of America," "collective defense within the framework of the North Atlantic Alliance," and other goals irritating to France. As a result, the defense component of the treaty remained stillborn until 1982. In addition, there was no headway toward the treaty's goal of increased Franco-German bilingualism,

---

79 Elie Marcuse, "Défense: une stratégie de trop," in *L'Express*, 30 October 1987, p. 22. The figure for 1985 is from "Interview with M. Roland Dumas, Minister for External Relations, Broadcast on West German Radio (*Südwestfunk*) 2 March 1986," Ambassade de France à Londres, 14 March 1986. The 1986 data are contained in a letter from Chancellor Kohl's office; they include neither the Tokyo Economic Summit nor the summits of European leaders.

80 See Claire Tréan, "L'affaire du Président," in *Le Monde*, 23 January 1988, p. 3.

81 See Luc Rosenzweig, "Quand un Français représente la RFA dans les réunions internationales," in *Le Monde*, 21 January 1988, p. 4.

82 See Elie Marcuse, "Défense: Paris va de l'avant," in *L'Express*, 22 January 1988, p. 44.

and English often serves as the lingua franca of Franco-German relations.[83]

Despite these setbacks, considerable progress was made in joint Franco-German weapons production during the 1960s and 1970s.[84] Projects included the Transall transport plane, the Alpha Jet combat plane, two anti-tank missiles (Milan and HOT), and an anti-aircraft missile (Roland). This cooperation faltered after the early 1970s, and more than fifteen years have now passed since a major new bilateral arms project was successfully completed. Meanwhile, several attempts at bilateral or multilateral weapons cooperation failed conspicuously. A joint tank project inaugurated in 1980 was

---

83 For example, English is used to communicate during Franco-German military exercises; see, Jonathan Steele, "If the Yanks go home: The end of the de Gaulle era," in *The Guardian*, 21 October 1986. Also see Luc Rosenzweig, "Une double épreuve de vérité," in *Le Monde*, 26-27 October 1986, p. 1.
English is the overwhelmingly dominant foreign language in both countries. In France, 79% of the youth have studied English compared to 29% for German (and Spanish), and in West Germany 75% have studied English compared to 35% that have studied French. This situation has deteriorated in France during the last two decades as more French students select English rather than German as their first foreign language and Spanish rather than German as their second language. Between 1958-59 and 1985-86 the position of English as the first language of French students increased from 76% to 85% while the German percentage fell from 21% to 13%. In the same period, Spanish rose as a second language from 30% to 47% while German declined from 33% to 27%. Philippe Bernard, "Le rendez-vous européen d'Expolangues," in *Le Monde*, 26 March 1987, p. 17.

84 See Lars Benecke, Ulrich Krafft, and Friedhelm Meyer zu Natrup, "French-West German Technological Cooperation," in *Survival*, Vol. 28, No. 3 (May/June 1986), pp. 195-207; Gustav Bittner, "La coopération franco-allemande en matière d'armement classique," in Karl Kaiser and Pierre Lellouche, eds., *Le couple franco-allemand et la défense de l'Europe*, op.cit., pp. 131-149; André Brigot, "Une coopération franco-allemande en matière de sécurité est-elle possible?" in Groupe d'études sur les Conflits et les Stratégies en Europe, *Sécurité et Défense de l'Europe: Le Dossier Allemand*, (Paris: Fondation pour les études de la Défense nationale, *Collection les sept epées*, No. 36, troisième trimestre 1985), pp. 149-227; Pierre Dussauge, *L'industrie française de l'armement: Intervention de l'Etat et stratégies des entreprises dans un secteur à technologie de pointe* (Paris: Economica, 1985), pp. 83-91; William Wallace, "Defense: The Defense of Sovereignty, or the Defense of Germany?" in Roger Morgan and Caroline Bray, eds., *Partnership and Rivals in Western Europe: Britain, France and Germany*, (Brookfield, VT: Gower Publishing Company, 1986), pp. 230-237.

abandoned in 1982, largely because France and the FRG preferred different production timetables.

France was also disappointed when the Federal Republic declined to develop a Franco-German optical reconnaissance satellite (Helios) following discussions held during 1983-84. Bonn argued that the project's success was jeopardized by frequent cloud cover over Central Europe, but some French experts also cited Bonn's disinclination to annoy Washington by entering the satellite field and wrangling in Bonn concerning which ministry would foot the bill.[85] As Jérôme Paolini has argued, the two countries' very different relationships to NATO led them to discordant conclusions. French military strategy is based on autonomous nuclear deterrence, and an independent intelligence capability was highly desirable, but the FRG follows an alliance strategy, and US intelligence "responded to her operational needs, was politically acceptable, and financially rational."[86]

A third significant failure was France's withdrawal in 1985 from talks with Britain, Italy, Spain, and the Federal Republic concerning a European Fighter Aircraft (EFA). France now plans to build an avion de combat europeen (ACE) based upon Dassault-Breguet's Rafale prototype while the other countries proceed with EFA. Although the Rafale project needs foreign partners to fill a reported budget shortfall of more than $1.5 billion, and Belgium rejected participation in February 1989, the French government has reiterated its intention to proceed alone.[87]

The principal ongoing Franco-German project is the combat helicopter program. First contemplated more than ten years ago, an agreement was signed in May 1984 to produce an anti-tank helicopter for the Bundeswehr and anti-tank and anti-helicopter models for the French from a single base. The lack of commonality among the three versions led to substantial cost escalation, and there

---

85 See François Heisbourg, "Coopération en matière d'armements: rien n'est jamais acquis," in Karl Kaiser and Pierre Lellouche, eds., *Le couple franco-allemand et la défense de l'Europe*, op.cit., p. 122.

86 Jérôme Paolini, "Politique spatiale militaire française et coopération européenne," in *Politique étrangère*, Vol. 52, No. 2 (Summer 1987), p. 443.

87 See "Rafale: le gouffre à millards," in *L'Express* , 23 September 1988, pp. 28-34; "Rafale: les extraits du rapport," in *L'Express*, 30 September 1988, pp. 8-10; and Jacques Isnard, "Un coup dur pour les Français," in *Le Monde*, 27 February 1989, p. 16.

were deep conflicts concerning design specifications.[88] These controversies are now resolved, and France will acquire 215 helicopters and the FRG 212 with deployment to begin in 1992-93. The program's high cost, more than DM 9 billion for the FRG and approximately FF 30 billion for France, made it vulnerable to political attack, but support for the project now appears firm as a symbol of Franco-German cooperation.[89] Other ongoing projects include a Franco-German tank recovery vehicle constructed on France's AMX-40 chassis and two missiles for battlefield reconnaissance, the Brevel and the CL-289 (which also involves Canada)

The armament markets of individual European countries are relatively small, so it is difficult to compete successfully against much larger American firms. Advocates claim that armament cooperation can reduce unit costs through economies of scale, maintain technological independence and competitiveness vis-à-vis the United States (and increasingly Japan), and strengthen institutions for European unification. The Franco-German experience illustrates how difficult it is to achieve these goals. Although François Heisbourg has argued that, "The cost of the next generation of weapon systems means that European arms cooperation is not only desirable but an absolute necessity,"[90] cooperative arms programs are not always cost effective. During the EFA episode, the

---

88 These included whether the crewmen would sit side by side or in line, whether an existing American targeting system would be used or a new system developed, and whether the aircraft's sights would be placed in the nose, on the roof, or on a strut above the roof. For a detailed analysis from a conservative French parliamentary perspective, see Henri Louet, Commission de la Défense Nationale et des Forces Armées, *La coopération industrielle franco-allemande en matière d'hélicoptères de combat* (Paris: Assemblée Nationale, troisième session extraordinaire de 1985-86), No. 249.

89 See Serge Schmemann, "France and West Germany to Set Up Joint Councils," in *The New York Times*, 14 November 1987, p. 3; Jacques Isnard, "Paris et Bonn s'engagent à construire en commun un hélicoptère de combat," in *Le Monde*, 18 July 1987, p. 10; "Un hélicoptère franco-allemand," in *Le Monde*, 18 July 1987, p. 1; "Determination to press on with anti-tank helicopter," in *The German Tribune*, 26 July 1987, p. 4 (translated from Süddeutsche Zeitung, 16 July 1987); and "Défense: l'hélico vole trop haut," in *Le Point*, 27 July 1987, p. 20.

90 Quoted in Diana Geddes, "Defense: more a liaison than a marriage," in *The Times* (London), 27 September 1986.

French defense minister claimed that joint programs often have higher costs and more delays than national programs;[91] this is plausible given the difficulty of coordinating the frequently incompatible needs, timetables, and doctrines of separate military organizations. For example, because of export considerations and out-of-area responsibilities, France often prefers lighter and cheaper weapons than the FRG whose concerns are limited to Central European contingencies. This influenced France's withdrawal from the EFA consortium which considered planes with sixteen possible weight and engine combinations. Furthermore, project failures can have negative political effects, and problems can metastasize if politicians compensate by approving questionable projects merely to advance the political agenda. As National Assembly deputy Henri Louet wrote of the helicopter program:

> If the needs were very different, it would perhaps have been wiser to recognize it and to refrain. Far from this attitude, the defense minister, Charles Hernu, needed a success following the abandonment of the Franco-German tank project and that of the fighter plane which was already outlined on the horizon ... the wish to succeed was so strong on the French side that the minister at the time was led to accept the unacceptable.[92]

Former French Defense Minister Giraud criticized both autarkic approaches and efforts to produce every weapons system through multinational programs. He advocated a division of labor among the European countries with each country specializing in weapons technologies where it possessed particular expertise, for example the Federal Republic might build tanks and France, aircraft. Giraud thought it absurd to seek a balance of national benefits from each individual program; instead, the equilibrium should be sought across

---

91 See Philippe Lemaitre, "Les membres européens de l'alliance atlantique pour une politique aéronautique à long terme," in *Le Monde*, 2 May 1986.

92 Henri Louet, Commission de la Défense Nationale et des Forces Armées, *La coopération industrielle franco-allemande en matière d'hélicoptères de combat*, (Paris: Assemblée Nationale, troisième session extraordinaire de 1985-86), No. 249, p. 23 and p. 66.

a range of armament projects.[93] Elsewhere in Europe, and particularly in the FRG, there is substantial support for the logic of this argument, but the domestic clout of arms manufacturers, and the lack of agreement among military chiefs of staff, persist as major hindrances to more rational armaments production.

Although the helicopter program now appears assured, and France remains the FRG's principal partner for bilateral projects and second partner (after the UK) for multilateral projects,[94] prospects for future weapons cooperation remain clouded. It is an open question whether armaments can reassume their earlier status as a leading sector of Franco-German security cooperation.

Bonn and Paris also cooperate on space projects. France is the principal proponent of European cooperation within the thirteen member European Space Agency (ESA). The Space Agency's attention is currently focused on three projects. The least controversial is Ariane-5 which involves the new and heavier version in the Ariane series of rockets for launching space vehicles planned for 1995 at a projected cost of nearly $4 billion. Hermès is a second and much more controversial program to launch a two-man space shuttle in 1998 at a cost approaching $5 billion. Some British detractors dismiss Hermès as no more than a Dassault-Breguet testbed for new fighter-aircraft technologies.[95] The third program, Columbus, involves a European laboratory for the planned American space station to be launched after 1996.

A stormy ESA meeting in November 1987 pitted France, which sought approval for all three projects, against Britain which opposed them. A German compromise, approved over vehement British objection, extended Hermès' research stage for three additional years at a cost of $585 million.[96] France is expected to finance 45 percent

---

93 See Jacques Isnard, "M. Giraud propose une <<charte de sécurité>> européenne," in *Le Monde*, 9 April 1987, p. 22 and "Le ministre de la Défense: concentrer les moyens," in *L'Express*, No. 1821, 6 June 1986, pp. 14-15.

94 According to German Defense Ministry official Lothar Rühl in a *Le Point* interview. See, "<<Une unité intégrée franco-allemande>>," in *Le Point*, 29 June 1987, p. 57.

95 See "Per ardua ad ESA," in *The Economist*, 7 November 1987, p. 93.

96 See Pearce Wright, "UK refuses to sign new European space plan," in *The Times* (London), 11 November 1987, p. 2; "Un <<oui mais>> allemand à l'Europe spatiale," in *Le Monde*, November 8-9 1987, p. 12; and "Out of Space," in *The Times* (London), 9 November 1987, p. 17.

of both Ariane-5 (FRG 22 percent, Italy 15 percent) and Hermès (FRG 30 percent and Italy 12-15 percent) without British participation. For Columbus, the French and German roles are reversed, probably because its link to the American space program makes it more attractive to Bonn but less attractive to Paris. Germany will contribute 38 percent followed by Italy (25 percent), and France (15 percent maximum).[97]

FUTURE RELATIONS

In just forty years, France and the Federal Republic have progressed from *Erbfeindschaft* to *relations privilégiées* with the German chancellor and the French president referring to a "community of destiny" between their countries and Chancellor Kohl declaring that "France and the Federal Republic can only master their future together."[98] This is a momentous achievement, and it is essentially true, as François Mitterrand has written, that "the only embryo of common European defense resides in the Franco-German Elysée Treaty."[99] Certainly the most probable scenario for European defense cooperation is the emergence of a Franco-German defense community which would then enlarge to include the other members of the Western European Union. This might occur as a "European pillar" within the Atlantic Alliance or as a substitute for NATO; in either case it would be profoundly important.

But is a Franco-German community probable considering the obstacles on both sides? France has finally discarded the option of nonbelligerency, but French leaders remain reluctant to sacrifice their residual autonomy. France refuses to rejoin NATO's integrated military structure, and the thorny issue of France's nuclear doctrine is unresolved. The Germans, while valuing the French connection, remain much closer to and dependent upon the United States and the Alliance. Although France is now more tolerant of the close German-

---

97 Jean-François Augereau, "L'Europe a affirmé sa détermination de ne pas <<jouer les seconds rôles>> dans la conquête de l'espace," in *Le Monde*, 12 November 1987, p. 9.

98 Quoted in François Mitterrand, *Réflexions sur la politique extérieure de la France: Introduction à vingt-cinq discours (1981-1985)* (Paris: Fayard, 1986), p. 104.

99 Ibid., p. 101.

American tie, the intimacy of this relationship remains an irritant between Bonn and Paris. There is also a gulf dividing French and German conceptions of European security.

The French are obsessed by fears of German neutralism and pacifism; these constitute the new French nightmare having replaced the old fear of German aggression.[100] Renata Fritsch-Bournazel has admonished that, "To speak constantly of a German drift, of a nationalist-neutralist temptation, is surely not the best way to convince the Germans of the sincerity of the sentiments of solidarity that the French feel toward their closest neighbor."[101] But the French cannot help themselves; they are trapped by the logic of Napoleon's dictum that, "The policy of a nation is in its geography." French fears are fed by the Greens' electoral strength (8.3 percent in the 1987 Bundestag election and 8.4 percent in the 1989 election for members of the European Parliament), the SPD's accommodationist defense policies, and German public opinion. A secret government poll divulged in May 1987 by the newspaper *Bild* showed that 71 percent of the population favored reunification of a nonaligned Germany,[102] and a February 1989 survey found that 79 percent of respondents "did not worry about the threat from the East."[103] The French were unnerved when even the FRG's most celebrated "hawk," the late Franz Josef Strauss, returned from his first trip to Moscow and said that, "We no longer have to fear the aggressive intentions of the USSR."[104]

France's commitment to European cooperation tends to intensify when the Federal Republic is perceived as drifting toward neutralism and pacifism. For example, in the early 1980s when West Germany confronted the contentious INF deployment decision, the long suspended defense component of the Elysée Treaty was implemented

---

100 For example, François-Georges Dreyfus speaks of "pacifist, neutralist, anti-nuclear propoganda" (François-Georges Dreyfus, "Les Allemagnes et le national-neutralisme," in *Revue des deux mondes*, No. 2 (February 1987), p. 356).

101 Renata Fritsch-Bournazel, "Interrogations stratégiques et quête d'identité," in Groupe d'études sur les Conflits et les Stratégies en Europe, *Sécurité et Défense de l'Europe: Le Dossier Allemand* , op.cit., p. 142.

102 See "Rumeurs à Bonn à propos de la réunification," in *Le Monde*, 14 May 1987, p. 2.

103 Source: *Der Spiegel*, 27 February 1989, p. 51.

104 Quoted in Yves Cuau, "Mars et Mercure," in *L'Express*, 5 February 1988, p. 23.

(February 1982), President Mitterrand supported the INF deployments before the Bundestag (January 1983), and the moribund Western European Union was reactivated by the Rome Declaration (November 1984). But as the INF crisis receded, and France became less fearful of German neutralism, the enthusiasm for new initiatives faded in both countries.[105] American behavior is also a crucial variable. Franco-German cooperation typically flourishes if the US is perceived as a weaker or less dependable ally, which is not surprising for both countries have relied upon the American military commitment throughout the postwar era.[106] It is the keystone of German defense but also fundamental to French policy, which depends upon America's contribution to overall European, and especially German, defense. Major changes in US behavior significantly affect Franco-German security relations, and the events of late 1986 (Reykjavik) and 1987 (double-zero) stimulated new interest in European defense cooperation.

The French, and to a lesser extent the Germans, were horrified by President Reagan's willingness at the 1986 Reykjavik summit to endorse possible elimination of ballistic missiles (some accounts said all nuclear weapons) by 1996.[107] Reagan seemed eager to abandon nuclear deterrence, which most Europeans believed had preserved the peace since 1945, in the total absence of prior allied consultation. This prompted British military historian Sir Michael Howard to describe "the approval at Reykjavik of arms reductions on a scale, and of a kind, which calls the defense of Europe into question."[108] As we have seen, the trauma intensified when the superpowers later

---

105 As Peter Schmidt has written of the WEU, "Much of the motivation for the relaunching sprang from the specific political situation in the context of the debate on the two-track decision and was thus of a limited nature." (Peter Schmidt, "The WEU - A Union Without Perspective?" in *Aussenpolitik* , Vol. 37, No. 4 (1986), p. 399).

106 See Karl Kaiser and Pierre Lellouche, "Le couple franco-allemand et la défense de l'Europe: synthèses et recommandations," in Karl Kaiser and Pierre Lellouche, eds., *Le couple franco-allemand et la défense de l'Europe* , op.cit., p. 313.

107 See Michael Mandelbaum and Strobe Talbott, "Reykjavik and Beyond," in *Foreign Affairs*, Vol. 65, No. 2 (Winter 1986/87), p. 226.

108 Sir Michael Howard, "Friends, foes and fears for the Alliance," in *The Daily Telegraph*, 2 December 1986, p. 14.

agreed to eliminate all Soviet and American nuclear missiles in the 500 to 5500 kilometer range.

Franco-German cooperation is also reinforced by French aspirations for national greatness, what Alfred Grosser describes as "a French ambition to exercise global responsibilities."[109] France controls only 4 percent of the global product and cannot fulfill her dreams alone; she needs the Federal Republic. As Stanley Hoffmann recognized many years ago, "It is through Europe that France can still pretend to a certain grandeur."[110] Or, as Paul-Jean Franceschini asserted, less tactfully, "Without Germany solidly fastened to her, France is nothing more than an ambition without means."[111]

When combined, France and Germany constitute 9.5 percent of the global product (close to the Soviet Union with 13 percent and Japan with 11 percent), while the whole EC produces 20 percent.[112] Therefore, by influencing West Europe, or at least the Franco-German tandem, France obtains access to the resources required to fulfill aspirations such as the European space program.

According to Jacques Chirac, France and Germany now confront "the same [question] General de Gaulle tried unsuccessfully to put to his principal allies: how to act so Europeans can, in the context of their alliance with the United States, take charge of their destiny."[113] There has been concrete progress toward this goal in recent years. Even in 1982, when the Elysée Treaty's defense component was belatedly implemented, virtually no one foresaw the subsequent achievements: French soldiers serving under a German commander during exercises deep within the FRG, a Defense Council established to harmonize military policy and operational plans, a permanent bilateral brigade serving under rotating French and German commanders, arms cooperation revitalized by the multibillion dollar helicopter program, and a revolution in French

---

109 Alfred Grosser, "Un optimisme mesuré mais légitime," in *Le Monde*, 23 January 1988, p. 2.

110 Quoted in Anthony Hartley, "The British Bomb," in *Survival*, Vol. 6, No. 4 (July/August 1964), p. 174.

111 Quoted in Ingo Kolboom, "La politique de sécurité de la France: un point de vue allemand," in Karl Kaiser and Pierre Lellouche, eds., *Le couple franco-allemand et la défense de l'Europe*, op.cit., p. 71.

112 See *Le Point*, 11 January 1988, p. 45.

113 Michel Colomès (interviewer), "Défense: la ligne Chirac," in *Le Point*, 5 October 1987, p. 28.

military doctrine as François Mitterrand and Jacques Chirac competed to reshape French policy concerning tactical nuclear weapons and the automaticity of French participation in Germany's forward defense.

Some observers disparage the alleged superficiality of Franco-German rapprochement. They dismiss Franco-German cooperation as a series of dramatic but ultimately empty gestures, what one German defense industry executive characterized as "purely symbolic bullshit."[114] This criticism has some substance, for as *The Economist* editorialized concerning the brigade and the Defense Council, "so far they will not add a man or a franc to Europe's defense."[115] The United States remains the ultimate guarantor, and it is Britain, not France, that continues to make the larger ongoing contribution to Central European defense. Nonetheless, Bonn and Paris have established the essential foundation for change.

De Gaulle erred in pursuing grand initiatives such as the Elysée Treaty and the Fouchet Plan without preparing the political terrain. The result was worse than failure: a residue of recriminations and the ossification of the European system for a generation. But now Paris pursues a policy which avoids forcing Bonn to choose between Europe and America. Criticism of Franco-German cooperation also overlooks the political import of symbolic acts. Prime Minister Thatcher (like Jacques Chirac) disdains symbolic gestures such as Chancellor Kohl and President Mitterrand joining hands on the Verdun battlefield in 1984, but that gesture graphically dramatized reconciliation between the nations after generations of hostility and warfare.

The significance of these accomplishments is obvious from the fact that they were only barely conceivable in the recent past. Considering this impressive headway, prospects for future progress should not be underrated, even though the new Defense Council

---

114 Quoted in David G. Morrison, "NATO Has Pre-Treaty Tremors," in *National Journal*, 28 November 1987, p. 3045. Yves Boyer has stated that, "when you leave the world of declarations and enter the world of action, I see very little progress and little prospect of real cooperation." (Quoted in *Insight*, 31 August 1987, p. 31). According to West Germany's commissioner for Franco-German cultural affairs, Lothar Späth, cooperation between the two countries consists primarily of friendly meetings between the countries' leaders rather than of substantive relationships. See *The Week in Germany*, 8 May 1987, p. 7.

115 "It takes two to decouple," in *The Economist*, 28 November 1987, p. 14.

confronts major obstacles to Franco-German defense cooperation. A principal impediment is Bonn's continued preference for its American guarantor and Paris' detachment from the Western Alliance. Bonn and Paris also have rather divergent perceptions of East-West relations and arms control, which many Germans consider the essence of security policy but which the French continue to view with considerable skepticism. Finally, with the nonbelligerency issue resolved, nuclear policy remains the true Gordian knot of Franco-German relations - especially the implications of French prestrategic forces and the possibility of French extended deterrence.

While the US maintains a sizable conventional troop presence in Europe and threatens, however incredibly, to defend Europe with nuclear arms, Germany will cling to the Alliance and France will hesitate to relinquish her residual autonomy. But these American commitments are being undermined by America's declining relative power as well as Mikhail Gorbachev's remarkable restructuring of Soviet foreign and defense policy. As the Soviet threat appears to recede, Americans are likely to perceive less need to continue large European troop deployments and to become increasingly loath to spend more to defend rich European allies than they spend to defend themselves. Already, NATO has endorsed President Bush's proposal to limit Soviet and American air and ground forces in Eastern and West Europe to 275,000 troops which would require an American cutback of approximately 30,000.

Even in the face of a diminished Soviet threat, Franco-German defense cooperation may expand with American disengagement. As the Federal Republic deepens its ties to the East, it serves both French and German interests to have Germany firmly anchored to the West. Considering existing patterns of political and military cooperation, it is therefore possible that a variant of the Franco-German defense community envisioned by former Chancellor Schmidt might evolve.[116] Eventually, the Franco-German nucleus

---

116 For example, François Heisbourg argues that if US troops are withdrawn, France should reconsider its refusal to defend a portion of Germany's eastern border. "If the 'hole' to fill were of limited size - equal or smaller than the 2nd Army Corps, for example, being about 50,000 men - and if some vacant infrastructures were available, it would be difficult for France to evade a West German request." (François Heisbourg, "Défense Française: L'impossible statu quo," in *Politique internationale*, No. 36 (Summer 1987) p. 148).

could even spawn a European defense community which embraces the nine members of the Western European Union.

7

West Germany and France: Convergent or Divergent Perspectives on European Security Cooperation?

Peter Schmidt

INTRODUCTION

Since the beginning of the 1980s West Europeans have witnessed an era of active bilateral and multilateral links in security matters:[1] the revitalization of Western European Union (WEU) occured in 1984; concerted action to achieve closer arms cooperation has taken place especially within the framework of the Independent European Program Group (IEPG);[2] efforts on the part of European Community member states to coordinate their foreign policy have culminated in the Single European Act which, through its ratification

---

1 For a more detailed discussion of the issue of Europeanization in the first half of the 1980s, see Peter Schmidt, *Europeanization of Defense: Prospects of Consensus?* (Santa Monica, CA: The Rand Corporation 1984); Peter Schmidt, The WEU - A Union Without Perspective, in *Aussenpolitik* (English edition) 4 (1986): pp. 388-399. For developments in the second half of the decade, see André Brigot, Peter Schmidt and Walter Schütze, eds., *Deutsch-Französische Zusammenarbeit in der Sicherheits- und Verteidigungspolitik* (Baden-Baden: Nomos 1989). This study is also available in French; André Brigot, Peter Schmidt and Walter Schütze, eds., *Sécurité, Désarmement et Politiques à l'Est* (Paris: Fondation pour les études de Défense nationale 1989).

2 During the June 1988 session of the Council of the IEPG, the Defense Ministers accepted an action plan to create a European armaments market.

by national parliaments in 1987, gives the European Political Cooperation (EPC) a contractual basis.[3] The starting point of all these efforts was the relaunching of the Franco-German Treaty of 1963, which began in 1982 at the end of Helmut Schmidt's chancellorship and at the beginning of François Mitterrand's presidency.[4]

This political context makes it clear that Franco-German relations cannot be seen as an isolated effort to improve bilateral links. The cooperation between these two important countries at the geographical heart of the continent must be interpreted within the wider context of Europe and the Atlantic Alliance. This was the basic idea which Foreign Affairs Ministers Genscher and Dumas had in mind when they designated 1987 as the year of "French-German relations for Europe." It was this same idea which prompted President Mitterrand and Chancellor Kohl to add an important extra clause to the Elysée Treaty of 1963 concerning the creation of the Franco-German Defense and Security Council in 1988.[5]

An analysis of Franco-German cooperation should start with a basic fact. The new "friendship" between the former *Erbfeinde* (hereditary enemies) is founded neither on a common or similar

---

3 See Alfred Pijpers, Elfriede Regelsberger and Wolfgang Wessels, eds., *European Political Cooperation in the 1980s. A Common Foreign Policy for Western Europe?* (Dordrecht, Boston and London: Martinus Nijhoff Publishers 1988). For the documentation concerning EPC-related provisions in the Single European Act, see the Annex.

4 For a broad discussion see Karl Kaiser and Pierre Lellouche, eds., *Le couple franco-allemand et la défense de l'Europe* (Paris: Economica 1986). This volume was also published in German; see footnote 23. For a more extensive work of the author, on which this article is based, see the following: Peter Schmidt, *Deutsch-französische Zusammenarbeit in der Sicherheits- und Verteidigungspolitik. Teil I: Der außen- und sicherheitspolitische Kontext* (Ebenhausen: Stiftung Wissenschaft und Politik 1987). Peter Schmidt, *Deutsche-französische Zusammenarbeit in der Sicherheits- und Verteidigungspolitik. Teil II: Entwicklung, Probleme und Perspektiven der militärischen Zusammenarbeit* (Ebenhausen: Stiftung Wissenschaft und Politik 1987).

5 For the text of the creation of the Council, see the Annex. For further documentation: Presse- und Informationsamt der Bundesregierung, ed., *25 Jahre Elysée-Vertrag* (Bonn: Presse- und Informationsamt der Bundesregierung 1988), pp. 44-49.

political culture nor on a great similarity in basic views towards security problems (as is the case, to some degree, between Great Britain and the US or France and Italy).[6] More striking are the political differences based on disparate histories and the diversified political consequences of those experiences:

Whereas France, defeated in 1940, suffered from negative consequences of pacifism and appeasement, Germany had to sustain the outcome of excessive use of power. Contrasting foreign policy styles in both countries are the result of these experiences.

Whereas France, under de Gaulle, decided to reestablish a strong central state and a presidential system designed to overcome contradictory social forces in order to avoid the social and political struggles which marked the pre-war era and the IVth Republic, the decision in West Germany was to project a presidential system and to introduce a parliamentary democracy with a strong federal element. These decisions determined the scope of action in foreign policy decision-making. Today, France enjoys more freedom of action in foreign policy matters than does the Federal Republic of Germany.

Whereas social forces in France are unified under the French national flag, reservations in Germany about too much national self-esteem or even nationalism still remain. One of the consequences is that France is still proud of its "grandeur" and independence, symbolized by its own nuclear force, whereas the Federal Republic has been interested in economic integration in Europe and military integration within NATO while renouncing the production of nuclear weapons.

Whereas France had the opportunity to reestablish "territorial integrity," Germany has remained divided. This occasionally evokes mixed feelings on the French side. On the one hand, the French "political class" believes that the striving for close relations between the two Germanies - or even reunification - is natural; on the other hand, reservations and even fears concerning such endeavours are still expressed.

---

6 For this observation see Michael Tatu, "Außenpolitik zwischen Ost und West," in Robert Picht, ed., *Das Bündnis im Bündnis*, (Berlin: Severin und Siedler 1982), p. 69.

This short enumeration of the main dissimilarities raises the question of the motives behind the "new friendship." Are there new converging assessments in security matters and a common strategy for how to react? If so, what are the consequences of such a policy approach for West Europe and the Atlantic Alliance?

This short analysis attempts to delineate the divergent and convergent motives in both countries by contrasting the basic principles in security policies in the 1960s and the 1980s, and to take a brief glance at the situation as the current decade comes to a close. It will be shown that, to a certain extent, both countries have changed their positions in the 1980s, relative to the 1960s, by assuming important features of the basic views and goals of the neighbor country. It was this very mutual interchange of attitudes which stimulated new Franco-German activities. An observation of some new convergencies concerning the basic foreign policy views of both countries at the end of the 1980s prompts the question of how such changes will influence further steps towards integration in the future.

CONTRASTING HISTORICAL PERIODS: THE 1960s AND THE 1980s

France: Fear as a Basis for Closer Cooperation

The 1960s: Preparing the Basis for Independence

In the 1960s, de Gaulle established France as an independent nuclear power with special intentions and views in security matters. Similar views are part of the new thinking of the Federal Republic of Germany in the strategic environment of the present day. De Gaulle's intentions were threefold:[7]

> To have France create an alternative European power center independent of the two superpowers; this meant the creation of a new European order extending from "the Atlantic to the Urals"

---

7 For this historical period read Michael M. Harrison, *The Reluctant Ally: France and Atlantic Security* (Baltimore and London: The Johns Hopkins University Press 1981).

by a process of *détente, entente, coopération* (détente, understanding, and cooperation) which downgraded the importance of the confrontation and competition of the two political and military blocs, namely NATO and the Warsaw Pact;

To enhance France's international prestige in terms of political influence within this new order by the existence of a French "force de frappe;"

To use France's nuclear force as an instrument to rebuild the belief in the French nation-state and its *grandeur* in order to harmonize domestic conflicts and to buttress France's international standing.

However, French security and defense policy has never been independent in the true sense. De Gaulle always emphasized that France left only the military integration of NATO but remained a loyal member of the Atlantic Alliance. He knew that Europe needed the presence and protection of American troops and the nuclear umbrella.

De Gaulle's policy assumed two other preconditions: the existence of a superior US and the belief that the Soviet Union is basically a satisfied power. These were expressed as follows:

As long as a clear American superiority continued over the Soviet Union and the US continually supported West European democracies by its sheer political and military weight, the Europeans were given, from the French point of view, more freedom of action than they in fact assumed.

De Gaulle's vision of a new European political order was conceivable only if there were no offensive interests on the Soviet side or if a superior America managed to contain the USSR. This first view lost credibility when troops of the Soviet Union and of four additional Warsaw Pact states (Poland, GDR, Hungary and Bulgaria) occupied Czechoslovakia in 1968; the second view could be called into question as the USSR achieved parity with the U.S on the strategic level.

It is misleading to some extent therefore, to describe the French position in terms of an evolution "from independence to interdependence."[8] France's independence was always borrowed from the Atlantic Alliance.

From the Beginning of the 1980s to the Late 1980s: Why France Became Interested in More European and Atlantic Solidarity

France's apprehensions in security affairs have always been strongly linked to the two pillars of France's "independence:" America's guarantees of protection and the perception of a satisfied USSR. From a French perspective, both pillars crumbled in the period between the late 1970s and early 1980s as a result of developments regarding the power ratio between the US and the Soviet Union and the growing peace movement in the Federal Republic of Germany. The military balance clearly appeared to be shifting in favour of the Soviet Union; this detracted still further from the credibility of American protection. The occupation of Afghanistan prompted a broad political discussion in France about the *Archipel Gulag* in the Soviet Union. At the same time, wide ranging political groups in France discerned what they regarded as a "neutral pacifism" in the German public - a pacifism which could set their most important European ally "politically adrift." These perceived developments endangered the pillars of French "independent" security and defense policy generally accepted by the domestic political spectrum since the end of the 1970s.

Another problem placed the French security concept under pressure. Having succeeded in developing their own national nuclear force, almost without any foreign aid, French officials now increasingly felt unable to develop the technological advancements necessary in important military and civilian fields. There was the great challenge of SDI and the rapid technological progress in the conventional field (Follow-on-forces-attack systems, reconnaissance means, etc.) which endangered the credibility of France's military and civilian technological standards. Also, France traditionally viewed military technology, a view shared by the United States, as

8 This is the subtitle of Robbin F. Laird, ed., *French Security Policy* (Boulder and London: Westview Press 1986).

an instrument to boost broad economic progress.[9] Thus, cooperation in military and civilian technology became an important issue for the French. It was this argument which led then French Prime Minister Pierre Mauroy to plead for the creation of a European pillar within the Atlantic Alliance through the common production of armaments.[10]

Theoretically, one solution to French problems would be reintegration in NATO's military structure in order to strengthen the Alliance and to cooperate in arms development and production. However, this is not a real option for France because of a general anti-superpower mentality initiated by the Gaullist legacy, and the political consensus in military and security affairs based on the acceptance of a nuclear strategy independent of NATO. France thus has to pursue an indirect strategy of strengthening its political and military ties within Europe, especially with the Federal Republic, in order to maintain the existing security structure. This development is also recognized in the US where one could read something like the following statement: "At a time when the German situation is in flux, Americans have a special reason to appreciate Mitterrand's France as a solid anchor of the West."[11] With respect to its attitude towards NATO, the position of Paris changed from *Saulus* to *Paulus*. The traditional French criticism of NATO almost disappeared and French policy started to support basic NATO policies without changing the essentials of de Gaulle's independent defense policy. However, it was not "Gaullism by any other name,"[12] as Stanley Hoffmann argues, but a policy of giving up the central political function of de Gaulle's "Gaullism" - the shaping of the European political order "from the Atlantic to the Urals." In this sense, France became more or less a power satisfied with the status quo in Europe.

Yet, it is on this very point that France found itself caught in a dilemma. On the one hand, it was loath to forfeit the domestic

---

9 Traditionally, more than 30 percent of all French research and development expenditures are spent within the military sector.

10 Speech at the Institut des Hautes Etudes de Défense Nationale in Paris. See *Le Monde*, 22 September 1983.

11 An Unexpected Anchor, in *Los Angeles Times*, 21 March 1984, Part II, p. 6.

12 This is the title of the article by Stanley Hoffmann in *Foreign Policy*, vol.57, Winter 1984/85, pp. 38-57.

consensus on security issues reflected by France's special role within the Alliance and its independent nuclear force. This consensus, for which de Gaulle fought unsuccessfully, was achieved by the renunciation of the critical anti-nuclear attitudes of the Communist and Socialist parties at the end of the 1970s. On the other hand, substantive offers to the Federal Republic of Germany could only go hand-in-hand with a complete or partial relinquishment of this special role. In response to this dilemma, the only instruments France had at its disposal were the following:

The simultaneous emphasis of solidarity within the Alliance *and* European identity;
The offer of far-reaching armaments cooperation as an integration vehicle;
The political-symbolic granting of consultations that would make the possibility of a new French security policy appear within reach;
The willingness to search for a consensus on important security issues, such as arms control, without giving up too much French independence.

What, however, really could be offered during the extensive consultation process? The following three French concessions surfaced during the first six years of this decade:

The foregoing of the still-existing marginal limitations of the Federal Republic of Germany's sovereignty in arms production stated in the WEU agreement;[13]
The restructuring of the French army[14] starting in 1983 in order to demonstrate French preparedness for quick support on German soil (establishment of a Rapid Deployment Force called

---

13 The list of the WEU treaty has been gradually cut down. The last limitations concerned the production of strategic bombers and long-range missiles. However, this is of no practical importance because the FRG does not plan to produce these types of weapons.

14 For a detailed discussion see David Yost, *France's Deterrent Posture and Security in Europe, Part I: Capabilities and Doctrine*, Adelphi Papers 194 (Winter 1984/85) and especially Diego A. Ruiz Palmer, "France" in Jeffrey Simon, ed., *NATO-Warsaw Pact Force Mobilization* (Washington, D.C.: National Defense University Press 1988), pp. 293-300.

F.A.R or Force d'Action Rapide) showing France's solidarity with the Federal Republic of Germany;

Consultations concerning the use of French tactical (prestrategique) nuclear forces on German soil offered by President Mitterrand in March 1986.

However, none of these concessions indicated a dramatic change in the basics of French defense and security policy:

The F.A.R. is a "multi-purpose weapon" and not confined to the European theatre. The discussion concerning the deployment of this force is in the tradition of the Lemnitzer-Ailleret agreement of 1967 which described some contingency plans for the use of French forces without any specific commitments. The maneuver "Bold Sparrow" (Fall 1987) demonstrated the capabilities of the F.A.R.; however, it was planned and carried out strictly outside the NATO framework.[15]

The envisaged consultations concerning the use of prestrategic weapons are very limited (considering the necessary promptness of the decision and its use on German soil[16]), and not comparable with the elaborate planning and consultation process within NATO. The French offer also incorporates some "symbolism" because there is not much sense in a bilateral consultation process during a crisis or war because Germany is defended within the multilateral framework of NATO and not by a defense union with France.

In conclusion, the French position is still split. On the one hand, it tries to demonstrate more solidarity especially with its partner on the other side of the Rhine in order to preserve the current structure of the Alliance. On the other hand, it makes an effort to maintain military autonomy as well as nuclear priority and independence. With respect to the Alliance and the overall European order, French

---

15 For a short analysis, see Wolfgang Bäder and Peter Schmidt, *Die deutsch-französische Heeresübung "Kecker Spatz"/"Moineau Hardi" vom September 1987* (Ebenhausen: Stiftung Wissenschaft und Politik 1987).

16 This raises the question of whether the term "German soil" includes the territory of the GDR.

policy changed from a reform-oriented position in the 1960s to a conservative position of maintaining the status quo in the 1980s.

The question now is why the Bonn government responded positively to the French initiative in the 1980s and negatively in the 1960s.

West-Germany: Opposing Views Urge a Negative Reaction in the 1960s and a Positive Response in the 1980s

The 1960s: The Federal Republic of Germany as a True Atlanticist

An evaluation of the first French attempt at close cooperation in security and defense matters, as symbolized by the Elysée treaty of 1963, would lead to the conclusion that it was a failure. The German parliament ratified an amendment to the treaty which contradicted not only the outstanding intention of de Gaulle to diminish European-American ties in favor of a new European order, but also other important French political objectives.[17]

The reasons for this failure were differences in important security interests, which still dominated the West German political scene despite the fact that Chancellor Adenauer had some proclivity to the French approach. It can be described as follows:

> There was no way to attain better relations without Soviet concessions changing the status quo.
>
> De Gaulle's vision of a "Europe of the fatherlands" reaching "from the Atlantic to the Urals" was contrary to the German aim of a politically and institutionally integrated West Europe. In a similar vein, the supranational aspects of European integration contradicted the traditional supremacy of the nation state still dominant in French political thinking.

---

17 The main political objectives of the Federal Republic as pointed out in the amendment opposing de Gaulle's views have been: close partnership with the US, the right of self-determination for the German people including the right of reunification; common defense within the Alliance fostered by military integration and the continuation of the European integration process within the EC framework following the inclusion of Great Britain. For the text of this amendment in the form of a preamble to the Franco-German treaty, see the Annex (Documents).

From the German point of view the Soviet Union was not defensive - as de Gaulle basically assumed - but rather a totalitarian and offensive political power threatening the Federal Republic (and West Europe) and preventing the territorial integration of Germany.

And last but not least, it was quite obvious to the Germans that France (and the other Europeans) did not have sufficient political and military power to protect West Germany. Therefore, nothing should further the view in America that the Europeans might be capable of relying on their own defense resources and thus no longer require American protection.

Because of this linkage policy, West Germany appeared in the 1960s as a stumbling block to the envisaged French (and American) détente policy. In opposition to de Gaulle's policy of looking for *détente, entente, coopération* within the framework of a divided Europe and Germany, the Federal Republic, until the late 1960s, sought to trade détente for progress in reunification. This policy was only feasible with a strong Alliance partner - the United States. The FRG had to avoid a forced choice between a German-American and a German-French axis as offered by France at the beginning of the 1960s.

The 1980s: Continued Ostpolitik

At the end of the 1960s, West Germany had to change its basic approach towards the East. It could not maintain a "brake-bloc" position against bilateral Soviet-American détente policy. The new German East-West policy, starting with the SPD-CDU/CSU-coalition (1966-1969) and reaching its climax during the years of the social-liberal government in the 1970s, basically accepted the status quo and aimed at improved East-West relations on the basis of the German separation. The new catchword was *Wandel durch Annäherung* (change by rapprochement). From this point of view, the "deutsche Frage" (German question) could only be diminished by détente. However, this policy can only be pursued if there is some basic understanding between the two superpowers. Superpower-détente became a prerequisite for the implementation of the German *Ostpolitik*. In this regard, German policy resembled French détente-entente-coopération-policy of the 1960s.

The same kind of countercurrent development can be observed in threat perception. At the end of the 1970s, culminating with the Soviet occupation of Afghanistan, France changed its perception of a satisfied and defensive Soviet Union to one of viewing the USSR as an offensive and totalitarian power. During the 1970s, Germany went the opposite way. Although the Soviet military build-up was not overlooked, one could increasingly detect the assumption that the leading communist power was basically a defensive one.[18]

The new German view of the Soviet Union influenced the German-American relationship especially in times of superpower tensions. Since the second half of the 1970s, West Germany has searched for partners who could influence American foreign policy to promote détente. After some disappointments during Giscard d'Estaing's presidency, the German proclivity towards European collaboration coincided with French offers to cooperate. However, this has not been the only reason for the positive German response to the French initiatives. The following additional motives, although somewhat contrary, influenced the positive German reaction to the French offer of close cooperation:

Domestic policy considerations called for a demonstration of a "European will" as a means of deflecting American criticism.[19] Pershing-IIs and Cruise Missiles, stationed on German soil, could too easily be denounced as instruments of United States hegemony.

Europeanites saw all attempts to assimiliate or coordinate basic political attitudes within Europe in a positive light.[20]

Atlanticists had some hope that the coordination process would prompt France to deemphasize its special role within the

---

18 See Walter Schütze, "Von de Gaulle zu Mitterrand - Die Entwicklung der französischen Entspannungspolitik," in Deutsche Gesellschaft für Friedens- und Konfliktforschung, ed., *DGFK Jahrbuch 1982/83, Zur Lage Europas im globalen Spannungsfeld* (Baden-Baden: DGFK 1983), pp. 91-111.

19 See especially the ideas of the Head of the Planning Staff of the Ministry of Foreign Affairs, Konrad Seitz, Deutsch-französische sicherheitspolitische Zusammenarbeit, in *Europa-Archiv*, Vol 37, No 22 (1982), pp. 657-664.

20 See Hans-Gert Poettering, Deutschlands und Frankreichs Interesse an einer europäischen Sicherheitspolitik, in *Aussenpolitik*, Vol. 37, No. 2 (1986), pp. 175-185.

Alliance and offer a clearer military commitment to the defense of West Germany.[21]

Finally, as a corollary to the French interest in fostering West Germany's ties with the West, important groups in the Federal Republic were interested in a stronger political commitment by West Germany to the West. The political wisdom is that West Germany must have connections with the East but must be bound to the West.[22]

In summary, despite the many incentives and motives behind the goal of Franco-German cooperation, there is still a great difference between political declarations and hard decisions. Pierre Hassner made the point in 1986 that never have there been so many initiatives for collaboration which bear such meager results.[23] It would seem that perceived political necessities are contrasted by "the devil in the details." The French and the Germans are still occupied with an intensive search to define common interests and to assume joint responsibilities which has not been very successful until present.

RECENT EXPERIENCE

Current Pressures in Favor of and Contrary to Franco-German Collaboration

Domestic Pressures

At present political pressures in favor of closer Franco-German collaboration can be found on both sides of the Rhine. On the German side the main advocate for closer European and Franco-

---

21 See the opinion of Manfred Wörner in his interview with *Frankfurter Allgemeine Zeitung*, 12 February 1987, p. 2

22 See Werner Link, "Die außenpolitische Staatsräson der Bundesrepublik Deutschland. Überlegungen zur innerstaatlichen Struktur und Perzeption des internationalen Bedingungsfeldes," in Manfred Funke, Hans-Adolf Jacobsen, Hans-Helmut Knütter, Hans-Peter Schwarz, eds., *Demokratie und Diktatur. Geist und Gestalt politischer Herrschaft in Deutschland und Europa*, (Bonn: Europa Verlag 1987), p. 410.

23 Pierre Hassner, "Achielleus, unbeweglich und gehetzt," in Karl Kaiser and Pierre Lellouche, eds., *Deutsch-Französische Sicherheitspolitik*, (Bonn: Europa Union Verlag 1986), p. 160.

German collaboration is the Minister for Foreign Affairs, Hans-Dietrich Genscher. In the eyes of the public, he plays a positive role by emphasizing détente and, at the same time, European security cooperation. After being forced to give up party leadership because he quit the coalition with the Social Democrats, Genscher was brought back into the power center of the Liberal party because of his views. However, these activities, which are mainly devoted to the cooperative aspects of East-West relations (common *Ostpolitik*, common views on the CSCE conference[24]), competed with the actions of Chancellor Helmut Kohl who gave more emphasis to the defense side of the cooperation by creating the Franco-German brigade and the Security and Defense Council. This kind of political rivalry seems to positively influence the political will required to take further steps in this field.

The main structural element which influenced French policy up to the last presidential election in June 1988 was the combination of a Socialist President (François Mitterrand) and a Conservative Prime Minister (Jacques Chirac). Some spoke of this situation as "cohabitation;" to others it was just "peaceful coexistence." Nevertheless, the president has been successful in defending his "domaine reservée" on major security and defense issues. The special political context within which Mitterrand had to act worked in favor of collaboration; he had to preserve his image of statesmanship because political conflicts with his European neighbors would be counterproductive. The result was pressure to coordinate views and to avoid conflicts with the Germans. Important political actions, like the acceptance of Helmut Kohl's proposal to create a common brigade, may be the positive outcome of this type of political rivalry.

In contrast, the present political situation in which François Mitterrand serves with a Socialist minority government under Prime Minister Michel Rocard seems to stimulate Franco-German relations to a lesser degree than the former Mitterrand-Chirac rivalry.

---

24 See the joint article of the French and the German Ministers for Foreign Affairs, M. Roland Dumas and Herr Hans-Dietrich Genscher, respectively, concerning the CSCE Conference in *Le Monde* and *Süddeutsche Zeitung*, 4 November 1986.

International Pressures

Another recent incentive for closer cooperation is the shifting attitude of the superpowers in the domain of arms control. The decisions of disarmament taken in Reykjavik by President Ronald Reagan and Soviet leader Mikhail Gorbachev raised many questions concerning the nucleus of the future security system and its military basis. After having just debated the possible shift from the Mutual Assured Destruction (MAD) principle towards Mutual Assured Security (MAS) using a strategic defense system (SDI), the Europeans have been under pressure to formulate a position on various denuclearization proposals and have been forced to accept the double-zero option which calls for the dismantling of the so-called INF systems. The insecurities involved, and the fact that the allies were surprised by this development, provided additional impetus to their efforts to find a common stance. One outcome of this complex political situation is the joint declaration on the zero-option issue for INF-systems by both political leaders, Mitterrand and Kohl, on 27 March 1987. Despite conflicting views, the two politicians endeavoured to find a common ground. France was not interested in a process lessening the legitimacy of nuclear forces that would endanger its own nuclear force and weaken the American commitment; neither were many German officials enamoured of a denuclearized military strategy.

The present situation is different. After having accepted the INF-Treaty and after some interesting disarmament proposals, including unilateral disarmament steps on the Soviet side[25], there is less pressure to achieve results in military cooperation. The coordination of views on *Ostpolitik* and disarmament may become more important.

The Outcome

Today, there exists a very extensive process of regular consultation between the Federal Republic of Germany and France which consists of the following:

---

25 See the speech by Gorbachev before the UN on 7 December 1988 where he announced, in addition to other proposals, the unilateral reduction of the manpower of Soviet armed forces by 500,000 men within the next two years.

Regular bilateral meetings of the Ministers for Foreign and Defense Affairs and high-ranking officials;

Regular bilateral encounters within the WEU-framework;

Regular meetings of the Ministers for Foreign Affairs within the EPC-framework (confined to political and economic aspects of security);

Several working groups and some subgroups (Committee for Security and Defense) which focus on agenda items such as political-strategic affairs, military cooperation and arms cooperation;

Consultations among the general chiefs of staff and commanders in chief of the services;

Exchange of civil servants of the Ministries for Foreign Affairs.

However, there are some differences between the extended consultation process and the political and military interests which include:

The French nuclear strategy remains basically national; there is no coordination with NATO's nuclear planning and decision-making process.

Cooperation involving conventional forces is underway with the goal of establishing more detailed plans for possible French military actions which would include not only the French forces in Germany but the entire First French Army and parts of the F.A.R. as well. But there will be no clear commitment of the French forces to forward defense.

Despite the French offer for consultations in the event of tactical nuclear weapons being used on German soil, and recent declarations of the French President that the French prestrategic weapons should threaten the enemy and not the German partner, Germany is not happy with the existence of these type of French nuclear weapons.

Despite close cooperation in CDE-matters (Conference on Confidence and Security-Building Measures and Disarmament in Europe), there are differences in "hard-ware" arms control (especially in conventional arms control)

Despite many political declarations in favor of arms procurement cooperation, there are deep-rooted problems concerning the main projects (Fighter 90, main battle tank). The decision to produce a common combat helicopter only clouds the lack of success in cooperative efforts.

In spite of all these contradictory developments, we have seen that the independent role of France during the last few years, while basically weakening the Alliance, can be a stabilizing element during times of political turmoil. France had to surrender its independent role to some degree in order to preserve the political framework within which this special role can only be realized. Nevertheless, there is little hope that France will rejoin the military integrated command structure of NATO. Closer European collaboration, however, seems to have become necessary during recent times, induced by possible dramatic changes in security principles (SDI, denuclearization offers). Nonetheless, the important question is not whether the Europeans should move closer together, but how this should happen.

The current European proclivity for a "European caucus" based on Franco-German collaboration that would save the Alliance includes some important pitfalls such as the following:

The complexity of the decision-making process on the European side complicates the dialogue with the US.

The tendency to escape hard choices and to establish some kind of division of labor between the "European caucus" and NATO. The Europeans tend to become specialists on "soft" issues, whereas the "hard" military decisions are to be made in NATO. This kind of development threatens the legitimacy of NATO in the long run. In this regard, the common brigade and the Security and Defense Council are, however, important countermeasures.

THE FUTURE

In view of all the problems of Franco-German and European cooperation in security matters, a great task lies ahead. The Europeans must find a way to escape the pitfalls and weaknesses inherent in current efforts to move closer together. The basic deficiency of the recent policy seems to be European avoidance of assuming more responsibilities within the Alliance. There is still some truth in Horst Mendershausen's words that Europeans "are interested everywhere but engaged nowhere."[26] This does not concern the traditional "burden-sharing" issue; the main point is political by nature and not (only) a matter of spending more money for military purposes. Are there some options? The former German Chancellor, Helmut Schmidt, proposed the creation of a common Franco-German conventional force; Chancellor Kohl is in favor of a European Army; the conservative member of the *Bundestag*, Jürgen Todenhöfer, raised the issue of a common European nuclear force. However, small steps are more likely. Recent Soviet foreign policy initiatives may hamper further progress instead of promoting increased West European defense collaboration. The grand political tool which could pry open the Pandora's Box of a new West European defense structure has yet to be found.

---

26 Horst Mendershausen, *Who Is Leading Whom in the Atlantic Alliance?* P-5465 (Santa Monica, CA.: The Rand Corporation 1975), p. 6.

8

West European Threat Assessment: An Instrument of Assertiveness?

Reinhardt Rummel

INTRODUCTION

During the 1980s a good many initiatives have been taken to develop closer security and defense cooperation among West European countries. They range from the intensification of Franco-German military cooperation at the beginning of the eighties, via the reform of the Western European Union (WEU) in the mid-eighties, to the plan for the establishment of a West European *Ostpolitik* at the end of the decade. Most of these initiatives are elaborated upon in other chapters of this volume. Their end results remain to be seen, but they all suffer from a major insufficiency, namely they lack a common focus in that they do not follow a joint West European orientation. Rather they try to fill gaps in the present security system, partially fix holes in the given defense network, or confuse symbolism with reality in strategic East-West relations.

This chapter does not attempt to discuss either those common goals which are lacking or the missing comprehensive strategy but reflects, instead, on a prerequisite for the latter, namely a *joint West European threat assessment*. These reflections start with the assumption that all follow-up stages in the process of intensifying West European security cooperation will require a common base for the West Europeans' views regarding what the common challenges are with which they have to cope.

Thus, the chapter deals with the motives and needs for a specific West European assessment capacity. It outlines the concept of an eventual West European "challenge assessment unit," analyzes the feasibility of establishing such a unit, and speculates on the effects and consequences it might have on the Western security structure. The conclusion of this chapter is that a genuine West European evaluation is a key factor to a better representation of West European interests in transatlantic as well as East-West relations. Yet, Europe, for the time being, has to be content with an insufficient technical, institutional, and political infrastructure with which to accomplish such a task. The West Europeans should, therefore, profit from the current external demands for such a capacity. They should gradually develop a challenge assessment unit of their own as an indispensable basis for any further step towards more West European self-reliance in security policy.

REASONS FOR A SEPARATE ASSESSMENT UNIT

When Europeanized threat assessement is proposed among Western security experts and officials, the first and foremost reply one hears (except in France) is that there is no real need for it, that things run well within the appropriate NATO bodies, that the West Europeans can trust the threat assessment of their leading ally and, in addition, that a separate West European evaluation will not change anything. This first reaction is understandable, but it tends to disregard and underestimate a widespread perception held by other experts and the wider West European security community who have accumulated doubts, suspicions and frustrations concerning the reliability of either a NATO- or US-based threat assessment.[1]

---

1 It is not only in France where people have publicly objected to the leading role of the US in intelligence collection and analysis within NATO.
Statements to this effect have also been made by prominent West Germans such as Helmut Schmidt. See Michael Charlton, *From Deterrence to Defence: The Inside Story of Strategic Policy* (Cambridge: Harvard University Press 1987), p.136.
Furthermore, the Zircon satellite affair in January 1987 demonstrated also Britain's reluctance to remain so dependent on US signals of intelligence. (See Spy in the Sky, in *New Statesman*, Vol. 113, No. 2913, 23 January 1987, pp. 8-12).

The Element of Trust in European-American Relations

While there is a high degree of transatlantic congruency on a number of commonly held fundamental beliefs, such as the Soviet military build-up (including naval forces) or Moscow's conventional superiority on the Central front, disharmony emerges among the Western allies when it comes to judging the strength of the Warsaw Pact as a whole, specific weapon systems at the forefront of Soviet military technology, or new arms control proposals.[2] The reasons for diverging Western assumptions on specific Soviet military capabilities can be objective ones, but time and again West European nations get the impression that the US military intelligence is abusing its strong and almost uncontrolled intelligence position for specific, individual purposes. It seems that the United States' greater capabilities lend an *a priori* greater weight to American judgements regardless of their quality.

West Europeans have learned that contradictory information can be part of day to day American foreign policy. Even in some albeit marginal cases disinformation (i.e. vis-à-vis Gadhdhafi's Libya) is part of Washington's foreign relations policy.[3] The US government certainly does not have the nerve to fabricate data, but it may exaggerate, minimize or otherwise distort new Soviet capabilities (see the original assessment of specific systems such as Mig-29 or Blackjack) or hold back information on certain developments in the Red Army (no picture of the SS-20 was published until the 1986 edition of *Soviet Military Power*). The appropriate choice of the most advantageous time to release new data is a powerful policy instrument. Former President Ronald Reagan, Defense Secretary Caspar Weinberger, and other government officials have reproached

---

2 There are many prominent examples for diverging transatlantic assessments, one of them concerning the quality of the WP army and NATO's sustainability in case of a conventional Soviet attack. Ironically, divergencies seem to be larger on NATO's own capabilities than on those of the Eastern bloc. This is also the reason why NATO's annual force comparisons are no longer published.

3 Bernard Weintraub, Reagan Confirms Secret Plan to Unnerve Gadhdhafi. Willingness to Plan "Disinformation" Tests Administration's Credibility, in *International Herald Tribune*, 5 October 1986, pp. 1f. For more examples, also concerning other countries, see Claude Julien, L'art de la désinformation, in *Le Monde Diplomatique*, Mai 1987, pp. 17-24.

the Soviets for cheating and, in other instances, breaking the rules of SALT II. The radar at Krasnojarsk was cited as proof that Moscow, who finally in 1989 admitted it as a mistake, had broken the provisions of the ABM treaty. Often Washington will protect the source of its information or, occasionally, will present interpretations which cannot be independently checked or verified.

It would be overstating the point to assume that Washington designs this kind of information policy just to mislead or irritate the West Europeans. Rather one can find a large number of reasons why military threat assessment is not a very transparent matter.[4] One reason is that the intelligence community has an inherent reluctance to disclose sources of information and that even the intimacy of the Western Alliance has not overcome these professional constraints. Another reason is that US military forces need a justifiable argument to convince Congress to approve of the acquisition of a certain weapons system. Here the American decision-making process tends to promote threat exaggeration. It also cannot be discounted that in certain cases Washington tries to impress both West European governments and the American people by issuing certain statements such as that which claimed the Soviet Union had deployed more medium range nuclear missiles than originally had been thought. The publication of *Soviet Military Power* by the Department of Defense fosters certain threat perceptions.

For West Europeans, who more often than not lack the intelligence capabilities and technological expertise with which to check all aspects of Pentagon and CIA reports on new Soviet weapons developments, it is disappointing and discouraging to voice doubts or present alternative figures, because their remarks will often be regarded as either incompetent, anti-American, or both. Therefore, the greatest potential value to West Europe of an independent assessment capability may well be political. Since the US can always assert that its assessments are based on data, methodologies, and techniques which the allies do not have, it is hard to argue with them. If the West Europeans had an independent capability, they would be in a much better position to enter into the debate as equals, and to voice contrary opinions when necessary.

---

4 All countries seem to have threat assessment techniques of their own. For Germany see Hartmut Pohlmann, Die Technik der Bedrohungsanalyse, in *Europäische Wehrkunde*, No. 11 (1980), pp. 557-562.

But the situation is more complex. Even if the allies employ good faith and endorse American data, the evaluation of this data offers another vast field of divergence and suspicion. This stage of evaluation has a technological-military and a politico-strategic assessment component. Both components provide ample room for either underestimation or exaggeration depending on the predisposition and the interests of the individual "interpreter," the evaluating agency, or the public audience. The debate between Washington and its Western allies on the criteria for technological-military equipment in the framework of COCOM demonstrated the difficulty of achieving a Western consensus. The politico-strategic assessment is even more subject to voluntarism. It is hardly governed by objectivity or assured knowledge but rather by political opinion or ideological belief.

Divergence of views on the assessment of identical military data is not a unique American phenomenon. When Helmut Schmidt resigned and Helmut Kohl assumed the Chancellery in the fall of 1982, the annual German White Paper on security policy, which was almost finished, was redrafted. Although identical data was used, this document presented a more alarming view of the Soviet threat than the original version. This type of reinterpretation tends to occur in almost all Atlantic Alliance nations. Its effects and repercussions have, however, far greater implications in the case of an American reassessment of the Soviet challenge. In this case, the problem for Washington's allies becomes a question of calculation and credibility, which is well known to them from other fields and instances where there has been a shift in US foreign policy.

West European Interests and Soviet-American Negotiations: the Case of Reykjavik

A good illustration of Europe's concerns was the so-called pre-summit of Reykjavik in October 1986, which provided a fresh impetus for worried West Europeans to organize and develop a common outlook concerning the challenges that follow the policies and intentions of Washington and Moscow. The Soviets made a proposal to remove medium range nuclear missiles from Europe within five years and agreed in principle to on-site inspections to verify the dismantling of the SS-20s deployed in the European part of the Soviet Union. Moreover, Mikhail S. Gorbachev conceded treaty provisions on the subsequent negotiations concerning those shorter range nuclear missiles deployed in the GDR and in Czechoslovakia to counter the Pershings and the Cruise Missiles. He no longer insisted that French and British missiles were to be included in the agreement.

When the Soviet-American accord on medium range missiles was concluded in December 1987, most of the West European governments voiced approval for the dismantling of intermediate range nuclear missiles. However, this agreement was not without mixed feelings. The West European perspective was that the two superpowers pursued the same goal, but for different reasons. The Soviet's primary aim was to give the impression that negotiations were held for the (American) denuclearization of Europe. By the same token, Moscow wanted the removal of weapons capable of striking parts of Russia, while trying to decouple the United States from Europe. Washington wanted a "showcase" for President Reagan's vision of a world without nuclear weapons in which space defense would serve as an insurance policy. Moreover, the dismantling of all land-based medium-ranged nuclear missiles would chiefly suit America's fundamental (though seldom publicly declared) desire to reduce its nuclear defense commitment in Europe. These may be misperceptions, but the fact remains that the Soviet-American INF agreement produced results. Some of the consequences of the accord, namely, indispensable build-up of short range nuclear forces and/or conventional forces were even harder to sell to the West European public than the former INF deployment decision.

There is a further West European concern which stems from the fact that the destruction of all short and long range INFs was never properly thought out in military terms. The degree of flexible response offered by Cruise Missiles, and the knowledge that the Pershing-IIs could destroy the Soviet command structure with pinpoint accuracy, has been crucial in NATO's ability to maintain the military balance. How then is the gap filled after this column in NATO's strategic architecture has been taken out? How is the remaining substance of the flexible response doctrine to be evaluated?[5] The communiqué of the NATO Nuclear Planning Group at Gleneagles in October 1986 contained both the conviction of the indispensability of Pershing and Cruise for reasons of politico-military doctrine *and* the plea to dismantle them as a follow-up to Reykjavik.

NATO may have to live with this type of ambivalence, but West Europe should try to get out of the particular Euromissile quagmire and start to work for a more consistent and durable position. The West Europeans (France included) are confronted with a wide range of strategic questions concerning their common interest. Given their geographic proximity to the Soviet bloc, West Europeans have to find out what prompts Soviet arms reduction proposals, the extent to which Moscow is willing to make concessions, and the direction of Gorbachev's European policy. Answers must be found to such questions as Who is going to construct "our common European home?" and Who determines the rules of the house? Furthermore, the West Europeans have to make sure that they understand the full meaning of the American motives for agreeing to the "zero-INF-treaty." It is fascinating that when an accord was within reach, US officials quickly started to reinterpret such crucial elements of the traditional transatlantic security consensus as flexible response strategy, the military, political, and psychological mechanism of coupling, and the seriousness of the conventional imbalance. Major shifts of assessment occured in a very short time.[6]

To deal more efficiently with changeable attitudes in the United States, West Europeans need to formulate a position of their own on these issues. With regard to the INF, it would have been appropriate that the five countries which agreed to the stationing of these missiles (plus France) had concerted their positions. France and Great Britain, in the long run, may need the support of those who were supported by Mitterrand during the INF deployment period.

---

5 The Western defense community has never really accepted, albeit supported the INF treaty. See Simon Head, The Battle Inside NATO, in *The New York Review of Books*, 18 May 1989, pp. 41ff.

6 Kenneth L. Adelman, Simple but True: We Agree to What We Asked For, in *International Herald Tribune*, 31 March 1987, p. 4. The INF Treaty, Hearing before the Committee on Foreign Relations, United States Senate (Washington, D.C. 1988).

Likewise, concertation of positions on SNF is crucial for all West European countries which either receive or possess such systems.[7]

To exert appropriate influence on the negotiations in progress and on the drafting of arms control treaties between the superpowers is only one albeit central goal of more joint West European activity. The West Europeans will have to play an equal (if not greater) role during the implementation and verification phases of disarmament. It will be of significant concern to them to verify whether the Soviets adhere to the treaty provisions, to evaluate resulting military reallocations in the Warsaw Pact, and - as early warning time will become more important in the new constellation - to watch Soviet conventional force developments more closely than in the past.

In summary, the post-INF world, which grapples with the replacement of outdated SNFs, and prepares for massive conventional disarmament should be incentive enough for the West Europeans to establish a politico-military assessment unit of their own.

ELEMENTS OF A "CHALLENGE ASSESSMENT UNIT"

The Idea and the Concept

To date, the West Europeans have only limited means available to them with which to reduce uncertainties stemming from the Soviet military build-up, as well as from the nature and political system of the leading Western power. They can, however, try to counterbalance what they perceive as American deficiencies and Soviet lack of transparency by developing a more substantial assessment capability of their own. Such a capability needs to be a more reliable and independent source of threat assessment, which would be capable of correcting American data and Soviet

7 Before her visit to Moscow in April 1987 to discuss the current arms control agenda with Gorbachev, the British Prime Minister Margaret Thatcher went to see both the French President François Mitterrand and the German Chancellor Helmut Kohl to coordinate views and policies. Two years later, in April 1989, Thatcher again met with Kohl. This time to coordinate positions on SNF and specifically the Follow-On To Lance (FOTL) systems. Both leaders disagreed sharply before and after their meeting.

information where necessary, and would introduce a "Europeanized" stand in the joint assessment of the Atlantic Alliance. Presently the European allies do contribute to the official NATO assessment individually, but their contributions are known to be rather "Atlanticized" within the Sixteen. The West Europeans often seem to have little choice but to agree to the US position, or at least to tolerate and respect it, if this is the course Washington prefers or if the overall NATO cohesion is claimed to be at stake. NATO needs a genuine West European input for joint assessment regarding most of the issues on the present East-West agenda. Such a joint assessment is also necessary for internal structural reasons in order to establish checks and balances within the alliance.

So far, the West European public must either deal with a national or a transatlantic threat assessment. It lacks a framework of reference and a possibility for identification, which would be commensurate with the security issues as viewed by the West Europeans. In other words, it is very difficult to build a West European security consensus based on a NATO threat assessment, as long as this, in turn, is mainly based on American intelligence sources. American evaluations may be sincere and factually sound, but some of them tend to sound remote and, at times, even alien to West European ears. It would be more natural if the West Europeans were more inclined to listen to their own collective assessment first, prior to entering the wider transatlantic framework.

The logic behind this reasoning is to push the publics in West Europe out from behind the frequently used alibi-position which tends to dump all the blame and burden on a supposedly ill-conceived American assessment of the Soviet Union. Once the West Europeans are responsible for their own assessment they will have fewer opportunities to shift responsibility to "NATO" or to "Washington." Their policies will have to reflect their own evaluations in a direct and explicit way. This can be of crucial importance to engender public support for the necessary defense efforts.

Threat assessment can be defined in a rather narrow way. It is the gathering of technical data, the military evaluation of such data, and the political interpretation of the military evaluation. The West Europeans need to strive for a more comprehensive assessment, which goes beyond merely understanding the nature and the dimension of the Soviet threat, but also includes the character of change within the Eastern bloc, the potential for destabilization, the scope of arms control, and East-West cooperation. This broadly extended evaluation can be regarded as a type of Harmel approach to threat assessment which combines the antagonistic and the cooperative elements of East-West relations to produce the creative tension inherent in challenge assessment.

A West European "challenge assessment unit" would need the means and the personnel to function independently of US capabilities. The West Europeans have neither a ready-made infrastructure nor a tradition for joint threat assessment outside the NATO framework. Eurogroup (which does not include France) has traditionally been too closely associated with NATO, while the EPC has been too removed from military matters to take on the burden of a West European security evaluation unit. Rather, the solution could be within the framework of the Western European Union (WEU) which parallels NATO except for its membership; France is a member whereas the United States is not. The revitalization of the WEU since 1984 has reoriented its functions and restructured its institutional structure. WEU, which now functions under the joint responsibility of the foreign and defense ministers of its member nations, could be chosen as the core of a West European assessment unit which could also draw on other West European agencies, as well as those European NATO countries which are not members of WEU. These countries are Denmark, Greece, Iceland, Norway and Turkey.

But a revitalized WEU does not go far enough. The Western European Union can elaborate a political platform on European security interests, as the 1987 document announced at The Hague clearly illustrates.[8] However, WEU needs to go beyond political assessment. This pertains mainly to data gathering and technological-military evaluation, also for the purpose of verification of arms control agreements. West Europeans will need technical sources of information such as observation satellites and electronic listening posts as well as technological experts who are familiar with state-of-the-art military equipment and the most modern research methods. In this regard, if not in previous instances, the establishment of such a unit raises the question of feasibility.

---

8 See the text in the Annex (Documents).

Implementing the Concept

The creation of a new full-fledged "challenge assessment unit" in West Europe may well be a desirable goal, but it could only materialize in the distant future. Yet, if the West Europeans were to start now, they could build on what already exists. In fact, some of the West European allies possess a fairly well-developed assessment culture of their own. France is certainly the front-runner here, partly because of its deliberate distance from the military structure of NATO, and partly due to its ambitious arms production and space technology programs. Recently, Paris has decided to purchase a number of AWACs to improve its reconnaissance and guidance systems. Nevertheless, France still has to rely heavily on US support in this regard.

Cooperation between France and West Germany has gradually improved in political as well as military matters. Bonn and Paris work closely together in such sensitive areas as the struggle against international terrorism which includes the sharing of intelligence. The two countries could be perceived as taking the lead in "Europeanizing" the national assessment activities of the West Europeans. The creation of a Franco-German defense council may be a first step in this direction.[9]

It is an open question whether France would accept sharing some of its surveillance capabilities for West European purposes. In this regard, Franco-German cooperation is certainly paradigmatic although its scope is not known to the public. The European Space Agency (ESA), an outstanding success story of West European integration, primarily has a civil orientation. However, it provides the West Europeans with a security (arms control) oriented option, if the need arises. In 1986 Paris proposed to consider threat assessment within WEU, but its partners believed this initiative to be a diversion from the hard core problems of cooperation.

Furthermore, NATO continues to collect data from national sources and to produce annual evaluations which the West

---

9 President Mitterrand said the council would strive to "coordinate decisions and harmonize analyses in the fields of security, defense, armaments research, the organization and deployment of joint units." in *International Herald Tribune*, 26 September 1987, p. 1.

Europeans could, and will have to, draw upon for their specific purposes. The EPC is well equipped to do part of the political assessment (witness its experience in the context of CSCE) while the Independent European Program Group (IEPG) and other agencies for arms cooperation are prepared to look at threat assessment from a "hardware perspective."[10] The core work will most likely have to be initiated and coordinated by the WEU. WEU's agencies have done some useful analysis recently on SDI, post-Reykjavik, CFE negotiations, and other issues. The Assembly of the Western European Union has a long tradition of analyzing security problems, in East-West perspective and that of critical Third World regions. It is relevant to note that in 1988 its Committee on Defense Questions and Armaments issued a report on "Threat Assessment."

Such factors attest to the foundation which exists for a "challenge assessment unit" in West Europe. To be effective, this foundation has to be developed more professionally and with more political support from major West European governments.

This support is not easy to win given the sensitivity of the matter and the unknown consequences such a step might entail. Ever since the failure of the European Defense Community in the mid-fifties, West Europeans have demonstrated very little solidarity in cooperating outside the NATO framework. A few exceptions are prominent, however. During Kissinger's Year of Europe in 1973, designed to revitalize Euro-American solidarity by a new Atlantic Charter, the West Europeans united to produce their Declaration of Identity. Other examples are related to security and East-West relations, such as the collective position on INF since the end of the seventies and the common West European stand on the COCOM rules in the early eighties. The West Europeans seem to need a pressing emergency, an almost-catastrophic event to initiate concertation among themselves. Interestingly enough, concertation is usually the result of a perceived external challenge.

In this respect the present challenge, which comes from a surprisingly unorthodox Soviet leadership, could turn out to be the expected external impetus which drives the West Europeans toward closer cooperation. So far, and especially since the "shock of Reykjavik," there has been an excess of rhetoric claiming more West

---

10 *Towards a Stronger Europe* (Volumes 1 and 2) (Brussels: IEPG 1986).

European assertiveness vis-à-vis the two superpowers, but it is difficult to see the substance in such declarations. Yet, there is still hope, as the challenge seems to be gaining rather than losing momentum.

The feasibility and the functioning of a West European challenge assessment will depend on a number of factors. The prerequisites of technological "hardware" and expertise are especially decisive. If the West Europeans remain weak in surveillance methods for too long, they risk confronting the type of credibility problems previously mentioned. On the other hand, the costs of West European intelligence and surveillance may seem discouragingly high, given the amount of Western redundancy which is likely to be produced. Then again, redundancy has its specific value in this context.[11]

Cost-benefit considerations will also apply to the outcome of an eventual joint West European challenge assessment. Even if all the technical installations were available and all the evaluation agencies were organized, a fundamental question remains. Would the West Europeans be able to talk sincerely and openly with one another in spite of the differences in status which exist among the various countries, the divergent nature of interests, and individual political cultures? In order to overcome their differences, West Europeans will have to confront each other with harsh realities. They may run the risk of revealing weaknesses, previously unadmitted, and of unmasking well-established but false perceptions concerning the reliability of allies and the "true" nature of Soviet strategy. Given these psychological background factors the West Europeans might come to the conclusion that the costs of "dismantling" their traditional behaviour are too high to justify the uncertain benefits of a collective intra-West European security assessment.

---

11 Nevertheless the question of costs is a crucial one. At various levels of cost, Europe would have to acquire different types and levels of capabilities. Therefore, as a good "technology assessor," one should eventually think through what capabilities could be bought at different costs, and assess what the value of that particular level of capability might be. It is possible that, on the margin, Europe could get enough political and assessment leverage without independent military satellites to make that level of investment worthwhile on political grounds, but that the marginal gain for a completely independent satellite capability would not be that great compared to the costs. These are the sorts of issues that need to be systematically studied if one is to figure out whether the plan of action for a European threat assessment is worth pursuing.

The same type of hindrance flows from the fear that the consequences of a separate West European assessment may turn out to be disruptive to the Atlantic Alliance. This factor, of course, should be watched as carefully as possible. Certainly, NATO has concealed part of the transatlantic (as well as West European) heterogeneity, and divergence is likely to come more to the fore in the new dual level assessment structure. But would there not be compensation for this effect by the establishment of more credibility within the Alliance? Such a prediction is difficult to make. Those Europeans who are convinced that reform of NATO is necessary, and that a redistribution of responsibilities calls for West Europeans to assume a larger share of the defense burden, may choose this option. Those Europeans who are convinced that NATO will never improve upon the status quo will shy away from any initiative which implies the risk of alienating the Americans. An erosion of the framework of the Alliance through suspicious actions, without the simultaneous creation of a compensatory structure, is not feasible in their view.

A compromise position could plead for a *supranational* assessment capability within NATO. This would be in addition to the traditional cooperation of *sovereign* states in the Alliance. The main reason is that some of the future information, guidance, reconnaissance and surveillance systems in the West will probably have a scope which exceeds the financial and technical ability of any single member country.[12] This is not a novel idea; the Sixteen have launched a number of common acquisitions in this regard, including communication ships and AWACs. Recently, NATO has ordered two military satellites designed to provide reliable military and diplomatic communication for the Alliance through the next decade. The British Defense Ministry's Strategic Electronic Systems Organization will manage the procurement of the NATO Communications and Information Systems Agency (NACISA).[13] These examples are not taken from NATO's assessment section. Yet, the following questions remain. Can we expect a breakthrough

---

12 See David M. Abshire, NATO's Conventional Defense Improvement Effort: An Ongoing Imperative, in *The Washington Quarterly*, Vol. 10, No. 2 (Spring 1987), pp. 49-60.

13 NATO Orders Two Military Satellites From British Firms, in *Aviation Week & Space Technology*, 26 January 1987, p. 27.

to transatlantic supranationality in general? Would such a result render obsolete any solution on the West European level?

The quality of a West European assessment will also depend on the dialogue between the public and the governments. Politicians have a tendency to retreat from an internationally agreed position if they face domestic pressure. How can West European government officials be united in a common position? Three different ways have been tried during the thirty years of the EC and the twenty years of the EPC experience:

(1) Political leaders should find it hard to deviate from joint public West European statements, but experience shows that they easily retreat to domestic priorities.

(2) The opposite approach would be a discrete understanding which would build upon a gentlemen's agreement among West European leaders, and could not be disregarded for reasons of diplomatic virtue.

(3) A third way to create a more reliable common West European stance is to extend and upgrade the security consensus within West European party families. This process needs to be implemented with greater speed within the European Parliament.

Yet, as past experience illustrates, in the field of security West European concertation efforts are more complicated and sensitive than in either the economic or foreign policy sectors. Therefore, the West Europeans will have to combine the above three approaches in the hope of reducing deeply rooted divergencies as well as spontaneous inconsistencies.

Considering those factors which work for or against the establishment of a West European "challenge assessment unit," it seems realistic not to expect too much too soon. The current arms control negotiations have redirected the focus of East-West relations to Europe. Upcoming decisions on SNFs, and in the conventional arsenal, will engage the West Europeans directly and raise their motivation for more security cooperation. Elements of cooperation (technical, political, and institutional) exist, but these need to be coordinated and focused on a common goal. In this perspective, the West Europeans are not in a hopeless situation. Instead of insisting on a new institution, West Europeans can coordinate their existing instruments and still achieve useful results. If a full scale common collection of data is too sensitive a task, the West Europeans could - in an initial attempt - pool the information of their individual intelligence sources, both national and European, and try to arrive at a joint military-strategic interpretation of these findings. The overall political interpretation, hopefully, should not be too touchy or complicated a question. A periodic West European White Paper could be one of the visible outcomes of such an enterprise.[14]

This plan could be moderated in another respect in order to make it more feasible. The West Europeans may concentrate on a few areas of the overall East-West challenge and - as part of a concept of division of labor within NATO - could shoulder the responsibility for meeting these demands i.e. verification missions in East Europe "on behalf" of the Atlantic Alliance. A moderate beginning does not exclude evolution if popular demand is evident.

CONSEQUENCES

At present a West European "challenge assessment unit" will certainly not disturb the Western security landscape, nor will it resolve overnight the problem of an underdeveloped common West European identity in security. However, it could, regardless of its size, provide some signs for development in the right direction. An assessment unit would dovetail nicely with the general process of the Europeanization of security policy, to which it would add some substance. It would also be timely as Europeanization has taken on new meaning following Reykjavik and the subsequent Soviet-American competition for the best and the most far-reaching military reduction proposal. French President François Mitterrand is only one of several West European leaders asking for a center of political power in West Europe in order to pool the strength of the West

14 See for this proposal Stanley R. Sloan, *NATO's Future. Toward a New Transatlantic Bargain* (Washington, D.C: The National Defense University Press 1985), pp. 188-191. The same proposal is made by the former French defense minister Paul Quilès: "Commençons alors par élaborer ensemble un livre blanc sur la sécurité de l'Europe. Les travaux de préparation de ce texte permettront de mesurer la réalité de l'existence d'une volonté commune, d'unifier les concepts stratégiques et surtout de répartir la responsabilité et la charge des grands programmes d'armement entre les différents partenaires." (*Le Monde*, 8 April 1987, p. 11).

Europeans and to harmonize their military means and policies. The former French president, Valéry Giscard d'Estaing, stressed the need for a "personalization" of West European security cooperation. Jacques Delors, the President of the EC Commission, offered a proposal to convene a West European Security Summit to deal with pressing security topics. An assessment unit, which would continually offer information and evaluation on arms control and defense issues as well as on questions of reform in East Europe, could become a useful instrument in connection with the above concepts.

Such a unit is also likely to stimulate discussions which have begun in the WEU and in Franco-German cooperation regarding the elaboration of a more cohesive West European posture and the identification of common goals in arms control and defense policy. The West European nations know that, if they want to enhance their influence vis-à-vis the superpowers, then they have no choice but to reduce their divergencies. In practical terms, this means the following objectives should be sought: better ways must be discovered to persuade France to accept an explicit West European role and perception for its defense forces; Great Britain's basically non-continental outlook requires some re-evaluation; and Germany's fixation on a Soviet surprise attack should be mitigated. Even if there are strong enough strategic interests to unite London, Paris and Bonn for a common approach, a number of almost insurmountable problems will remain on the periphery of that triangle.[15] One example is sufficient to illustrate this point: Greece will certainly hold a threat perception which is not in the mainstream of West European assessment, and Athens may not want to pass any intelligence or military procurement data to Turkey.[16]

A continuous joint West European challenge assessment will not only help to adapt and develop national strategic thinking, it may also pave the way to a new relationship between governments and their public in security matters. Since the eighties, it has become more difficult in some West European societies to guarantee a large

---

15 James M. Markham, Europe's Triangular Initiative, in *International Herald Tribune*, 3 April 1987, p. 2.

16 In fact, since 1986, NATO has been unable to publish its annual force comparisons because of the Turco-Greek dispute in the Aegean. The other NATO members will have to publish their figures individually. For the European NATO members a collective approach could be sought in the WEU context.

security consensus. Often, opposition groups have criticized NATO or a particular government for its security policy without presenting credible alternatives. An inordinately large number of these groups have been given too much free reign.[17] Until the present time, the West European nations have independently defined how they perceive the threat, and how they view the likelihood for greater East-West cooperation. A joint West European capacity for challenge assessment would avoid some of the deficiencies of purely national and, predominantly American, assessments in NATO. A more realistic security debate may follow. Certainly, a West European assessment will also have its deficiencies. Deliberate concealment of important military information may not be excluded. Furthermore, the temptation to abuse information policy certainly exists within West Europe, as well. But in the case of a European assessment capability, independent of the United States, the West European electorates have the possibility to hold their governments accountable for such discrepancies and to vote for a change in such an event.

The other expected consequence, depending on the results of the internal concertation process, is that the West Europeans may partly alter their relations with the superpowers. A common West European challenge assessment, combined with technological capabilities for surveillance and verification, would probably foster, for the West European nations as a group, a more direct security dialogue with the Soviet Union and East European countries.

The more immediate impact, however, is likely to occur vis-à-vis Washington and within the Alliance. Two independent sources of assessment within NATO do not (necessarily) mean a restructuring of the Western defense structure. Instead they can provoke a more realistic transatlantic debate on the perennial, yet newly posed, question of how to cope with the Soviet Union and the Eastern bloc countries. In this perspective, a West European challenge assessment would reorient the transatlantic debate

---

17 There are signs that the problem of trust within the Alliance is an ongoing problem - not only confirmed by the examples already mentioned, but reflected in the collapse of the previous defense consensus in Britain and West Germany and - to some extent in the US - and in the formulation of alternative assessments - the von Bülow type of analysis, for example. See Andreas von Bülow, *Die eingebildete Unterlegenheit* (Bonn: C.H. Beck 1986).

regarding both the burdens and the benefits associated with the Western Alliance.[18]

---

18 James B. Steinberg, Rethinking the debate on burden-sharing, in *Survival*, Vol. 29, No. 1 (January/February 1987), pp. 56-78.

PART III: West Europe in the Transatlantic Bargain

The chapters in Part III assess the economic and strategic transatlantic environment in which the West Europeans struggle to achieve assertiveness. Several of these chapters use case studies to illustrate the definition of stakes, for the United States as well as for the West Europeans, within the Atlantic system.

An era in American foreign policy on transatlantic relations resulted in a qualitative leap forward for the process of West European "self-recognition." External events which profoundly influenced West European interests, but over which the Europeans had little control, provoked - as *David Allen* and *Michael Smith* state in their chapter - a re-evaluation of national priorities. In such areas as arms control and the Middle East, the West European states tried to make a collective response through the mechanism of European Political Cooperation. *Vera Erdmann-Keefer* explains that, while the United States is generally supportive of the European integration process, economic disputes are bound to arise over shares in global markets. Such conflicts of interest further define the emerging West European identity, in its institutional and commercial manifestations, as one separate from that of the United States. As West Europe seeks to establish its separate identity, European misperceptions about American policy formulation can hinder the process of assertiveness. In his chapter on strategic initiatives, *David Rubenson* argues that a West European understanding of the ways in which U.S. institutions function is essential to preserve healthy transatlantic relations. The chapter by *Stanley Sloan* considers the need to modernize transatlantic relations in the next decade in order to shape a new transatlantic bargain which reflects the increased economic and political potential of West Europe.

Such a policy framework would capture a blend of "continuity and change" as the United States would be called on to maintain a strong defense, an effective deterrent posture, and an active pursuit of improved relations with the East, while simultaneously facilitating structural transition within the Atlantic Alliance. Such a transition would undoubtedly require an American leadership which is willing to understand the complex institutional machinery of the European Community, to tolerate the ways in which the EC institutions may gradually begin to shape a European consensus within NATO, and to accept a fair amount of West European initiative within East-West relations.

9

West Europe in Reagan's World: Responding to a New American Challenge

David Allen and Michael Smith

INTRODUCTION

United States policies and policy-makers were largely responsible for the creation and the consolidation of "West Europe," both as a concept and as an international force. It is thus hardly surprising that since at least the early 194Os American concerns, American initiatives, and American responses have formed a crucial if not a dominant element in the consciousness and policies of West European governments. The threat of a hegemony exercised from Washington has been interwoven with the fear of abandonment if the forces of isolationism or insularity should once more take hold in the US, to form a continuing, if often muted tension, in the fabric of transatlantic relations. Academic analysts, as well as political leaders and officals, have identified and exhaustively dissected the issues - economic, ideological and strategic - around which the Euro-American system has revolved and evolved. There are thus powerful and persistent reasons for studying the ways in which US policies have impacted upon and evoked responses from the West Europeans. When, as was the case with the first Reagan administration, these policies have been assertive and contentious, the case for assessment and evaluation is self-evident.

It is far from self-evident, however, what was the net effect of the initial Reaganite challenge on the policies and policy-makers of

West Europe. To be sure, the emergence of an assertively globalist American administration, staffed by committed ideologues and dedicated to a policy of confrontation based on massive military strength could be seen as posing a series of problems for "civilian power Europe," but it is not clear to what extent this constituted a fundamental or even a significant discontinuity with European-American relations before the 198Os. In order to explore this puzzle, it is necessary both to identify the nature of the Reaganite challenge to West Europe and to locate West European responses within a more general analysis of the Atlantic system. On the basis of this kind of analysis, some provisional judgements can be made on a number of important issues. One of these is the problem of foreign policy in West Europe itself, and in particular the tension between policy-making at the national level and the emergent elements of a "European foreign policy" or a "European identity." Insofar as the dimensions of this problem changed during the early 198Os, to what extent did this represent a move in the direction of a common foreign policy, and to what extent a reassertion of national priorities and procedures? If meaningful judgements can be made on these changes, two further questions follow. First, can the changes be seen as in any way the consequence of Reaganism and its distinctive implications for West Europe, or were they a reflection of semi-autonomous trends or tensions within the international role of West Europe? Second, what might be the likely future evolution of West Europe's role within the Atlantic system, and what might the consequences be for the system itself?

This chapter sets out to deal with the issues outlined above by moving from a general assessment of West Europe's position within the Atlantic system to a more specific and empirical treatment of Reaganism and West European responses to US foreign policies during the early 198Os. First, it will identify some of the organizing assumptions of the Atlantic system and some of the models of Atlanticism to which they give rise. Second, it will expose some of the particular problems raised by the role of West Europe within the Atlantic system, in the context of the system's development during the last forty years. Third, the argument will focus on the distinctive challenges posed for West Europe by Reaganite foreign policies between 1981 and 1986. Fourth, there will be an assessment of developments in two major areas of European-American interaction: East-West relations and the handling of extra-European conflicts.

Although there is a rich vein of material relating to economic interactions between the US and West Europe during the 198Os, this is not our focus here: our concern is to explore the nature and import of West European responses within the broad area of diplomatic and strategic relations on the assumption that it is there that evidence of significant movement towards or away from a common West European stance can be found.

ATLANTIC RELATIONS: A FRAMEWORK FOR UNDERSTANDING

In order to locate the position of West Europe within the Atlantic system, it is necessary first to identify some of the underpinnings of the system itself. The approach here makes no pretensions to be comprehensive or theoretically watertight: rather, the intention is to highlight some qualities of the system and to draw from them some questions about the nature of the West European "presence." Four qualities of the Atlantic system seem to be relevant to the discussion: first, levels of mutual dependence and the stakes held in the system by its members; second, conceptions of roles and the relative statuses of members; third, policy styles, conceptions of the legitimacy and desirability of actions and the mutual responsiveness of policy-makers; finally, the mangement of the system, its "rules" and their impact on the behavior of members. The distinctions between these qualities, both analytically and empirically, are often blurred, but they provide a useful starting point for analysis in the present context.

The first of the four qualities builds on the undoubted fact that there are high levels of mutual dependence between the members of the Atlantic system, and that as a consequence they have a considerable stake - individually and collectively - in the system's perpetuation. But the quality of mutual dependence and common stakes is by no means uniform or unchanging. A "bottom up" view of the Atlantic community would emphasize the common interests of the peoples of the North Atlantic area, together with the cultural, commercial, and elite transmission belts that have been strengthened by the advent of mass and rapid communications. Other views of the system take a markedly different line of attack, and stress the unevenness of mutual dependence both in the strategic and in the economic domains. In this perspective, it is a combination of power and fear that holds the system together - the power of the US and the fear imparted by a perceived Soviet threat. It is apparent, though, that these forces cannot mask the fundamentally disparate stakes held in the Atlantic systems by members as diverse as the US and Belgium, Denmark and Greece, the UK and Turkey. Nonetheless, the system persists, and at least in part this is a reflection of its heterogeneity: it is neither an amalgamated community nor an arena for the free play of purely national interests and national power. This means that calculations of the stakes held and the risks run by the members of the system are inherently complex and indeterminate, and that no exercise of political will, coercion or persuasion is guaranteed to produce the expected results.

Within this heterogeneous and indeterminate arena, a second feature demands attention. Alongside the diverse patterns of mutual dependence and stakes in the system already noted there exist factors of role and status which can have powerful effects on political activity at the national and the international levels. Sometimes it is assumed that the impact of intense mutual dependence at the level of populations as well as that of governments will gradually wash away distinct conceptions of national roles in the Atlantic system and substitute a kind of integrated cross-national pluralism. Such a process will at best only be very gradual, though, and it could powerfully be argued that the Atlantic area is characterized by the remarkable vitality and persistence of national role conceptions. If that is the case, then such national conceptions create important possibilities of tension when they are brought into confrontation with the undoubted disparities of national status within the system, and when they are asked to coexist with the institutions of a nascent transnational community. Given these tensions - actual and potential - the problem of role is central to an understanding of the Atlantic system, and the capacity and inclinations of the members to perform their roles a persistent source of uncertainty. Not the least of the issues raised is the role of "Europe" within a Euro-American system or Atlantic partnership, and this issue will be explored later in the chapter.

Given the qualities of complexity, diversity, and potential tension that underly the Atlantic system, it becomes important to focus on the criteria and priorities which guide the conduct of policy and shape its style. What is possible, acceptable, or desirable in terms of behavior within the Atlantic system is by no means self-evident - or at least, what is legitimate at one level or in one context may very well not be in another coexisting or overlapping domain. If one subscribes to the notion of a transnational Atlantic community, then national or sectional policy priorities may dissolve in the face of an almost instinctive or automatic convergence underpinned by elite and popular responsiveness. There is very little evidence that such a process is well-advanced in the North Atlantic area: indeed, some would argue that convergence of policy styles has more typically reflected patterns of domination and subordination which grow out of the uneven mutual dependence and disparities of status already described. Convergence in this view is an inappropriate term: submissiveness or compliance matched by hegemony and privilege are the true character of the Atlantic system. Again, though, the texture and structure of the system defy easy categorization, and it can persuasively be argued that policy-making for the North Atlantic area is bound to be hard work. It entails the reconciliation of many layers, of many constituencies and of many targets in a process of hard bargaining both within and between countries. This is especially the case if there is any requirement for policies directed outside the Atlantic area itself, since there the diversity of stakes and roles can have far freer rein.

A final component of the Atlantic system is the mechanisms by which the system is maintained and managed. Much of what has already been said bears upon this aspect of the argument, but it is important to pay specific attention to the ways in which Atlantic relations are "run": the institutions, rules and procedures that fit the needs of the members, express their mutual dependence and obligations, and govern their expectations and behavior. The Atlantic area is well provided with multilateral arrangements and institutions, but this does not represent in full the ways in which the system is run. It is in fact both more and less than a true picture: more, because despite the impressive array of Atlantic institutions their capacity to affect events may be relatively limited; less, because the persistence of the system expresses informal factors that may be a much more powerful source of coherence and intelligibility than the most elaborate of organizational structures. For some commentators this underlying condition of coherence and integration is fundamental to an idea of Atlantic community, forming an indissoluble regime to which the institutional architects can give expression but which they cannot by themselves create. Others, though, would argue that this image of Atlantic solidarity is a convenient myth, and that the real explanation of the way the system runs is to be found in the distribution and exercise of power between its members. As has already been noted, the Atlantic system contains considerable unevenesses of stakes and status, and this has found its expression both in the period of open US hegemony and in the period of its erosion. By some accounts, the erosion or fragmenting of hegemony should make the underlying regime more fragile and the uncertainties of life in the Atlantic system more pervasive, but this can be challenged on two grounds. First, and substantively, it can be argued that despite the fragmentation of hegemony the US can assert its dominance when and where it matters. Second, it can be argued that even when substantive hegemony is eroded there remain substantial incentives for the members of the Atlantic system to play by the rules. The impression thus is of a rather uneasy halfway house between hegemony and polyarchy, in which the unease reflects not only the cracking of the power structure but also the disparities of mutual dependency, stakes, statuses, and policy foundations already noted.

A number of initial conclusions can be drawn from this brief review. In the first place, given the diversity of the Atlantic system and the tensions - actual or potential - within it, no single model or image can do justice to its evolution or provide a reliable guide to its future development. There may have been times at which the system approximated the "ideal types" of Atlantic community, partnership, or empire, but as the system has persisted it has diverged more and more from the dictates of any analytical or ideological norm. Second, and relatedly, it is apparent that the notion of an Atlantic system itself has often been a weapon or a stake in political combat, and that the political contestability of the idea has reflected the operational uncertainties of the Atlantic arena. Finally, and most importantly for the argument in this chapter, it is evident that the contestability of the Atlantic system has significant implications for the position of West Europe as expressed through the individual or collective circumstances of its societies and policy-makers.

WEST EUROPE IN ATLANTIC RELATIONS

Throughout the history of the postwar Atlantic system, the place both of the West European states and of any such entity as "West Europe" itself has been fundamentally ambiguous. At one level, this ambiguity expresses the divergence between aspiration and reality, which has had two typical manifestations. The first of these has been American in origin: the tendency to wish into being a united or potentially uniting West Europe, and to suffer inevitable disillusionment when the aspiration evokes ten or a dozen distinctive national responses, often cloaked in the rhetoric of the unity from which they detract. This, of course, mirrors the European end of the conundrum, since within the half-continent itself there has often been relatively little in the way of consensus on its actual or potential future development. From the earliest days of "European unity" there has been tension not only between the national level of action and capacity and the aspiration for supranational amalgamation, but also between the idea of an "Atlantic Europe" and the more limited and regional preoccupations often of those most in favor of integration itself. The great reappraisals and crises of the Atlantic system have often grown out of this basic uncertainty, on both sides of the Atlantic, about what the necessary, possible, or appropriate position for West Europe should be. From the European Defense Community through the Kennedy-de Gaulle confrontation to Vietnam, Nixon, and the "Year of Europe" the history of West Europe, its trials and successes, its achievements and limitations, have been pivotal to the Alliance, to the European Community and to the states involved on both - or many - sides.

It was noted earlier that despite aspirations for the growth of a transnational Atlantic community, national role conceptions have been remarkably resilient and influential in the system as a whole. At the West European level, it has been evident throughout the postwar era that the reconstruction of national political and economic life produces not only high levels of interconnectedness and mutual dependence but also a reinvigoration of national consciousness. Indeed, one of the most potent elements in this kind of reinvigoration has on occasion been the presence, posture, and actions of the US in its role as protector or hegemon. For the major countries of West Europe, the relationship with the US has in each case been "special," but very different national responses and attitudes have flowed from this central reality. The British have had the painful but generally gradual task of adjusting to loss of status and to an erosion of the easy assumptions once made about the "Anglo-Saxon alliance"; by the 198Os it could fairly be said that there was more than ever going on between the British and the Americans, but that more and more - *pace* the Reagan-Thatcher ideological affinity - relations fell into the normal range of interactions between advanced industrial societies. The French have had a far more turbulent passage as members of the transatlantic crew, but it cannot be denied that their orientation to the international world has been fundamentally affected by the American connection. Tensions between the desire for restoration of national status and prestige and the imperatives of geostrategic and economic engagement have produced some spectacular squarings-off as well as many more subtle mutual adjustments in Franco-American relations, but by the mid-197Os there appeared to have emerged a *modus vivendi*, with France as a nonconforming but relatively amenable ally. For the third country in the West European "Great Power triangle," the Federal Republic of Germany, events have taken a different course again: initial subordination almost as a condition of international existence has given way to a far more equal - but also nuanced and subtle - relationship with the US. Through the 196Os an emerging West German consciousness of their distinctive position and national needs intersected with the changing international framework and the shifts in American policy to produce a complex and potentially troublesome "partnership," both economic and political. The 197Os saw a full flowering of the contradictions with the impact of détente and the onset of recession, and it became apparent that the Bonn-Washington connection contained inherent conflict as well as accustomed intimacy.

In the case of the "Big Three," but also in relation to other West European countries, it is apparent that the American - and thus the Atlantic - connection has had a pervasive, complex, and diverse impact. One effect of the transatlantic relationship has been to make the US a factor in both the domestic politics and the foreign policies of the countries concerned. The results for the Atlantic system have been paradoxical and often - especially in American eyes - perverse. Although the mutual dependence of the US with each and all of the West European countries has grown, so has an awareness in West Europe and its capitals of the diversity of national positions. To use the terms deployed earlier in the paper, it is apparent that West European countries have a heterogeneous set of national stakes, roles, policy styles, and interpretations of the rules by which the Atlantic system can and should be run. This assessment is clearly vital to an understanding of the ambiguities attending the West Europeans' positions at the level of national policy. Just as important is its bearing on the West European capacity to operate collectively, either within the Alliance or through the European Community.

It has often been noted that the development of a European "voice" was an important and often publicly stated condition of American assistance during the 194Os and 195Os. Equally often it has been concluded that insofar as there has grown up any West European presence on the international stage, this has by no means been reassuring or even to the liking of the US. There are effectively two dimensions to the problem: first, the willingness and ability of the West Europeans to play their allotted roles within the Atlantic system, and second, the potential for the emergence of something resembling a West European "foreign policy." On the whole, the first of these issues characterized the 195Os and 196Os, whilst the second has been more apparent during the 197Os and 198Os. In both cases, the trends established in West Europe intersected with significant phases of US foreign policy, especially as it affected the Americans' status within and commitment to the Atlantic system.

The earliest pressures for construction of a West European entity within the Atlantic system came in the economic domain, with the conditions attached to the Marshall Plan and the European Recovery Program. Whilst these led only imperfectly and indirectly to the establishment of a "uniting Europe," there was at least progress to report. In the strategic sphere, with the fiasco of the European Defense Community, it could be argued with the benefit of hindsight that the potential for any kind of relatively equal partnership within the Alliance was fatally undermined. A combination of the tensions between West European national positions and the structural dominance of the US was potent enough not only to prevent the establishment of a European defense entity but also to perpetuate a fractious political asymmetry that found expression on several notable occasions in the late 195Os and the 196Os. At the same time, the growth of European economic integration, whilst producing solid institutional and technical achievements, appeared unable to move beyond a somewhat introspective and instrumental stance. Not surprisingly, when President Kennedy called in 1962 for progress towards an Atlantic partnership, the results in both the strategic and the economic spheres were decidedly ambiguous. It appeared by the end of the 196Os that the Americans had overestimated their capacity to set the terms of debate within the Alliance - considerable as it was - but that they had also overestimated the potential for development of any "Europe" that was not a mere "civilian power." This tells us something about the lack of clarity and responsiveness in US policies, but also indicates the limited and essentially conditional nature of the West European entity with which they found themselves dealing.

It was during the 197Os that both Americans and West Europeans found themselves dealing with the implications of a nascent "European" foreign policy mechanism. Although there were a number of fora in which the development of distinct West European collaboration could be observed, it was the mechanism of European Political Cooperation (EPC) that most fully expressed the new tendency. Two features of this phenomenon should be pointed out immediately: first, although it is tempting to draw analogies between EPC and the foreign policy of a putative West European state, it is in reality an often uncomfortable halfway house between national foreign policies and an integrated multinational stance; second, since EPC is centred on attempts to define what is specifically a European Community position, it will almost inevitably do this in such a way as to emphasize any areas of distinction between a "European" and an American posture. Neither of these features is particularly comforting for policy-makers in Washington, and as a result there grew up in the 197Os a considerable fund of less than constructive interaction between the US and EPC. On the European side, it is clear that in the early years of EPC, the policies and attitudes of Nixon and Kissinger combined with the force of events in the Middle East and elsewhere to provide some of the most tangible impetus to enhanced collaboration.

This is not, though, to draw a simple connection between European-American disagreements and the elaboration of foreign policy collaboration in West Europe. That collaboration is itself multi-layered, and has to accommodate considerable variations in size, geopolitical position, and interests between member states of the Community. However much the "Big Three" of Britain,

France, and Germany might wish to coordinate their policies on specific questions, the interests of countries such as Greece and Ireland can introduce complicating and frustrating diversions. Equally, the restricted nature of participation for smaller members in the great issues of the day can produce resentments. Particular problems arise over the extension of EPC to any areas that could be defined as strategic in nature, since these by definition are the areas that most members will want to keep most firmly within their national control - quite apart from the fact that the Irish are neutral and thus sensitive to any such expansion of the agenda. Nonetheless, the increasingly intimate connection between economic and security questions in the world of the 197Os and the 198Os has meant that the EPC agenda has had a growing security content. As one commentator has put it, however, "European defense cooperation may be back on the agenda, but it is not in the cards."

Although it is clear from this brief sketch that West European foreign policy collaboration is inherently limited, this does not mean that it is without significance either in itself or in the context of Atlantic relations. It has already been noted that any "European" foreign policy stance is likely to be defined in ways that emphasize its distinctiveness from that of the US, even if this is only at the declaratory level. It is also clear that both members of the Community and third states often find it convenient to work through a collaborative mechanism when more purely "national" methods might be unpalatable either to domestic or to other forces. When this kind of procedure is added to the diversity that characterizes West Europeans' engagement in the Atlantic system at the country level, it is plain that we are dealing with an extraordinary nuanced and often mercurial set of actions and interactions. American policies are and have been a major conditioning factor in the operation of this multi-layered system, but in order more precisely to gauge their impact during the 198Os it is necessary to explore the challenges posed by the theory and practice of Reaganism.

THE CHALLENGE OF REAGANISM

Just as the status and roles of West Europe have been a constant source of ambiguity in the Atlantic system, so has the position of the US itself. It would be tempting and convenient to assume that the perceived stakes held by the US in the system, its anticipated and actual roles and its orientation towards policy-making and management formed a constant factor, a source of continuity and order. It is clear from the history of Atlantic relations that such an image of the US's position and orientation is at best only tangentially related to reality and at worst grossly misleading. At the structural level, there have been considerable fluctuations in the pervasiveness and extent of American dominance - a dominance that may have been eroded in some areas of activity but which is still enshrined in at least some of the institutions and mechanisms of the Atlantic system. A situation of fragmented or fragmenting hegemony such as has characterized the Atlantic area during the 197Os and 198Os provides a shifting and unpredictable backdrop to relations between the US and West Europe. This impression of fragmentation and unpredictability is reinforced by the rhetoric and the actions of US administrations. Once again, this factor has a long historical pedigree: the question "what kind of US?" has been implicit in the development of Atlantic relations since their inception. At the level of rhetoric, the propensity of policy-makers in Washington to announce grand designs and to play to the domestic audience as well as to the allies has created some of the more notable tensions in European-American relations, with John Foster Dulles, John Kennedy and Henry Kissinger all implicated to various degrees and to diverse effects. At the level of action, the style of American policies with a potent combination of unilateralism, interventionism, globalism, and insularity has provoked West Europeans to successive reappraisals of Washington's commitments, expectations and anticipated future behaviour. It is within this broad context - and particularly within the context of the late 197Os and early 198Os - that the Reaganite challenge to the West Europeans should be evaluated.

It is possible to see "Reaganism" - the cluster of beliefs, practices, and policies associated with the US presidency in the early 198Os - as a response to two interconnected trends. The first of these is the changing position of the US in the international arena, with the erosion of American hegemony, the rise of new actors and the problems of interdependence which beset successive administrations during the 197Os. The second trend is one of domestic change: a shift in the foundations of policy-making which changed the basis for policy legitimacy and created a demand for new solutions to long-established problems. Reaganism in effect constituted the manifesto for those expressing dissatisfaction and demanding change in the style and substance of American policies both at home and abroad: the promise was that of a new set of values (or the reassertion of neglected values), their translation into a new policy agenda, and a re-establishment of coherence and consistency in policy-making. In the particular context of the Atlantic system, the initial implications of this program were hard to discern. Reassuring commitments to the Alliance and to the interests of the allies went along with a promise of the kind of assertiveness and globalism that had caused much agonizing in the past. Not only this, but the implied domesticism of much of the Reagan agenda - a kind of muscular insularity which promised to make the Americans feel better about themselves - held the potential for Atlantic disjunction as much as Atlantic unity.

The remaking of US foreign policies promised by the incoming administration was thus far-reaching but unpredictable when viewed from a West European standpoint. By elevating ideology and long range goals, and calling for a new spirit of assertiveness, it questioned the rather pragmatic and instrumental approaches that have been a feature of much European foreign policy-making, and thus seemed likely to demand a reappraisal of priorities at the national and the collective levels. By stressing globalism and a universal contest between the forces of good and evil, it challenged the regional and parochial obsessions of most West European countries and of their mechanisms for policy coordination whilst threatening to politicize a wide range of issues that had been allowed to lie fallow during the 197Os. Not least, the Reaganite emphasis on strength and will was at odds with the rather ambiguous diplomatic proceduralism beloved of West Europeans. It appeared that the combination of domesticism and universalism was potentially disruptive in two dimensions: first, by emphasizing the disjunction between domestic demands and the need for responsiveness and consultation in alliance relations; second, by stressing globalism at the expense of attention to nuances and national preferences in areas such as West Europe. The gains to be anticipated from a restoration of coherence in foreign policy-making were to be welcomed in principle - and the installation of the "Atlanticist" Alexander Haig as Secretary of State could be seen as a specific earnestness of intent

- but the ability of the administration to carry through its "revolution" was at least open to question.

From the vantage point of the late 1980s, the Reagan administration's foreign policy record between 1981 and 1986 appears uneven to say the least, and this unevenness carried with it major implications for the Atlantic system and its West European members. In general, it can be argued that US foreign policy from 1981 fell into three phases: an initial unravelling, a period of relative stability, and a descent into renewed confusion. During the first eighteen months of the administration, the predominant feature of policy-making was confusion and contradiction whilst the substance of policy was marked by rhetorical inconsistency and behavioral immobility. The problems of policy-making arose largely from the disintegration of the seemingly united policy-making community, with Haig at the epicenter of successive upheavals. This process was aggravated by the domestic preoccupations of the administration, which meant that much of its foreign policy output was directed at audiences within rather than outside the US. Although the sinews of economic and defense policy were being ostentatiously refurbished, there was evidence that the process would not be untroubled and a considerable lack of clarity about the purposes to which any new-found strength might be applied.

The inner fragility of Reaganite foreign policy was exposed in the summer of 1982, with the successive upheavals in Central America and the South Atlantic, the Middle East, and East-West relations. It could be argued that only with the fall of Haig and his replacement by George Shultz did the administration finally acquire an effective foreign policy: only then was there an attempt to match means and ends in a consistent and appropriate way. The problem was, though, that a lot of momentum had built up behind certain elements of the Reaganite program in general, and this made it extraordinarily difficult to make any meaningful change of course. Although early Reaganite foreign policy had achieved little, it had raised expectations, generated suspicions, and constrained the freedom for maneuver of its inheritors.

There was thus a paradoxical quality about the stabilization of US foreign policy between 1982 and 1985. Almost everyone noted a change of style and tone - a movement from overblown rhetoric to more measured approaches symbolized by the new Secretary of State - but equally it became apparent that the gap between grand strategy and on-the-ground developments was still dauntingly wide. The inter-departmental competition generated by the early years did not go away; Congress showed an increasing inclination and capacity to insert itself into the oversight of foreign policy; and external clients or adversaries demonstrated an annoying disinclination to be impressed simply by the piling up of US capabilities. Thus, the "strategic consensus" in the Middle East was abandoned in a piecemeal fashion, but this did not do away with the entanglement of American interests. Equally, involvement in Central America was constrained, but remained costly and problematic. The Soviets were accepted increasingly as adversarial partners, but the "new arms race" seemed to possess a life of its own. Although it was suggested after the election victory of 1984 that "Reagan II" would be more interested in the fruits of statesmanship than the continued assertion of national virility, it was not clear that the weight of the past four years could so easily be sloughed off.

Perhaps inevitably in the light of these mutually offsetting forces, 1985 was a curiously indeterminate year in the evolution of Reaganite foreign policies. At the declaratory level, the tone seemed to be set by George Shultz's assertion that the refurbishment of America's strength and position during the first Reagan term had established the basis for real gains in the international arena. Now, it appeared, was the time for the US to move forward and build concrete achievements on the ground already laid. Such an impression was reinforced by evidence that Shultz had moved to consolidate the State Department's hold on the policy-making process and that the White House "hawks" were on the defensive. It was also apparent that both friends and adversaries of the US saw the opportunity for new initiatives with the opening of the new Reagan era. But by the end of the year, there was precious little evidence of a great leap forward in US foreign policy; indeed, there was a discernible loss of momentum in many areas despite the renewal of contacts at the summit with the USSR. As some commentators argued, the achievements of Reaganite policies up to 1985 had in many respects been cost-free and built on foundations laid by earlier administrations, which had enabled the President and his advisers to look strong from an essentially negative position. The challenge of moving onto the offensive and confronting the real difficulties inherent in creating new structures still remained, and if it was not accepted then the danger was of a purely reactive policy stance.

By these criteria, 1986 was the year in which Reaganite foreign policy was tested and found wanting. Not only was the American administration unable to move beyond obstruction into the realm of creation and innovation; it also experienced the disintegration of some of its central assumptions in a way that further accentuated the gulf between words and deeds. Perhaps the first casualty - and one already apparent in 1985 - was the domestic consensus on the merits of a "policy of strength." At the level of resources and appropriations, there was increasing reluctance to acccept the implications of a defense spending "binge," expressed in Congress and through more general budgetary pressures. At the level of action in the international arena, it became possible not only to question the prudence of the White House's choices but also - in the cases of Libya and Iran - to impugn the integrity of the policy-making process itself. Nor was this simply an echo of the early Reagan years, of the turmoil emerging from the "on the job training" of the administration; this was the kind of thing that creates lame duck presidents and paralysis of the foreign policy machine. The whole mess was accentuated by the intractability or perversity of international events, particularly those in the Middle East and Central America and at the Summit. Although it was possible either to praise or blame the administration for the intent of its actions, it was difficult to be enthusiastic about the purposefulness or the coherence of the actions themselves.

In many ways, the combination of policy fragmentation and international turbulence which emerged during 1986 and persisted through 1987 and 1988 spelt the end of the Reagan era in American foreign policy. It foreshadowed a period of "hangover" in which reactiveness and often passivity replaced the earlier assertiveness and muscularity. This is not to say that nothing of significance occurred during these years: rather it is to point out that many of the landmarks were more the ending of previous lines of policy than the initiation of new directions. The INF Treaty, signed in December 1987 and ratified by mid-1988, thus represented the culmination of the processes already noted rather than the beginning of a new era of negotiations, since the natural tendency of Soviet and many American policy-makers was to wait for the new administration.

American policy awaited a new infusion of vigour and direction, but it was not clear from whence it would eventually come.

The events of 1986 and after raised important and intriguing questions about the future of Reaganite foreign policy, but these are not the central concern of this chapter. It was argued earlier that the unevenness of the Reaganite record carried with it major implications both for the Atlantic system and for its West European members, and these should be stated here before more detailed evidence is considered. In essence, the problem can be expressed as the uneasy coexistence of "rhetorical" and "practical" Reaganism. It was noted earlier that the rhetoric and the theoretical program of Reaganism, with its emphasis on ideological stridency, assertion of strength and a strange mixture of domesticism and universalism, was such as to pose immediate problems for the West Europeans (and indeed for others closely concerned with the American posture). But the problems turned out to be by no means as simple as this might imply, since the evolution of "practical" Reaganism created a dynamic, fluctuating and often elusive set of challenges. In the first place, it was apparent that the gap between grand statements of ideological intent and the practical adjustment of interest which was fostered by the fragmentation of domestic American opinion and the White House machine, posed considerable challenges for those such as the West Europeans who had major stakes in a consistent and fathomable US policy posture. Secondly, the predictable disjunction between domestic demands and the requirements of alliance politics was sharpened both by the administration's initial obsession with getting the economy right and the arms buildup off the ground and by the need to attend to the demands of congressional and other constituencies. Finally, the instability of policy implementation fostered by lack of coordination and control in the administration, coupled with a rather erratic unilateralism, heightened a long-standing fear of the West Europeans, that they would be the victims of White House accidents as much as the subject of systematic manipulation or coercion.

Such conclusions, though, are interim and abstract, raising as many questions as they answer. The remainder of this chapter will attempt to put some flesh on the bones of the general argument by examining two case studies in West European responses to Reaganism between 1981 and 1986 - East-West relations and regional conflicts outside Europe. On the basis of this evidence, we can hope to draw more specific conclusions about the status and roles of West Europe in the Atlantic system of the late 198Os.

A FIRST CASE STUDY: EAST-WEST RELATIONS

West-West problems over East-West relations predated Reaganism and will assuredly outlast it. Since the 195Os there have been conflicts about the balance between diplomacy and coercion, commerce and economic warfare, strategy and alliance. It was apparent throughout the 197Os that on significant issues there were substantial differences between European and American perspectives. To put it crudely, Americans - with some variations under the Carter administration - were increasingly prone to see the USSR as expansionist, unamenable to persuasion, and responding most to tactics of coercion and linkage. West Europeans, on the other hand, had a view of the Soviets which emphasized their pragmatism, the complexity of their predicament, and their openness to bargaining. Nowhere was the contrast more sharply expressed than in US and West European versions of détente: more and more during the 197Os, the Americans had come to see détente as instrumental, a means to an end, whilst Europeans in general saw it as desirable in and of itself. As has already been noted, Reaganism was largely founded on a view of the world that could only heighten this underlying disparity of perceptions.

Such a crude contrast, however, does much less than justice to the subtleties and variations of positions within West Europe itself. Whilst there may be a general tendency for Europeans to think more in terms of balance than bipolarity, of diplomacy rather than coercion, of commerce rather than warfare, this conceals a wide spectrum of national or sectoral orientations. Such orientations reflect in their turn variations in responsiveness, perceived stakes and domestic pressures of the kind noted earlier in the chapter. Not all West Europeans - governments or peoples - are responsive in similar directions or degrees to American or Soviet policies: here the spectrum has to cover both an instinctively Atlanticist Britain and an incorrigibly nationalist France, as well as a West Germany fated to give a high priority to détente in almost any circumstances. Nor do all West Europeans have equal stakes in East-West relations, whether the stakes are conceived of as moral and ideological or in the more tangible form of trade and other transactions - transactions which for example enmesh the West Germans more than any of their European partners. Finally, the domestic forces shaping West European policies are often as variable within the half-continent as they are distinctive from those operating within the US. Governments hold power not in terms of a standard contract with their electorates but in terms of fluctuating popular, party-political, and constitutional processes. East-West relations for fragile coalitions have different implications from those felt by single party governments - as do peace movements, popular protests, and the pressures of lobbies.

European-American relations in the East-West arena are thus inherently complex, and intra-European relations especially so. A policy stance such as that initially assumed by the Reagan administration can be liberally endowed with simplifications, but the real world of diplomacy is bound to modify it, perhaps profoundly. In the same way, West European governments confronted Reaganism in 1981 with some broadly shared perceptions, but with wide variations in detailed stances - variations which were accentuated by the development of European-American diplomacy during the next six years. Nonetheless the immediate prospect of the new administration called forth a substantial amount of coordinated diplomatic activity in the first half of 1981. Essentially, all West European leaderships felt the need to channel at least some of Reaganism's energy into the diplomatic mode, and the device of European Political Cooperation helped in the concerting of policies. A number of trends in the remainder of the first Reagan administration, and in the first half of the second term, made such levels of convergence difficult to sustain, chief among them the mercurial nature of policy-making in Washington and their own internal or "European" problems.

Three overlapping patterns of West European diplomacy became increasingly visible in the 1981-86 period. First, there was a proliferation of bilateral East-West contacts, encouraged both by the development of US policies and by the maneuverings of the Soviets. Whilst Moscow was often accused of trying to divide the West, it is fair to say that the demands imposed first by the insularity and then by the external projection of Reaganism had important limiting effects on the development of any coordinated West European effort. Secondly, it became apparent that in East-West relations in particular the existence of a variety of "West-West" diplomatic channels provided convenient bolt-holes, escape hatches, or negotiating fora. Indeed, many such channels were sought out and cultivated by West Europan governments in the attempt to communicate concerns to Washington, especially during the early years of the administration. Finally, when the Reagan White House at last started doing what West Europeans said they wanted - that is, negotiating with the Soviets after 1984 - a new problem emerged. Perhaps it is better seen as an old problem in a novel form, since this was not the first time that active Soviet-American links have threatened to "crowd out" West European concerns or pressures. Suddenly the idea that West Europe could act as a link between the superpowers, either bilaterally or multilaterally, was subject to all the old doubts and fears of condominium. When this was added to the other factors noted above, it is clear that the process of West European insertion into or isolation from East-West diplomacy was a significant background condition in responses to the Reaganite challenge. But it is important to move from this general level of assessment to the handling of specific East-West issues. Two such issues are especially salient: first, East-West trade, and second, arms and arms control.

East-West economic links have been a focus of European-American relations since the inception of the Marshall Plan. During the 196Os and 197Os the clash between those who espoused embargoes and "economic warfare" and those who believed in the therapeutic qualities of commerce was generally muted, but the politicization of economic transactions during the 197Os had an inevitable spillover into Atlantic dealings. This came into the open with the crises in Iran and Afghanistan, which created American demands for sanctions and a number of burning issues even before the Reaganites took over the White House. Two central questions characterized debate and conditioned responses to US policies in West Europe: in the first place, were economic relations a weapon with which to coerce miscreants or a set of incentives with which to tempt them? Secondly, could economic dealings in some way be insulated from political or strategic judgements, or were they inextricably intertwined with them? From the late 197Os on, it was apparent that West European policy-makers were coming up with a variety of often contradictory answers to these questions. Three essential positions could be discerned on the spectrum of response.

At one end were those - especially the FRG - who were heavily engaged in East-West trade and thus constrained by social and economic imperatives, quite apart from the belief that trade and finance were an essential prop of détente. In the center of the spectrum were those who held a more pragmatic view of the matter, and who in a sense were able to see trade as more of a two-edged sword - a stance most often taken up by the French. At the other end were those who (perhaps because the material stakes were lower for them) could afford a certain ideological stridency, but who were nonetheless beset by commercial interests who could voice their interests quite forcefully. The British and the Italians are best placed in this position. For all West European countries, the tension between ideology and commercial advantage, and between their "European" and Atlantic priorities was well established before 1981.

Economic sanctions and economic warfare were early on the agenda of European-American relations in 1981, but remained relatively muted. The British and the West Germans let it be known that they were opposed to the lifting of the grain embargo imposed by the Carter administration, but also that they would oppose any sanctions directed at the Soviet-West European gas pipeline project - an early target of Reaganite "hawks." There was little discussion of the issues at the Ottawa economic summit, where the participants were much more concerned with domestic problems. It was in December 1981, with the imposition of martial law in Poland, that the question, and the contradictions to which it gave rise, really came to the fore. For the Europeans, a pattern of response was fairly quickly established, both at the national and the collaborative levels. The West Germans gave priority to the economic and social aspects; the French stressed their right to decide as they saw fit; and the British focused on the need to stave off a possible "West-West" crisis. Both the French and the West Germans found the issue sensitive within their governing coalitions, and thus a political "hot potato," whilst the British and the Italians were rather more relaxed except where specific commercial interests were at stake. These variations were not, it appeared, a matter of intense interest given the relatively unassertive initial response from Washington. Haig was credited by some with preserving some space for the West Europeans to deviate, but it may also have been that the lack of order in US policy-making prevented any assertive American response.

Whatever the cause, West European movement towards the US position was glacial to say the least until mid-1982.

Everything changed in June and July 1982, and the crucial element was a shift in the American policy process. The advent of William Clark as National Security Affairs Advisor and the increasing harassment of Haig had led since the spring to escalating attacks on those who were seen as appeasers - or to put it more kindly, those who favored multilateral as opposed to unilateral diplomacy. The Versailles economic summit was the last hurrah of the multilateralists: within two weeks Haig was gone, and the hard line was dominant. On East-West trade, Versailles had been a fudge: although West Europeans and the Japanese had been left in no doubt about strong US feelings, they had also been led to believe that deals could be done, especially on the pipeline. But during July it appeared that the US declared economic war on its allies as well as on the Soviet bloc - and it must not be forgotten that the East-West issue was superimposed on a number of other festering trade disputes between the US and the EC. One immediate feature of West European responses was their diversity both at the declaratory and at the operational level. The West Germans tried their best to ignore the sanctions; the French expressed nationalistic outrage and resistance; the British protested both their Atlantic solidarity and their determination to protect their interests, if necessary by legislative means. In these cirumstances, European solidarity of a positive as opposed to a negative kind was difficult to discern. Although the EC summit of June 1982 issued a declaration, the British were suspected of neutering it, and the formal protest issued and documented in August was less dramatic than the flights and speeches of individual West European leaders.

During the autumn of 1982 a number of processes combined to diffuse - but not to fundamentally resolve - the conflict. First, it became apparent that a number of powerful interests in the US did not like the sanctions: their influence over the succeeding two years was to produce a gradual erosion of the measures at the US national level. Second, the influence of George Shultz - an old economic hand - produced a negotiating process involving the major stakeholders and culminating in an agreement on general principles by the end of the year. Third, the problem was "rerouted": studies in the framework of COCOM, NATO and the OECD diluted the crisis and produced an impression of routine technical adjustment.

This did not please everybody - by 1984 the Pentagon was increasingly worried about West European computers and telecommunications equipment, whilst the irksome restrictions of the COCOM denials list were still a source of aggravation to the Europeans. It was noticeable, however, that on occasions during 1983 and 1984 when the Americans could have raised the stakes afresh, they refrained from doing so. Meanwhile the Europeans had moved into line in areas such as subsidised export credits, whilst resting firmly on their well-established hostility to US dictation.

The peaks and troughs of European-American conflicts over East-West trade cannot be divorced from broader disagreement over trade policy. Nor can they be decoupled from the next area of concern here: armaments and arms control. Two points must be made at once about this issue: first, like East-West trade, it has a long and tangled history; second, more than East-West trade, it demands of the West Europeans an answer to the question what kind of Europe. The historical context is vital to an understanding of the 198Os, since it reveals a consistent tension between European and American images of the desirable and the practicable in security matters. On the one side, there is the problem of US commitment - a problem summed up for the West Europeans in Michael Mandelbaum's juxtaposition of twin dangers, "entrapment" and "abandonment." On the other, for the Americans, there is the problem of the West European contribution. The "nuclear alliance" has to be rationalized for US domestic audiences, and it is no help to policy-makers in Washington if it appears that the Europeans are backsliding, hedging, or appeasing in the face of the enemy. The problems are compounded by the nature of defense debates and defense policy-making in the US: often it is unclear even to those in the know whether American policy is driven by technological momentum, by the demands of the domestic audience or by intellectual debates which run the risk of being disconnected from reality in all but their impact on the outside world. These uncertainties underline the difficulties for West Europeans, since it is hard to define a position if the scenery is constantly in a state of flux. But quite apart from this, Europe has an identity problem. Having arguably grown fat on its status as a "civilian power," what are the costs and benefits of going beyond that at the European level? This tension is implanted in national as well as multinational interests for West European leaders, and thus cannot be overcome by simple acts of will or faith.

Developments in the late 197Os and early 198Os compounded the problem. The December 1979 "twin-track" commitment on intermediate-range nuclear forces (INF), stimulated by West European pressure, heightened the "abandonment-entrapment" tensions at an elite and a popular level. Ronald Reagan came to office committed to the INF decision, but also rejecting SALT II as "fatally flawed" and dedicated to a policy of strength before negotiation. His administration, and Haig in particular, proclaimed their determination to consult the European allies, but consultation in these circumstances ran the risk of exacerbating the structural and political divergences we have noted. Within the West European context, there was a world of difference between the UK - a nuclear power on the fringes of Europe - and West Germany, the original "front-line state" with no autonomous nuclear capability, a territory festooned with other peoples' warheads and a large indigenous peace movement. Add in Greece, Italy, and the Benelux, and it was clear that one was dealing with more than mere nuances on the surface of a broad consensus.

On the whole, though, the first year of the Reagan era did produce a substantial degree of convergence among West European views. This was particularly noticeable on the central issue of arms control negotiations, which the US "policy of strength" seemed to discount as a policy option. To many in West Europe, there appeared to be a danger that the "dual-track" policy could become a "one-track" policy - producing an arms race in Europe without the essential consultations or negotiations which could render it controllable or explicable to European publics. Thus there was fairly constant European pressure for talks; but it was also apparent that different European leaders perceived the priorities differently. For the West Germans talks were vital, not least because of the strength of domestic feeling on nuclear policy. For the French, who shared some parts of the Reaganite response to Soviet threats, the key aim was not to become over-identified with US initiatives. The British, dependent on the Americans for nuclear hardware and conscious of the vestiges of a "special relationship", were loyal but discreetly critical. All were alarmed by the decision to produce the neutron bomb, taken in mid-1981 by Washington (or by the Defense Department) without consultation.

It became clear by the end of 1981 that Europeans and Americans had rather divergent views of the linkages on which arms control should be built. The Reagan line was simple: build up strength and offer talks to the Soviets as long as they behaved. West Europeans could not afford to be so unconstrained: they wanted talks for pressing domestic or regional reasons. Whilst Haig might have responded to these needs, it was increasingly unlikely that he would win out in this area of policy. Over the winter of 1981-82, it appeared that West European pressure had less influence over US policies than domestic budgetary demands and the desire in the White House to choke off the nuclear freeze movement. Although the President's "zero option" offer to the Soviets in the context of the INF talks was broadly supported by the Europeans, it also became apparent that when talks actually started they might further distance the US-Soviet dialogue from the allies, leaving them as concerned bystanders and little more.

In this context, the events of 1982-83 assume a peculiar importance both for European-American relations and for the developing needs of the West Europeans themselves. Essentially, a new "dual-track" process appeared: on the one hand, the Europeans continued to press their demands for shifts in US policy and for consultation. On the other hand, there emerged a series of moves towards a more formal "European identity" in the security field, raising important questions about the relationship of such an identity both to the US and to national policies in Europe itself. The first of these trends built to a climax as the deadline for deployment of Cruise and Pershing approached, and as popular pressures in West Europe - with the notable exception of France - became more insistent. There is evidence that the Europeans' pleas were heard in Washington: the assiduous attempts to carry the West Europeans along through such devices as the NATO Special Consultative Group, along with the frequent presence of US emissaries in "sensitive" countries, testify to the concern in the White House. There still remained, though, the nagging feeling that the US commitment to INF deployment outweighed its readiness to negotiate - and especially its readiness to link talks on strategic and theater weapons. For many West Europeans, the US appeared more concerned with internal debates and rhetoric than with the impact of policy on the outside world or with the preoccupations of its allies.

If European fears of US neglect were the negative side of the picture during 1982-83, the positive side was the increasing attention to possibilities for security cooperation on a European basis. One aspect of this trend focused on the European Community, with the publication in late 1981 of the Genscher-Colombo plan for a "European Act;" amongst other things this would have extended the discussion of security issues in an EC context. By the spring of 1982 two lines of further development could be discerned, but both underlined the difficulties attending any such plans. Whilst the British evinced considerable reluctance to subscribe to grand projects for European Union, the French and West Germans began actively to pursue avenues of further defense collaboration. Both trends threatened to dilute any EC initiatives, and established a continuing conflict between plans for a "European identity" and the realities of national orientations. Reaganism as expressed in US policies on NATO and nuclear weapons certainly confirmed a place on the agenda for security issues, but there was considerable ambiguity about the capacity of West European governments to respond at the European level. The ambiguity was confirmed by the events of the next three years.

Whilst it could be claimed that the deployment of INF in the UK, Italy and West Germany from December 1983 was a victory for dogged allied and Atlantic solidarity, it was clear that the process raised questions about the future linkage of strategic and theater nuclear policies. The threat of "decoupling" or "Europeanization" was underlined by the re-emergence of US doubts about the value of their troops in Europe, especially in Congress, where the Nunn Amendment tied a threat of troop withdrawals to perceived European failings on defense expenditure. At the same time, discussion of "emergent technologies" in the conventional field provided further food for thought in West Europe, the potential battlefield. The centerpiece of the developing Reagan strategy in 1984-85, though, was the Strategic Defense Initiative (SDI), which promised - or threatened - to neutralize strategic nuclear weapons through the deployment of technologies which were not only "emergent" but hardly on the drawing board.

The emergence of SDI as a central agenda item in European-American relations may have appeared like a bolt from the blue, but the problems it raised for West Europeans were in many respects long standing. Once again the threat of "decoupling" appeared, with supreme irony in the light of the all too recent battles over INF. Alongside it went the threat of decisions that would affect the status of West European nuclear forces and renew the domination of the continent by Superpower strategies - decisions which were likely to be taken for US domestic reasons and then issued to the allies for their reactions. Renewed technological dependence and the likelihood of a "brain drain" further complicated West European responses. To some European leaderships, however, the new challenge supplied yet further justification for the construction of a European defense identity. Although Genscher-Colombo had raised the question of EC-centered security policies, the keystone of the new identity which evolved during 1984 was the near-moribund Western European Union (WEU). The French were its key proponents, especially in the context of their attempts to revive collaboration with the West Germans. By mid-1984, it was widely agreed among West European governments that the WEU could and should be revived, but it was far from clear what the purpose or thrust of the revival should be. Its major members - the UK, France, West Germany and Italy - appeared to agree that WEU was a convenient forum, free of the niggling presence of the Irish and Danes which complicated EPC. But when it came to more positive and material commitments the members parted company to varying degrees. The French appeared to see WEU as a means of asserting West European separatism without espousing integration. West Germany could not decide whether it should be a means of expressing European separatism or a means to counter threats of "Europeanization" in NATO. The British, as always, qualified their enthusiasm with the warning that WEU must not be seen to undermine NATO. Whereas the fragility of EC and EPC collaboration might well have been exposed by a rejuvenated WEU, it was far from clear where the new identity might lead.

By mid-1985, therefore, the status of the West Europeans - individually and collectively - vis-à-vis the security dimensions of European-American relations was marked by continuing ambiguity and uncertainty. The nature of interests, the channels of communication and the conceptions of role relating to West Europe in East-West politics were distinctly confused and questionable. Developments in both American policies and in US-Soviet relations during 1985-86 were such as to underscore the confusion, and three issues in particular stand out: SDI, arms control and the summits.

The most obviously corrosive factor for a European defense identity during 1985 was SDI, both as a program and as a focus of debate in domestic or international politics. While the Americans were busy working out what SDI meant for the strategic posture, their budgets and their relations with the Soviets, the Europeans were able to do little but spectate. "Star Wars" was apparently non-negotiable with the Soviets, but also with the allies, as successive rebuffs dealt to European leaders in Washington appeared to demonstrate. At the same time, the program itself was inherently divisive, in two main ways. First, the implications of defense against Soviet strategic missiles suggested a wasting away of British and French capabilities, and an exacerbation of the problems attending the strategic-theater link, whatever reassurances might be offered by administration spokesmen. Although the touting around of anti-tactical ballistic missile systems (ATBMs) was a feature of 1985/86, it cannot be pretended that this offered any immediate or substantial cause for West European relief, and the problem of linkage offered fertile ground for Soviet diplomacy. Second, the technological impacts of the SDI program created major dilemmas for West European governments: should they scramble for a piece of the action (either directly or through private firms), or should they link their participation to the political and strategic qualifications already noted? Several European governments concluded framework agreements for SDI collaboration, but the benefits in cash and kind did not prove to be easily calculable, and the calculations were rendered even more delicate by the impact of US domestic restraints on the SDI program. At the European level, there was no indication of any European Defense Initiative: the Eureka program remained debatable but in any case not intended to fulfill such a role either for Europeans or within an Atlantic framework.

Developments in arms control and at the summit were the most taxing for West Europeans during 1986, reflecting as they did both the evolution of Soviet-American relations and the growing uncertainty of US policies themselves. A continuing theme was furnished by the growing pressures on central pillars of the established arms control regime: SDI placed into question the continued efficacy of the Anti Ballistic Missiles Treaty (ABM Treaty), and the continuing US military buildup exerted growing pressure on the observance of the unratified SALT II agreement. It was notable that the efforts made by European leaders to communicate their concern over both these issues were largely on a bilateral basis, without the attempt at a concerting of policies on a cross-national basis. Where there was an attempt to elevate broader European concerns, this was largely focused on the field of conventional weapons, with calls for the extension of the CSCE "umbrella" to cover conventional force reductions - a call met with very little enthusiasm in Washington.

As noted earlier, the development of closer Soviet-American dialogue has always posed a problem for West Europeans; while they may be in favour of it as a general principle, there is always the fear that decisions may be taken on their future without their involvement. During 1985-86, the practice of Soviet-American summitry not only rekindled these fears but also linked them potently to concrete issues of arms control in ways that threatened a major Atlantic crisis. The roots of the immediate problem lay in the combination of US willingness to negotiate on the basis of their perceived strength (but with severe reservations about the status of SDI especially) with the new mobility of Soviet diplomacy under the leadership of Mikhail Gorbachev. While both leaderships placed a high priority on moves towards a summit in November 1985, they adopted differing postures towards the West Europeans. US policy seems only reluctantly and at the last gasp to have conceded a place to the allies, whereas the Soviets actively worked to stress the European focus of their diplomacy and to communicate their concerns to West Europeans in particular. The consequences of the Geneva summit were on the whole acceptable to the West Europeans, although the subsequent propaganda battle of competing arms control plans was far less reassuring: once again it appeared that European concerns might be marginalized or traded away. Much more concern, amounting to a full-blown Atlantic crisis, was generated by the October 1986 Reykjavik summit. Although initial European reactions stressed support for the meeting and disappointment at its failure, it gradually dawned on leaderships all over West Europe that their interests had all but been bargained away. Proposals to eliminate nuclear weapons in Europe and to cut strategic arsenals with a view to their abolition threatened to destroy the coupling of European and US strategies, to place renewed pressure on the British and French deterrents and to lay the Europeans open to coercion from superior Soviet conventional forces - and this only three years after the INF deployment struggle.

Not surprisingly, national leaderships in West Europe were quick to scramble for reassurance, either in Washington or within the European framework (the French were heard again to urge the beefing up of WEU). The problem was that they found themselves dealing with an embattled and increasingly unsure American administration, assailed by the fallout of Reykjavik, the adverse results of the mid-term elections and the policy-making chaos unleashed by "Irangate." It was not apparent that this Atlantic crisis would be quick to disappear.

A SECOND CASE STUDY: REGIONAL CONFLICTS OUTSIDE EUROPE

The history of European-American relations is punctuated by a number of episodes which arise from conflicts outside the Atlantic area and which raise the question of the limits to alliance. One of the major initial stimuli to the building of the Western alliance, the Korean War, was essentially an extra-European phenomenon that had repercussions within Europe; and during the 1950s and 1960s there was a succession of greater or lesser pressures from outside the Atlantic system - especially in the Middle East and Southeast Asia - which challenged the solidarity of its members. One of the factors thrown into relief by these episodes is the contrast between the increasingly regional concerns of the West Europeans and the globalism of US foreign policies - a contrast which was to be underlined by the advent of the Reagan administration. But it is also apparent that as in the case of East-West relations there are significant differences of emphasis between the interests and the orientations of the West Europeans themselves. Partly these differences grow out of distinctive and powerful historical experiences, particularly those of the ex-imperial powers; partly they also grow out of and reflect the diversity of political and economic dependencies that attaches to each of the West European states; and partly they are an expression of the ways in which West European regimes react to the global extension of superpower tensions. Whatever their origins, it is important to recognize the potential for contradictions and divergence which is inherent in the connections between the Europeans and the world beyond the North Atlantic area.

During the 1970s and 1980s, American policy-makers have had frequent recourse to the argument that whereas the US is a global power with world wide responsibilities, the states of West Europe, both individually and collectively, have been reduced to secondary, regional status. From Henry Kissinger in 1973 to Lawrence Eagleburger in 1983, there have been repeated declarations that both the inclinations and the potential of the West Europeans disqualify them from effective participation in questions of wider world order, wherever these might manifest themselves. West Europeans themselves, on the other hand, have found in the extra-European theater a growing opportunity to express themselves collectively. Such a coincidence of attitudes and trends holds in it the possibility of considerable tensions, and on the face of it these would be especially severe given the proclivities of the Reagan administration. The record of the early 198Os gives some support to this presumption, but as in the case of East-West relations the conclusions are far from cut and dried.

The Middle East forms the longest standing area of interaction beween the US and the West Europeans, both individually and collectively. Quite apart from the major historical and contemporary involvements of several West European states in the region, this has been an arena in which the Europeans have sought to develop collective policy stances - and in which as a result they have consistently fallen foul of American efforts. During the 1970s the growth of the Euro-Arab dialogue, which was important to the early years of European Political Cooperation, also had the effect of outraging Henry Kissinger. As the 1970s wore on, the movement towards the Camp David Accords again saw the Europeans at odds with the attempt to construct a collective Western position, but the underlying tensions only surfaced fully with the Venice Declaration of the EC countries in July 1980. Essentially this sought to widen the basis of any future settlement, in particular by including some consideration of the Palestinian case. Given the wide range of views that West European states hold on the Arab-Israeli conflict, and given the hostility of the US towards anything that put Camp David into question, the Venice Declaration constituted something of a triumph for West European collaboration. So loud and vehement were the protests from Israel in particular that it appeared the West European stance could have a material impact on the dispute.

As soon as the Reagan administration came into office in 1981, it was apparent that US policies might diverge even more substantially from those expressed in the Venice Declaration. To the Reaganite way of thinking the Soviet Union constituted the major threat to the Middle East, and the way to deal with it was to build a "strategic consensus" with those states in the area who were seen as moderate and potentially responsive. There was no room in this conception for the historically based European diagnosis, nor was any consideration to be given to the Palestinian case. As many commentators have noted, the underlying assumptions of this strategy were flawed and led the Reagan administration into turbulent waters. From the European point of view, however, the dominating problem was that the Venice "manifesto" could not be translated into meaningful action. To be sure, fact-finding missions by successive EC Presidencies were mounted, but these lacked the credibility which would have been given by a "real" foreign policy. In addition, the tendency of the British and the French especially to assert their national interests was a severe handicap to collective efforts; at the inception of the Mitterrand presidency in France, the new Foreign Minister, Claude Cheysson, went so far as to claim that "Venice is dead."

During 1982, it appeared that the Europeans were first of all won back to the American position and then overtaken by it. Partly this seemed to reflect a shift in the European perception of the problem (although it was difficult to be certain given the nuances imparted by successive presidencies of the Council of Foreign Ministers), but more importantly it grew out of the renewed purposefulness of US policy under the influence of George Shultz. In September, President Reagan for the first time advanced proposals that seemed to take account of the Palestinian problem. The "Reagan Plan" proposed security for Israel, autonomy for Palestinians in association with Jordan, and an end to annexations of Arab territory. It appeared that there was no longer any significant difference between the European and the American positions, and in formal terms at least, this remained the case until the last days of the Reagan presidency. Certainly the Reagan Plan took much of the impetus away from the Europeans' desire to involve themselves in the peace process, although there still persisted a dogged European inclination to include the Palestinians in any negotiations.

More material than the peace process, and more disruptive for the West Europeans, was the process by which the US became an increasingly active participant in the Middle East conflict. In a sense this dated back to the Camp David agreements, under which the supervision of Israeli withdrawal from the Sinai and the provision of economic and military aid made the US into an active sponsor of the settlement. But during 1985 and 1986, the US's role changed in significant and to some observers ominous respects. The "sponsorship" phase in fact saw the West Europeans actively engaged with the US, providing contributions to the Sinai Peacekeeping Force. As the US also became embroiled in the Lebanon during 1982-83, Britain, France and Italy, too, contributed to the multilateral force established to oversee Israeli withdrawal; but here the consequences of involvement in a turbulent situation without a clear political or strategic rationale were brought home not only to the Americans but also to their European helpers.

Although the Americans managed to extract themselves from the Lebanon during 1984, it was apparent that their entanglement in the Middle East - as participant and potential target - could not so easily be liquidated. The events of 1985 and 1986 demonstrated that the untidiness and unpredictable violence attending participation in Middle Eastern politics could impose severe strains on US policies; from the point of view of this paper, it is also important to note the implications for the West Europeans. The escalation of terrorist activity directed towards Americans, and the US tendency to define this as a form of aggression demanding retaliation if necessary by military means, was both more demanding and more fragmenting of West European responses. During 1985, the hijacking to Beirut of a TWA Boeing 727 and the *Achille Lauro* affair created an increase in tension which in several respects had direct implications for the West Europeans. At the national level, the Greeks and the Italians especially felt the force of US demands that they should be more vigilant against the terrorist threat, but this also connected with an assumption on the part of the Americans that the Europeans collectively could and should do something about the problem. Whilst the Europeans were very willing to contemplate action in general to enhance security, they were much less happy with the idea of direct punishment for those deemed responsible. The airport bombing of Christmas 1985, and the US identification of Gadhdhafi's Libya as the source of support for the terrorists brought these conflicting pressures to a high pitch. Significantly, the inability of the Europeans to agree on strong collective action was cited by some as a reason for the Americans' resort to force in the bombings of Tripoli during April 1986. The raids certainly had important effects on the West Europeans' stance, in two conflicting ways: first by forcing them to recognize that their lack of collective action had exacerbated the problem and undermined any restraining influence they might have exerted over US policy; secondly, and in a contradictory sense, by underlining the gulf between respective European leaderships' responsiveness to demands from Washington. In simple terms, the British willingness - albeit reluctantly - to assist the US, contrasted with the distinct hostility shown by others such as the French. The slowness of the EPC process in the face of a clear determination by the US to act, and the essentially reactive European stance even in the aftermath of the uncovering of the "Syrian connection" during late 1986, only served to underline the well-documented gap between declaration and action in European foreign policy. In these circumstances, the revelation through "Irangate" of a similar and more damaging gap in US policy towards Iran could have encouraged some European complacency, but it promised additional problems arising from the turmoil of US policy-making.

Another region in which the West Europeans and the Americans found their policies in somewhat uneasy coexistence was the Western Hemisphere, encompassing in this instance both Central America and the South Atlantic. The first episode that demands attention is the Falklands War of 1982, in which both the US and the Europeans had a number of conflicting interests. On the European side, the support given to the British in the shape both of declarations and of sanctions represented a step forward in collaborative policy-making, although it was not without its problems. The speed of the collective European response contrasted significantly with the debacle following the Soviet invasion of Afghanistan, not to mention the Iranian episode in 1978-79. For once the EPC mechanism and the EC process meshed well together, to provide substantive support at a time when US policy-making was in a certain amount of disarray. Although, as the conflict developed, both Ireland and Italy found it necessary to drop out of the collective measures, the impact of European solidarity was marked, and was contrasted with the length of time the Americans took to commit themselves. This delay in fact had damaging effects, since the amount of effort the UK had to put into bringing the Americans round was seen by some Europeans as leading to neglect of their needs and a taking for granted of the collective support once it had been achieved. That support did, though, neatly turn the tables on a US which had been wont to stress its principled stand on regional conflicts, yet found itself in the South Atlantic having to balance precisely the kind of conflicting stakes and roles which are often seen as a fatal flaw in European policy-making.

The picture is somewhat different in an area of intense US foreign policy and domestic interest - Central America. The Europeans broke new ground in 1984 by declaring their collective support for the Contadora peace initiative and by holding a ministerial meeting with both the Contadora group and the five Central American Republics. In supporting a peace plan that called for the removal of foreign advisers from Central America, an end to arms shipments from outside and a halt to support for guerrillas attacking one country from another's territory, the Europeans put themselves into direct confrontation with US policies. Although for a variety of domestic and other reasons the Reagan line on Central America tended to be more assertive in rhetoric than in fact, there was no doubt that it ran directly counter to the Contadora process, and it was no suprise that US reaction to EC involvement was very negative. Attempts to exclude the Nicaraguans from the talks with EC ministers were overt and resented, and Sir Geofffrey Howe was heard to reassure the Nicaraguan foreign minister that "the EC does not accept orders from the US." Such drama - albeit on a minor scale - has not been repeated, although the EC continued to meet periodically with both the Contadora states and the Central American Republics and initiated an economic assistance agreement with states in the region. It cannot be claimed that these actions have played a role in restraining US policies - the major limiting force there seems to be domestic and congressional opposition - and indeed, the EC stance was attacked by Washington as being the kind of empty gesture that shows all the worst aspects of European collective action. The extent to which the US takes EC views into consideration on Central American affairs was perhaps best demonstrated by the Grenada episode in 1983, when European collective and invididual outrage was decidedly uninfluential.

On a third regional conflict - that in Southern Africa, and particularly South Africa - the fact of the matter is that neither the US nor most West European countries have a vital interest in developments, although on both sides of the Atlantic there are powerful forces arguing for action on the grounds of humanitarian, economic or world order interests. The Europeans and the Americans have followed similar lines towards South Africa partly as a reflection of this and partly as an expression of their relatively limited abilities to affect events unilaterally. In both the US and the European case also, there is a conflict between geostrategic and other interests that militates against decisive action. During 1985 and 1986, however, there was more evidence of the kinds of tensions that emerge when real action, with costs and risks entailed, might have to be taken. The reluctant conversion of Reagan to limited economic sanctions in 1985, and their reinforcement by congressional action, contrasted quite strongly with the inability of the Europeans to arrive at a collective position that carries any real punch. The strong divergences of economic and political interests that exist especially between the British and other EC members operated during 1986 in such a way as to severely limit the economic sanctions that could be agreed, and also to restrict the scope for collective European diplomatic efforts. Whilst a coordinated US-EC stand on sanctions would clearly be a powerful incentive for the South Africans to reconsider their position, this kind of Atlantic cooperation seems rather unlikely to occur in the circumstances of the mid-1980s.

CONCLUSIONS

This chapter started from a series of propositions about three major elements of Atlantic relations, with particular reference to the 198Os and the impact of Reaganism. In the first place, it was argued that the nature of the Atlantic system raised persistent problems for its members - in shorthand terms, the problems of "stakes," "status and role," "policy styles and responsiveness" and "management and rules." Secondly, it was noted that in the light of these factors and of historical trends, the position of "West Europe" in the Atlantic system has been consistently ambiguous: in particular, that the tensions between West Europe's allotted role and its ability or inclination to perform it, and between the national and international levels of West European policy-making, are a potent source of uncertainty within the Atlantic areas. Finally, it was suggested that an overlapping set of ambiguities and tensions emerged from the position of the US, and that the foreign policies of Reaganism gave these problems a particular prominence, especially through the coexistence of "rhetorical" and "practical" Reaganism. In the light of our two case studies, we can now attempt to reassess some important questions that arise from the study of Atlantic policy-making during the 1980s: what kind of challenge did Reaganism pose for the West Europeans? Did West European responses confirm or modify the historical ambiguity of their position in the system? What might the future development of the system hold in the light of the trends manifested in the period under review?

It seems clear both in general and from our two case studies that Reaganism had substantial impact on the definition of stakes within the Atlantic system: to put it baldly, US foreign policy in the early 1980s sharpened the issues and heightened perceptions of risk for the West Europeans. In the first place this arose from the Reaganite program, but the picture was confirmed by Reaganism in practice. The earlier discussion suggested that this tension of rhetoric and reality would point up the contradictions in West Europe's position, particularly the tensions between national and collective modes of action. On the face of it, this happened, and West Europeans often did not know which way to turn. But there were important variations: whilst on East-West relations Reaganism sowed uncertainty and resulted in significant intra-European fragmentation, the picture in respect of extra-European issues was less clear. Could it be that where the direct stakes are lower and the challenge to tangible values less open, there is more room for the furthering of "West European" collaboration, especially at the declaratory level? Experience in the Middle East, the area of highest stakes outside the European theater, seems to bear out this evaluation.

Reaganism in theory and practice can also be seen as a challenge to comfortable assumptions about the role of West Europe in the Atlantic system. By emphasizing the US role in an assertive and putatively hegemonial fashion, Reaganism led to questions about the ability of West Europeans to fulfill their individual or collective roles. There is no doubt that the early 1980s saw continual debate about the past, present and possible future of a West European "identity," and that this coincided with the Reagan era - but coincidence does not mean causation. Here again, it is possible to contrast findings in our two case studies. In East-West relations, the impact of Reaganism in theory and in practice seems to have contributed both to the generation of debate about a West Europan identity and to the subversion of moves towards such an identity by its invocation of special relationships with particular European governments. This may not have reflected conscious design on the part of the Americans, but the impact was no less powerful for that. Outside East-West issues, Europeans seemed more capable of defining a role - often in juxtaposition to that of the US - but there was evidence of centrifugal forces when "real" policy commitments were demanded.

Behind at least some of the problems about stakes and roles lay the factor of policy styles, especially as expresed through different levels of national responsiveness within West Europe. The assertiveness and unilateralism of Reaganism, and the feeling that the US had become less amenable to external influence during the 1980s, have certainly changed the climate of Atlantic relations. For West Europeans, and particularly on East-West issues, these feelings were translated into a search for effective channels of communication and influence, by no means all of them at a collaborative "European" level. The heightening of tensions and the raising of stakes in the "new Cold War" certainly produced evidence of this pattern, but it is also clear that the erratic détente of 1985 and 1986 made its contribution. Very often, the problems thus manifested have affected the domestic political climate in West European countries, and thus arguably made the attainment of collective European positions even more difficult; arguably too, American efforts at consultation on East-West issues also undermined European collaboration. Outside Europe, it is notable that differential levels of West European responsiveness to US policies also played a role - particularly in those episodes where declaratory unity had to be translated into operational effort.

Finally, it appears from the evidence of the early 1980s that the management of Atlantic relations remains untidy and often intractable. Reaganism in prospect implied management on the basis of strength and renewed leadership from Washington, but the reality was often disruption, with Atlantic relations functioning as a subset of events in Washington or between the superpowers. What is clear is that no West European capacity to join effectively in the management of the system has either developed or shown any signs of developing at the strategic level. Of course, this can be blamed on US policies; but it is at least as likely that it reflects fundamental limitations to the achievement of collective West European consciousness or mechanisms. Even if the Americans showed willing to let the Europeans in on the act, it is very doubtful whether they could come up with the goods. This is not to say that there were not areas of limited collaborative "Atlantic" management, but the record both on East-West relations and on the extra-European scale was distinctly patchy.

Definitive judgements on the implications of Reaganism for the evolution of West European foreign policies will be a long time coming, and certainly cannot be made on the basis of the evidence assembled here. But there are a number of ways in which the events of the early 1980s give added point to some general questions about the evolution of the Atlantic system, and of West Europe's place within it. First, it is clear that development of a distinct European consciousness is more notable than the development of West European policies. In this process, Reaganism undoubtedly played a major role: it has sharpened the collective mind of the Europeans and pointed up debates about the appropriate role for them within the Atlantic system and the wider world. Second, it is apparent that this process infused national policy-making as well as European collaboration with the sense that things are changing and that Atlanticism is not the only possible direction for West European development. Such feelings were reinforced by political debate at the domestic level, which raised questions about the shape of "Europe" itself either at the level of the European Community or within the context of the superpower alliance structure. Reaganism, in its theory, its practice and its apparent disintegration, thus played a central catalytic role in what might come to be seen as a historic phase of West European "self-recognition."

In focusing on the challenge posed by Reaganism to West Europe, this chapter has confined its main attention to the period up to 1986. The rationale for this is simple: this was the period in which the assertiveness and the insular muscularity of Reaganism created a positive challenge and a demand for self-recognition on the part of the West Europeans themselves. As noted earlier in the chapter, the post-1986 phase represents as much as anything else a playing out of the tensions and uncertainties created in the "Reagan era" proper, but this is not to deny its potential significance for the further development of a West European consciousness. The INF Treaty and its aftermath had the effect not of ending an era of arms control, but rather of opening up an entirely new agenda, centered on the problems of short range nuclear forces. In this, though, the most active role was arguably played not by any Americans but by the West Germans and particularly the Soviets, who directly and indirectly contributed to a wider debate about the future shape of Europe broadly defined. In the Middle East and the Persian Gulf, the American presence continued to demonstrate ambiguity and to generate often unsuspected risks both for Europeans and for Americans - a situation in which the historical contradictions of much European policy-making were often underlined. In the last days of the Reagan administration, in December 1988, the recognition of the PLO by what had hitherto been its staunchest Western adversary, created a new reality in which the diplomatic skills and cohesion of the West Europeans would be taxed again. The catalyst which had been introduced in the early 1980s by Reaganism, and whose action had been modified by the unfolding of complex events, was still at work in the final months of the decade, but its effects were still difficult to discern or to evaluate.

10

The "Corn War": A Euro-American Trade Dispute

Vera Erdmann-Keefer

INTRODUCTION

Since the inception of the EC and its Common Agricultural Policy (CAP) Atlantic relations have repeatedly been shattered by serious disputes over trade with agricultural products. Some of these clashes occurred in connection with the gradual expansion of the EC and turned out to be test cases for opposite dynamics: West European assertiveness as well as American power politics. The accession of the Iberian countries to the Community on 1 January 1986 was no exception to the rule.

The Treaty of Accession of Spain and Portugal to the EC included three points American farmers considered especially harmful to them. First, the Treaty regulates the Portuguese soybean market by setting import quotas according to the domestic consumption. The Americans used to "own" the Portuguese oilseed market and are now still major suppliers although they have to share the market with Brazilian and Argentinean competitors. Second, the Treaty would reserve a 15.5 percent share of the Portuguese cereals market for Community suppliers. The Americans used to dominate the Portuguese import market for cereals. Third, the variable levy scheme of the CAP was extended to Spanish agricultural imports. Hence, American exports of corn and sorghum to Spain - between 2 and 4 million tons annually - would become more expensive due to higher tariffs.

President Reagan found these measures to be illegal under the General Agreement on Tariffs and Trade (GATT), unreasonable, and a burden on US commerce. Accordingly, he took action under Section 301 of the Trade and Tariff Act setting quotas for European imports and suspending tariff concessions under GATT. The Presidential Proclamation of 15 May 1986 set a deadline for 1 July 1986 for negotiations over compensation for the EC enlargement. In case the deadline was not met, tariff increases would be imposed. The deadline was not met but Europeans and Americans were able to work out an Interim Agreement over the access to the Spanish feed grain market for six months. When the new deadline, set for 31 December 1986, was also missed, the Americans, on New Years Eve, announced that the planned tariff increases on brandy and white wine - among other products - would actually be enacted. This last American attack eventually led to the temporary agreement of 30 January 1987 over the access to the Spanish feed grain market.

The Press coined the term "corn war" for the incident outlined above. This label will be used throughout the chapter although one might argue against the use of martial vocabulary in connection with trade conflicts or point to the fact that while the arsenal of weapons (tariff increases, quotas, etc.) was ready on both sides it was never fully put into action. "Corn war," admittedly, also has a certain provocative attraction. There are three good reasons, however, to take a closer look beyond this attractive label at the incident itself.

First, the "corn war" is yet another example of the paradoxical relationship between the US and the EC. During the "corn war," Senators and the President repeatedly emphasized that the US was indeed in favor of EC enlargement. The Americans saw Spain's and Portugal's entry into the EC as a way to strengthen the young democracies in the two Iberian countries. After all, both countries had had only a decade to recover from dictatorship. In the case of Spain, EC-membership was closely connected to NATO-membership and in a referendum the Spaniards voted, as expected, to stay in the North Atlantic Alliance. The vote occurred on 12 March 1986 - only a few weeks after Spain had officially become an EC member state. But despite these strong American interests in the enlargement the very same Senators and the President also emphasized that this should not be "at the expense of American farmers." Again, the American attitude towards the EC was marked by a general political "yes" but a strict "no" once economic interests, and those in the agricultural field in particular, were threatened. This dual approach can be identified throughout the 30 years of EC-US relations.

The constant tensions which marked those relations could in fact be predicted. In 1957 the Europeans founded a "Common Market" with the goal, among others, of strengthening Europe economically. This "Common Market" or economic unification should eventually lead to the higher aim of political unity. If the undertaking is successful, the Americans, although very much in favor of European unification, necessarily have to face an economic competitor. Likewise, if the Europeans enact a Common Agricultural Policy aimed at enhancing productivity and increasing self-sufficiency rates, conflicts with an export-oriented American agricultural policy arise. The "corn war" is nothing but another manifestation of a fundamental divergence between the EC and the US. The transatlantic relationship will be marked by agricultural conflicts as long as the Europeans, on the one hand, insist on the CAP as a "bedrock of European integration" and the Americans, for their own domestic political reasons, insist on securing US farmers' export markets overseas. The tension will not hinder the US from being an outspoken proponent of European unification. Rather they will continue their pursuit of forming a coherent group of allies.

The second reason why the "corn war" merits attention is that it is also an indication of the crisis of agricultural markets worldwide. While Europeans and Americans squabble over one another's agricultural policies, both are attacked for these very policies by the group of "Free Traders." In August of 1986, fourteen countries, among them Australia, Canada, New Zealand, Brazil and Argentina, adopted the "Declaration of Cairns" which is aimed at the removal of market barriers in agricultural trade, and at a considerable short term reduction followed by abolition in the long run of all subsidies with negative effects on agricultural trade. The signatories also agreed to put pressure on those countries whose agricultural policies interfere with the rules of international free trade. In the current round of GATT, subsidies in the agricultural field are among the most prominent topics. President Reagan already let it be known that the US was willing to cooperate in an elimination of agricultural programs.

Finally, the third source of interest in the "corn war" is that the academic treatment of agricultural trade conflicts between the US and the EC seems insufficient so far. Ever since the CAP was enacted in 1962 the United States and the EC have frequently met in agricultural trade battles named after their targets of attack - chicken, wheat, corn, pasta. Government officials involved with the problem[1] and academics have generally accepted that domestic policies on both sides, and agricultural policy in particular, are the main cause of these conflicts. Influential farm lobby groups have seen to the persistence of high levels of government support that, combined with the technological progress witnessed in the farm sector, has generated large surpluses on both sides of the Atlantic. The academic discussion over these trade conflicts, while acknowledging the political conditions that have engendered the surpluses, gives less consideration to the importance of these conditions than to the evolution and resolution of the conflicts themselves.

The academic discussion has normally treated EC-US agricultural trade conflicts descriptively, following diligently the course of each encounter and the nature of the "ammunition", i.e. tariffs and quotas, used.[2] The trade conflicts have been treated in a "European" or "American" way, as scholars have concentrated on the problems of one side to the exclusion of the other.[3] Finally, the conflicts, with respect to GATT, have been treated in a purely legalistic way.[4] In some of these studies the problem of domestic

---

1 For example, see Hintergründe amerikanischer Aggressionen gegen EG-Agrarpolitik, in *Agra Europe* 41/86 (13 October 1986) based on a speech given by Dr. Wilhelm Schopen, former agricultural attaché at the West German embassy in the U.S.

2 Ross B. Talbot, *The Chicken War*, (Ames: Iowa State University Press 1978), admitted, p. 147: "What are the theoretical implications of this study? Limited, one might succinctly and accurately answer. The study is a reasonably accurate description of the perception, decisions, and actions of two general sets of political actors, one on each side of the North Atlantic."

3 J. Goldstein, Stephen D. Krasner, Unfair Trade Practices: The Case for a Differential Response, in *The American Economic Review*, May 1984, pp. 282-287. Stefan Tangermann, What is Different about European Agricultural Protectionism? in *The World Economy*, March 1983, pp. 39-58.

4 The most comprehensive survey is by Edmond McGovern, *International Trade Regulation, GATT, The United States and the European Community*, (Exeter: Globefield Press 1986). Garcia Bercero, Trade Laws, GATT and the Management of Trade Disputes between the US and the EEC, in *Yearbook of European Law* 5 (1985), pp. 149-89. William H. Boger III, The United States - European

policies and surplus production has been vaguely mentioned as the origin of the trade conflicts.[5] Less attention, however, has been given to the solution of these conflicts and the question of how current internal politics on both sides affect the course and outcome of the negotiations that resolve trade conflicts. Indeed, the overwhelming influence of farm lobbies and mountains of surplus production that are mentioned in the literature as giving rise to conflicts would also seem, if these forces are equally strong on each side, to prevent any resolution of them. Hence, while it was acknowledged that the conflict does have internal causes this assumption was neither detailed very elaborately nor followed up through the course of the conflict.

Taking as an example the "corn war," this chapter focuses on internal political factors on both sides that determined the outcome of the negotiations. To foreshadow the general conclusion, due to specific internal conditions the Americans are in a better bargaining position while the Europeans, mainly due to the institutional structure of the Community, have to play the game with a handicap.

The chapter includes three parts. The first is devoted to a brief description of the Spanish and Portuguese market with respect to American agricultural trade before the enlargement in January 1986; this market was at the center of the "corn war." This part also outlines changes after these countries joined the EC, providing the background for the conflict and indicating the scope of the issues at stake during the "corn war." The second part gives the history of the trade conflict, beginning with the initial reactions of American farm lobby groups to the agricultural accommodations that the EC made to the entry of Spain and Portugal in the beginning of 1986 and extending to the first preliminary agreement that was reached in January of 1987. The third part gives an analysis of internal political issues at crucial points during the conflicts and their relationship to the bargaining positions assumed by the negotiators. By way of conclusion, general factors determining the trade conflicts are defined and a strategy for easing these conflicts in the future is suggested.

Community Agricultural Export Subsidies Dispute, in *Law and Policy in International Business* , 16 (1984), pp. 173-238.

5 For a brief listing see Dieter Loesch, Current EC-US Economic Conflicts, in *Intereconomics* (March/April 1984), pp. 51-56.

AMERICAN AGRICULTURAL EXPORTS TO SPAIN AND PORTUGAL BEFORE AND AFTER THE EC ENLARGEMENT

Both the Spanish and Portuguese markets for agricultural products are of considerable interest to US suppliers. In fiscal year 1985, the year before the "corn war," they exported products worth 502 million dollars to Portugal and 826 million dollars to Spain.[6] In 1985 they held a 50 percent share of the Portuguese agricultural import market, a share that dropped to about 35 percent in 1986. In 1986, US agricultural exports to the smaller of the Iberian countries declined to 428 million dollars. Nevertheless, the US is still Portugal's main partner in agricultural trade. [7] Principal among Portuguese imports from the US are grain (mainly corn) and oilseeds; together they represent approximately 92 percent of all US exports to Portugal. US suppliers used to dominate and even entirely own the market for these two products. By 1985, however, Argentinean and Brazilian suppliers had accumulated a 50 percent share of the oilseeds market, Canada had entered the wheat market, and Argentina also entered the corn market. Having seen their strong position so recently eroded, US suppliers were particularly concerned about changes after the integration of the Portuguese agricultural market into the EC.

The Spanish market is also of importance, especially to American corn and sorghum exporters. American sources indicate that feed grains worth 282 million dollar were exported to Spain in 1985.[8] The recent general decline of American agricultural exports further accentuated the American concern over losing market shares as a consequence of the enlargement.[9] American agricultural exports to the EC dropped from 8.640 billion dollars in 1984 to 6.442 billion in 1986 while EC exports to the US rose in the same period. This resulted in a diminishing US surplus in agricultural trade with the EC from 5.128 billion dollars in 1984 down to 2.327 billion in

---

6 United States Department of Agriculture (USDA), Economic Research Service, *Foreign Agricultural Trade of the United States* (November/December 1985).

7 Homer Sabatini, Portugal's Accession: How Will It Affect Trade Ties with the U.S.?, in *Foreign Agriculture*, October 1986, pp. 4-9.

8 See note 6.

9 USDA, *Outlook for U.S. Agricultural Exports* , 2 December 1986.

1986. While the EC can still call itself the "best" customer of the US the Europeans are clearly not the excellent customers they used to be.

The Treaty for the accession of Spain and Portugal to the EC was signed on 12 June 1985 and became effective 1 January 1986.[10] Article 292 of the Treaty calls for a control mechanism for

> the quantities of oil seeds and oil fruits, as well as of flour from which the oil has not been extracted and of all vegetable oils, with the exception olive oil, intended for human consumption on the Portuguese domestic market, in order to avoid any worsening of the conditions for competition between various vegetable oils.

Prior to the accession a complex system of licenses governed the Portuguese market which encouraged the increase of imports of oil seeds, especially soy and sunflowers. Portuguese oil consumption, however, was relatively small. Hence, the Portuguese increasingly exported the oil extracted from the seeds.

After the accession, tariffs for these products were to drop considerably. Over a period of ten years the tariffs for oilseeds and oleaginous fruit-derived products were to be abolished between the EC and Portugal. Towards third countries the old Portuguese tariffs were to be lowered to the level specified in the Common Customs Tariff, which for American soybean imports was zero.[11]

In order to prevent the Portuguese market from being flooded with foreign oil due to these more favorable tariffs the EC decided to monitor imports for a transitional period of five years and to set quotas for these products.[12] The domestic consumption of soy oil was estimated at 50,000 tons for 1986 by the Management Committee, by adding 20 percent to previous years' consumption. Under the new import regime, since 1 March 1986, 42,000 tons of oil imports would be admitted to the Portuguese market without restriction. Imports above this quota are only permitted provided that

---

10 OJ L 302 (15 November 1985). For most of the agricultural measures the effective date was 1 March 1986.

11 Article 243 of the Accession Treaty, OJ L 302/94.

12 Reg. No. 476/86 (25 February 1986), OJ L 53/51 (1 March 1986).

the produce is re-exported. The import regime does not discriminate between EC and third country imports.

Until 1986 the Portuguese cereals market was dominated by the Empresa Publica de Abastecimento de Cereais (EPAC) which held a marketing as well as an import monopoly for cereals. Under this monopoly 96 percent of Portugal's cereal imports came from the United States (about 74 percent being corn). Articles 319 and 320 of the Accession Treaty provide for a gradual dismantling of the monopoly over a four year period. In addition Article 320 (c) states:

> If imports of products of Community origin do not represent, per year, a minimum quantity of 15 percent of the total quantity of cereals imported during that year, EPAC shall buy during the following year, in the Community as at present constituted, the quantity lacking in relation to the 15 percent quantity referred to above.

This 15 percent share was increased by another 0.5 percent that had to come from Spain.[13] Spain's entry into the EC triggers the variable levy system of the CAP. Each year the Council of Ministers of Agriculture sets target prices for principal agricultural products. These target prices are considered essential in guaranteeing the income of the European farmer. In order to keep the target price at its fixed level inside the EC, intervention agencies are obliged to buy surplus commodities at a rate close to the target price (called the intervention price). In order to preserve this target price for European farmers even in external trade, export restitutions are paid out of the European Agricultural Guidance and Guarantee Fund (EAGGF). The European farmer can sell his products at a - usually - lower world market price while he receives the difference from the EC internal price as an "export refund." On the other hand, in order to protect the European market from cheaper imports which obviously would destroy the system of fixed prices, importers have to pay a variable levy (tariff) on their products. The levy offsets the difference between the lower world market (import) price and the EC internal price. It "varies" with the world market price.

Until 1984 Spain had its tariffs for corn and sorghum bound under the General Agreement on Tariffs and Trade (GATT) at a 20

---

13 Reg. No. 3792/85, Art. 7 (20 December 1985), OJ L 367/9.

percent rate. Then a system of regulating duties,[14] similar to the EC system was introduced to the cereals sector for a transitional period of three marketing years. After the accession and effective 1 March 1986 the variable levy scheme extended to Spain, increasing considerably the price of agricultural imports into Spain. In addition to the Spanish price of 200 ECU per ton for corn a levy of 42 ECU would have to be paid. The price of 200 ECU is the final price under Spain's own transitional variable levy program.

American sources are somewhat at variance with these European estimates since they use as a benchmark the 20 percent tariff on imports into Spain that prevailed prior to the transitional scheme.[15] They claim that after 1 March 1986 the tariff would go up to 100 percent due to the variable levy system. Because of the previous Spanish obligations under GATT the Americans demanded negotiations for compensation according to Article 24:6.

THE "CORN WAR": ANATOMY OF A TRADE CONFLICT

In the beginning of 1986 the United States Trade Representative, members of Congress and various interest groups protested strongly against the European measures accompanying the accession of Spain and Portugal to the EC. To defend their products the American Soybean Association (ASA) launched a crusade through Europe sponsored by the American Cyanamid Company, a producer of herbicides.[16] Soybean producers and manufacturers of inputs into soybean production perceived the European measures as a first step to the dismantling of the GATT provision that held soybeans free of duties (the so-called zero-binding condition), to the American soybean farmers one of the free trade islands in the sea of European protectionism. Upon his return from Europe, ASA president George Fluegel and National Soybean Processors

---

14 Real Decreto 1031/1984 de 23 de mayo, por el que se establece la normativa de regulacion triennial de mercado en el sector cereal, BOE No. 129, 30 May 1984.

15 *White House press release*, 31 March 1986.

16 American Soybean Association, press releases of 29 January 1986 and 21 February 1986.

Association chairman Jack Reed sent the following telegram to President Reagan and other US officials:

> European Community (EC) will impose March 1 GATT-illegal soybean import/consumption restrictions on Spain and Portugal. EC is taking action without consultation with US as required by GATT, a blatant violation of zero-duty binding as negotiated in 1962, the largest single trade concession ever received by the US through GATT. EC told ASA official in Brussels that US government in Washington appeared unconcerned about these restrictions. US failure to act decisively now could lead to similar restrictions in all EC, thus jeopardizing US export market that absorbs 1/4 of all US soybean production with a value of 3.5 billion dollars annually. It is absolutely imperative US government take strong immediate action to prevent EC soybean restrictions. Urge you tell EC in strongest terms that retaliation is certain if EC continues present course. We urge your immediate action to help our nation's 450,000 soybean farmers and overall soybean industry.[17]

In addition to their worry that these quotas were precedent for the EC wide establishment of soybean quotas and would extend longer than the announced five year period, American soybean producers were also concerned that these quotas would impede them from regaining their previous dominant market position. This was so because the quotas were based on the previous years' figures when US soybean exports to Portugal were at a nadir.

Congressional statements supported the position of the soybean farmers. Doug Bereuter, Republican Representative from Nebraska accused the European Economic Community of "[...] using its same old tactics again. The Community is taking another in a depressingly long series of unfair steps which hurt the American farmer and the United States."[18]

In an exchange of letters between Jacques Delors, the President of the EC Commission, and Commissioner Willy DeClerq, whose responsibility is EC external trade and Clayton Yeutter, United States Trade Representative (USTR), and Secretary of State George

17 American Soybean Association, press release of 21 February 1986.

18 *Congressional Record*, 6 February 1986.

Shultz, US concerns already expressed by the lobby group and Congress were made official. While reassuring the Europeans that the US was generally in favor of European integration and indeed in favor of the enlargement, the Europeans were reminded of their obligations under GATT. Two points in particular were taken up. First, the quotas on the Portuguese oilseeds and vegetable oil market were considered illegal under GATT. Second, approaching the problem of the enlargement more generally, the Americans accused the EC of completing the enlargement and enacting measures before negotiating over compensation according to Article 24:6 of GATT. This article regulates "compensatory adjustment" for trading partners in the event a customs union is formed or changed. The EC interpretation of this article states that it is not necessary to start negotiation over compensation before the enlargement is completed. Nevertheless, the Europeans emphasized their willingness to fulfill their GATT obligations and offered to initiate negotiations after the enlargement was enacted. A GATT working group had already been established on 12 February 1986.[19]

Not at all convinced by the European line of argument President Reagan announced on 31 March 1987 that he would take action against the EC under Section 301 of the Trade and Tariff Act of 1974.[20] This instrument triggers "mandatory responses to unfair distortion of international trade." It authorizes the President to take action against foreign trade practices that violate international trade agreements or are unjustifiable, unreasonable, or discriminatory and burdensome or restrict US commerce. The President's action under Section 301 may encompass duties, fees or restrictions on products and services of the respective trading partner. The goods do not necessarily have to be related to the goods and services which are the subject of the complaint. In this specific case the Portuguese measures of the EC were found illegal under GATT from the very moment the 301 action was announced by President Reagan. One and a half months, when the actions were specified in detail and made official, both the Portuguese and Spanish measures were considered "unreasonable" and "a burden on US commerce."

President Reagan responded to the Portuguese oilseeds and vegetable oil problem by introducing quotas with an equivalent

---

19 GATT/*Airgram*/ 2246 of 18 February 1986.
20 *White House press release*, 31 March 1986.

restrictive effect on EC imports into the US. The answer to the Spanish problem, caused by the introduction of the variable levy system for corn and sorghum imports into Spain was twofold. The US notified GATT that it would cease to recognize GATT limits on tariffs of certain US imports (that is, it withdrew tariff bindings) of comparable value to those exports affected by the levies imposed in Spain. The second step would then be the implementation of tariff increases on those products if the EC would not provide compensation under GATT by 1 July 1986. According to American estimates, the EC measures resulting from enlargement could affect as much as one billion dollars of US farm exports. The President's press release states that

> The US has been fully supportive of the enlargement of the European Community to include Spain and Portugal. We do not, however, believe that the EC should use this occasion to impose new trade barriers. Americans should not have to pay for the benefits which EC member states enjoy.[21]

This general announcement of countermeasures did not target specific products. Rather, the American administration published a Retaliation List of products to be considered for the implementation of quotas and tariff increases.[22] They were to be discussed at a Trade Policy Staff Committee (TPSC) hearing where American as well as some European interest groups testified. The US countermeasures were finally made public in the Presidential Proclamation 5478 of 15 May 1986 and came into effect on 19 May 1986.[23] The Proclamation specified quotas effective until 31 December 1986 for chocolate, candy, apple or pear juices, beer, and white wine valued over four dollars per gallon, as well as subsequent annual quotas for the same products. However, these quotas were set at a level high enough not to affect EC imports. They were based on the quantities imported in 1985 plus an additional share of 20 percent and for white wine an additional 40 percent. The quotas responded to the

---

21 Ibid.

22 *Federal Register*, 3 April 1986.

23 Imposition of quantitative restrictions on imports of certain American products from the European Economic Community, *White House press release*, 15 May 1986.

two "Portuguese Problems" - namely, quotas for oilseeds and vegetable oil and the 15.5 percent share of the Portuguese cereals market that the EC reserved to itself.

For a second group of products American tariff concessions granted under GATT were to be suspended after 30 days in response to the Spanish corn and sorghum problem. The list of products included pork, blue-mold cheese, Edam and Gouda cheeses, endive, carrots, olives, white wine up to four dollars per gallon, brandy, cordials, liqueurs, Kirschwasser, gin and hops. Any tariff increase, however, would be held back until 1 July 1986 while the EC and the US negotiated over the Spanish problem.

Neither the generous quotas nor the postponed tariff increases had an immediately restrictive effect on EC-US trade (although the quota system did cause costly delays at customs) but were instead designed as a warning to force the Europeans to the negotiating table to discuss concessions for the consequences of EC enlargement. The reactions of the US, however, show clearly which of the two problems, access to the Portuguese or to the Spanish markets, was more important to the Americans.

The American measures elicited an immediate response from the EC Commission. Willy DeClerq claimed that the EC had "scrupulously respected" its international commitments during the enlargement. He accused the United States of an unfriendly action, needlessly aggressive and difficult to understand.[24] The Commission issued a list of products considered for counter-measures. Like the Americans, the Europeans shaped their reaction into three categories of measures. The first included sunflower seeds, honey, wine, and bourbon; the second fruit juices, beer and dried fruit. The third group, directed at the Spanish problem, included corn gluten feed, soy cake and meal, wheat, and rice. However, these were mere announcements by the Commission which yet needed the approval of the Foreign Affairs Council made up of the foreign ministers of the member states. It took some time until an official counteraction was decided upon by the Europeans.

---

24 As quoted by Donna Vogt, Jasper Womach, "Tension in United States-European Community Agricultural Trade," in *Congressional Research Service Report No. 86-112*, p. 23. See also H. Peter Dreyer, US, EC exchange threats on trade; both sides prepare lists of goods targeted for restrictions, in *Europe*, May 1986, p. 13.

The Foreign Affairs Council of the EC, in its meeting on 21 and 22 April 1986 in Luxembourg, decided to take up GATT negotiations under Article 24:6 for compensation over the enlargement. This step had been discussed between the Commission and the USTR before and had been announced to the Americans earlier. The Council also expressed its determination to defend EC interests in the upcoming conflict over the enlargement. A month after the Presidential Proclamation 5478, in its session of 16 and 17 June 1986, the Foreign Affairs Council decided to take up the fight over the enlargement at last. It gave a mandate to the Commission to work on countermeasures regarding the imports of corn gluten feed, rice and wheat that were to come into effect simultaneously with the American proposals. With regard to the Portuguese problem, the Council introduced surveillance of American imports, a measure frequently employed by the EC. Without being immediately restrictive this measure allows the EC to have an eye on the imports in question and facilitates restrictive measures later on. In this specific case such measures would be taken once the American quotas began to restrict European exports to the US.

After last minute efforts of EC officials on a visit to Washington at the end of June, an interim agreement was reached between the two trading partners on 2 July 1986 - one day after the deadline set in the Presidential Proclamation. The interim solution, designed to avoid US retaliation and to gain time for GATT negotiations, was aimed at the Spanish problem exclusively. The Portuguese problem, at one point the major sticking point because of the agitation of the American Soybean Association, was again neglected. A new deadline was set to complete these negotiations by 31 December 1986. Both the EC and the US promised a "cease fire" until this date. The US would not implement the announced tariff increases and the EC would not retaliate with measures against corn gluten, rice, and wheat. For the period of this half year, US exports to Spain of products affected by the changes after the enlargement would be reviewed. The EC would make sure that among other imports, corn and sorghum would reach an average of 234,000 tons per month. In case of a shortfall imports of these products into other EC member states would be encouraged with a reduced levy.

Parallel to the bilateral agreement between the EC and the US, negotiations under GATT started in Geneva. The opponents met there on 2 May 1986 for the first time to discuss compensation according to GATT article 24:6. Only the Spanish problem, i.e. variable levies on imports of corn and sorghum, was to be treated under this heading. The Portuguese measures would not qualify for Article 24:6 negotiations because the Americans considered them illegal under GATT rather than a case for compensation after the enlargement of a customs union.

After several meetings in Geneva, the EC came up with an offer for compensation on 30 July 1986. The Europeans proposed quotas based on the average importation level of the last three years (1983-86) for oilseeds, non-grain animal feed (corn gluten, for example) and salmon. For these quotas US exporters would be treated according to the old tariff schedule prior to accession which meant that most of their exports would remain duty-free. In addition, the quotas would be increased by an amount equivalent to traditional imports into Spain of cereal products whose tariffs had been unbound following accession, i.e. barley, corn, and sorghum.[25] The Europeans had made the quota offer because it would encourage US sales of cereal substitutes to Spain and Portugal which had not been traditional importers of these products so far. The quotas were designed to provide non-sectorial compensation for losses in the corn and sorghum sector that, in the eyes of the Europeans, had shown signs of decline for American exporters in recent years anyway.

The Americans protested strongly against this solution. They claimed that sales of cereal substitutes to Spain and Portugal were possible without quotas. In fact, the quotas would put a ceiling on US exports expected to expand in the next few years. The Americans also demanded compensation in the same sector, i.e. corn and sorghum, as the case in question. In detail, quite different requests for compensation were expressed. The Administration had asked the EC for duty-free imports of 13 million tons of feed grains. The US Feed Grains Council, however, considered a gradual phase-out of EC export subsidies for feed grains as the best form of compensation. In a letter to USTR Clayton Yeutter and Secretary of Agriculture Richard Lyng they explained, "The US would be

---

25 Farm Groups Blast EC Efforts to Set Quota for Soybeans, Corngluten; U.S. Feed Grains Council Rejects EC Compensation Offer as "Unreasonable"; EC Proposes Duty-Free Quota without Growth on Key U.S. AG Exports; in *Inside U.S. Trade*, 15 August 1986.

exchanging the Spain/Portugal feed grains market for the elimination of EC export subsidies to third markets."[26] This elimination of export subsidies would also have a positive effect in restraining EC surplus production.

The American Soybean Association reacted more aggressively to the European offer. It saw the proposed quotas as yet another attack on the unlimited access for American soybean suppliers to the European market at a zero tariff rate. The ASA wanted to initiate another Section 301 complaint on these grounds. Again, as in February of 1986, when the quota scheme for the Portuguese oilseed market became known, they strongly defended their right to a European market share. Similar reactions came from the National Corn Growers Association.

As the 31 December 1986 deadline set in the interim agreement approached, little progress in negotiations over compensation was made. Minor changes were agreed to by both sides. The EC increased the level of quotas on soybean oil. Consequently the US increased the quotas on ale, port and stout beer effective 29 October 1986. By the end of November the EC had made a new offer suggesting free access for soybeans and corn gluten feed to the twelve EC member states as compensation. The US rejected this proposal, again, for not being sector identical with the original complaints. This stubborn insistence by the Americans on sector specific compensation rendered the European strategy for the Article 24:6 negotiations of global compensation impotent. They pointed out that, while the US had disadvantages in the agricultural field as a result of the enlargement, the Americans would benefit in the industrial field where Spanish and Portuguese Tariffs dropped from an average 15 percent level to the 5 percent level of the Common Customs Tariffs of the EC. The Americans not only did not accept this strategy of negotiation of trading off agricultural losses and industrial gains but denied the benefits to their industrial exports in the first place. They claimed that the favorable effect of the tariff decrease would be offset by more intensive trade between Spain and other EC member states at a zero tariff rate which would finally displace US products.

---

26 U.S. Feed Grains Council Rejects EC Compensation Offer as "Unreasonable", *Inside U.S. Trade*, 15 August 1986.

The Foreign Affairs Council of the EC, in its meeting on 24 November 1986 took note of Commissioner De Clerq's report on the GATT 24:6 negotiations. It encouraged the Commission to continue to search for a mutually acceptable solution by the Council's next session in December. By the time of its 15 December meeting, however, no agreement had been reached. Some of these meetings were part of the diplomatic routine of EC-US relations. Officials from the EC and the US meet regularly to discuss economic questions. Since 1981 one of these meetings per year is a "high level talk." On 12 December 1986 it was Secretary of State George Shultz who saw the President of the EC Commission Jacques Delors in Brussels. This high level consultation did not prevent the Americans from riding yet another fierce attack in the "corn war" immediately afterwards - as the Europeans later would mention bitterly.

The failure of any results to emerge from the December negotiations rendered the deadline set for 31 December 1986 utopian. The Council asked the Commission to negotiate, as suggested by the Commission, over an extension until 31 January 1987. It agreed with the Commission's view of the American request as being unjustified and emphasized again that the Community would take unilateral measures to defend its interests.[27]

In the US, the Feed Grains Council and other farm lobby groups showed signs of discontent with what they called the "conciliatory" attitude of the US Administration. They pressed for an immediate confrontation:

> It is almost inevitable that we will have a confrontation with the EC and it is better to have it now than in five years when the US position in international markets is further eroded.[28]

In addition, the Feed Grains Council showed concern over the implementation of the interim agreement concluded on 2 July 1986. The agreement guarantees 1.4 million tons of US feed grain sales to

---

27 Relations Communauté-Etats-Unis: Conclusion du Conseil, *Presse 204* (Foreign Affairs Council of 15-16 December 1986 under the presidency of Sir Geoffrey Howe, United Kingdom).

28 Yeutter Sees Less Than 50% Chance of Settling AG Dispute with EC, in *Inside US Trade*, 9 December 1986.

Spain over a period of six month (234,000 tons each month). However, five months after the agreement had come into effect, only about 200,000 tons of this quota had been used up. The guaranteed EC purchase of feed grain accelerated during December of 1986, the last month of the interim period. By 22 December a shortfall of 700,000 million tons, which amounts to half of the entire quota was recorded.[29]

The pressure exerted by the farm lobby resulted in a new round of the trade war. In a Press Conference in Palm Springs, California on 30 December USTR Clayton Yeutter announced that tariff increases of up to 200 percent ad valorem on products like gin, white wine, cheese and brandy would soon be enacted.[30] Taken together the EC exports were estimated to be approximately 400 million dollars which is the amount of losses the Americans calculated to have per year as a consequence of the enlargement. Yeutter called the offer made by the Community for compensation "grossly inadequate":

> We rejected that offer and concluded regrettably that we had no choice but to follow through with the protection of our interests, as presented in the action that's being announced by the President today.[31]

In an immediate response the EC Commission proposed a 30 to 50 Ecu levy on imports of corn gluten feed and rice worth equally about 400 million dollars.

The American measures, announced on 30 December 1986, became official with the Presidential Proclamation 5601 of 21 January 1987 announcing tariff increases for those articles on which tariff concessions under GATT had been suspended in May: pork, blue-mold cheese, Edam and Gouda, Endive, carrots, olives, white wine, gin and brandy.[32] For these products the EC had between 85 and 95 percent of the US market. The enormous tariff increase up to

---

29 U.S.-EC Grain Talks Fail, *The Journal of Commerce*, 22 December 1986.

30 The White House Office of the Press Secretary, *Press Briefing by Ambassador Clayton Yeutter*, United States Trade Representative, Palm Springs California, 30 December 1986.

31 Ibid.

32 *Imposition of Increased Tariffs on Imports of Certain Articles*, Presidential Proclamation 5601.

200 percent ad valorem was intended to stop the European export of these products "in its tracks."[33] Although the Americans tried to hit member states of the European Community evenly, France would be the main victim of the retaliation. About one quarter of French exports to the US were affected, brandy and white wine being a major share of those exports. The tariff increases scheduled for 30 January 1987, however, were never applied. The trading partners were able to find another solution in the few days between the Presidential Proclamation of 21 January and the final deadline of 31 January. After further negotiations between DeClerq and Frans Andriessen, Commissioner for Agriculture on the one side, Clayton Yeutter and Secretary of Agriculture Richard Lyng on the other side, a temporary agreement was concluded on 30 January 1987.

The Foreign Affairs Council undertook the first step to this agreement in its meeting on 26 January. The Council conceded to postponement of the application of Article 320 of the Treaty of Accession until 31 December 1990. The article would have introduced the variable levy system for cereals to the Portuguese market and reserved a 15.5 percent share of the market to suppliers from other EC member states. In the contract of 30 January 1987 the EC agreed to lower tariffs and additional access for 26 products from the US to the twelve member states. The main part of the agreement, however, provided for a minimum annual purchase of 2 million tons of corn and 300,000 tons of sorghum by Spain either through a reduced-levy quota or through direct purchases by the Community on world markets. Imports of non-grain feed (i.e. corn gluten, brewing and distilling dregs and waste, citrus peels and pellets) were to be deducted from the corn and sorghum quotas. The agreement applies until 31 December 1990. Both Clayton Yeutter and Richard Lyng noticed with satisfaction that "this is the first time that the US has received full compensation following an enlargement of the EC."[34] In exchange for these European commitments the Americans withdrew the pending tariff increases proclaimed on 21 January.[35]

---

33 Yeutter, note 30.

34 Office of the United States Trade Representative, *Statement by U.S. Trade Representative Clayton Yeutter, 29 January 1987;* Department of Agriculture, *Statement by U.S. Secretary of Agriculture Richard E. Lyng*, 29 January 1987.

35 *Federal Register*, Vol. 52 No.23 (4 February 1987).

The concession of 2.3 million tons feed grains per year seems modest compared with the American request of 4 million tons at the outset of the final negotiations. Compared to the concession granted under the Interim Agreement of July 1987 - 1.4 million of feed grain for six months - the Americans lost 0.5 million tons on a yearly basis. They also had to share the Portuguese feed grain market with other exporters because the agreement left the quota open to all non-EC member states. According to estimates of the US administration in January 1987, US suppliers would take up about 1.9 million tons of the quota.[36] The whole Spanish import market for corn actually absorbed 2.7 million tons in 1984 and about 3.9 million tons in the following year.[37]

With the temporary agreement of 30 January 1987 a lid was put on the Pandora's box that was opened a year before when the Americans became aware of the details of the Treaty of Accession. The agreement offered a preliminary solution to the problem of American feed grain exports to Spain. It explicitly did not resolve the principle conflict over the interpretation of GATT Article 24:6. And there were other items left in the box. Although the Europeans had agreed to postpone the claim for a 15.5 percent EC share of the Portuguese cereals market, the Americans had not lifted their quotas directed at this Portuguese problem.

FARM INTERESTS IN A TRANSATLANTIC CONTEXT

In the one year course of the "corn war" a few crucial incidents and major points of conflict emerged. Spain and Portugal became members of the European Community on 1 January 1986. Only shortly afterwards did American farm lobby groups take action against the agricultural consequences of the enlargement. On 31 March 1986, President Reagan announced retaliation measures for the first time against Portuguese soybean quotas, community preference of 15.5 percent for the Portuguese cereals market and the

---

36 Art Pine, Wendy L. Wall, U.S., EC Settle Trade Dispute on Agriculture, in *The Wall Street Journal*, 30 January 1987, p. 1.

37 Food and Agricultural Organization, in *Monthly Bulletin of Statistics*, Vol. 10 (March 1987).

variable levy on corn and sorghum imports into Spain. The measures were quotas and tariff suspensions specified in the Presidential Proclamation of 15 May 1986. The Proclamation set a 1 July 1986 deadline for the negotiations over compensation under GATT article 24:6. This deadline, however, was not met and an interim agreement concluded on 2 July, created a grace period until 31 December 1986 and granted the Americans access to the Spanish feed grain market meanwhile. By the end of December the Americans found that the Europeans had not made any satisfactory offer. Consequently they announced that they would enact the planned tariff increases and set them at a threatening rate of 200 percent ad valorem. Further negotiations led to the agreement of 30 January 1987 granting non EC members a 2.3 million ton quota for corn and sorghum exports to Spain and implying that the Americans would take a big share of the quota.

On both sides, farm interest groups pursued a solution to the problem that would provide them with maximum gains. The Feed Grains Council requested the phase-out of European export subsidies on feed grains in exchange for the Spanish and Portuguese market - a solution which, of course, would have touched the very principles of the CAP and its variable levy system. On the other side, the European Committees of Professional Farmers, the Committee of Agicultural Organizations in the EEC (COPA) and the Committee of Professional Agricultural Organizations (COGECA), pursued a general approach to the compensation problem meaning that losses in the agricultural field should be counted against gains in the industrial field.[38] Neither of the two sides would win entirely during the negotiation process. And both sides vividly expressed their disappointment after the conclusion of the agreement.[39] However, American farm interests were better defended in this trade conflict than European interests.

---

38 "Globalitätskonzept" von COPA und COGECA gefordert: Verrechnung von Agrarverlusten mit Industriegewinnen, in *Agra Europe* 51/52, Europa-Nachrichten, p. 10.

39 Berufsstand kritisiert Handelsabkommen mit den USA, in *Agra Europe* 6/87, Europa-Nachrichten, p. 51. Anne Swardson, U.S. Rescinds Plan for Tariffs on European Imports, in *Washington Post*, 30 January 1987, p. A3, quoting Alan Tank, assistant vice president of the National Corn Growers Association: "They should have walked away from this agreement before they got to this stage [...]. We may have needed a little trade war."

What was at stake for the farmers on both sides? The enlargement, as originally regulated in the Treaty of Accession, would grant EC cereal suppliers a 15.5 percent share of the Portuguese market; they would also benefit from a higher external tariff (variable levy) on corn and sorghum imports into Spain. However, these were additional benefits to the European farmers while, on the other side, American farmers had to defend themselves against losses. They had previously held almost the entire Portuguese cereals market and had exported between 2 and 4 million tons of corn into Spain every year - a market they valued at $400 million in 1986. The threat to their current exports, rather than the promise of expanding them, was the crucial motivation of American farm groups that was not shared by European farmers in this particular conflict. At a time when US farm exports were generally in decline American farmers fought over what they believed to be their piece of a shrinking pie while the Europeans only had to expect future benefits which could enhance their situation in the long run but were not considered vital at that very moment.

It is not surprising, then, that the trade conflict was initiated as a result of agitation by American farm lobby groups. It was the American Soybean Association that apparently started the retaliation process. They toured Europe in the beginning of 1986 and upon return vigorously expressed their concern about the consequences of the enlargement to the President and the Congress. Throughout the whole negotiation process the ASA acted as a watch dog, barking every time the Europeans even mentioned "quotas" and "soybeans" in the same sentence. This reaction was mostly political and not so much based on an immediate economic threat. The ASA equated "quota" with a violation of the zero-duty binding (duty exemption) for soybeans negotiated between the EC and the US in 1962 during the Dillon Round. It was not self-evident, however, that the particular set of quotas at issue in the current conflict would in fact harm US exports. If the quotas themselves were indeed harmful, American negotiators would have more strongly pressed for compensation on this end, as well.

The influence of American farmers on American policy-makers was especially high at this time due to the nationwide elections of 4 November 1986. Americans voted for their Representatives in the House and for one-third of the Senators. The latter race, especially, was important because the Republican majority in the Senate was in jeopardy and President Reagan was confronted with the possibility (that became reality) of dealing with a Congress dominated by a Democratic majority for his last two years in office. This election provided an extra incentive for Senators and the President "to stand up for the rights of the American farmer"[40] in a transatlantic trade conflict. In the principal corn producing states in the US eight senators stood for election. The Midwestern states of Iowa, Illinois, Nebraska, Indiana, Minnesota, Ohio, Wisconsin, South Dakota, Missouri and North Dakota together produce about 80 percent of US corn.[41] With the exception of Nebraska and Minnesota, all of these states held elections for the Senate. In the competition for the crucial votes in the farming states the senators' only option was to press for retaliation. To take no action against the EC would not have brought them any votes. Once they had initiated the retaliation and gained the votes in the 4 November 1986 election their goal was reached. They would not have to be concerned about European counter-retaliation. Any harmful consequences of a trade war for American farmers would not harm a newly-elected Senator.

These points suggest that American farm interests were voiced rather strongly in the transatlantic trade conflict. The European farmers were in a different situation altogether. As mentioned above, they were expected to be less aggressive since, unlike the Americans, the issue for them was not diminishing market share but rather future market gains. Their pressure lacked the special effect that electoral events could have brought to bear because only France had an important national election, but it was held in March and the great political compromise of cohabitation between the Socialists and Chirac's party was introduced before the "corn war" entered a serious stage. A situation parallel to the US, where eight Senate seats representing eight major corn-producing seats were being contested, could have been duplicated only if the main agricultural producers among the member states, Germany, Italy, France, the Netherlands and the UK, had held national elections in this period.

In general, the institutional set up of EC puts the Europeans at a disadvantage in negotiations with the Americans. While negotiators on the US side, e.g. USTR Clayton Yeutter, are only responsible to

---

40 Pete Wilson, R-California, in a Senate floor debate, in *Congressional Record*, 17 April 1986.
41 USDA, *Agricultural Statistics*, 1985.

the President, Commissioners on the European side depend on the approval of the Council made up of ministers of twelve member states. Commissioners virtually fight on two fronts: defending European interests against American attacks and defending Community interests against attacks from member states as expressed in the Council and various preparatory committees during the decision making process (Committe of Permanent Representatives to the European Communities, Art. 113 committee). Given this institutional set up, the Community has two specific disadvantages. First, it cannot react as fast as the United States. During the "corn war" it was the Commission that was always ready to attack the US with retaliatory measures using tariffs on wheat, corn gluten feed, and rice. These announcements had to pass the Council to become enacted which usually involves a delay of several weeks. The Council would often edit them and adopt a softer version. While President Reagan announced his first retaliatory step on 31 March and countermeasures proposed by the Commission were published in the press immediately, the Council took three weeks to merely agree on "defending European interests" in general. Detailed counter-counter measures were finally specified by the Council in mid-June.

Second, because any decision of the Europeans is a compromise of twelve member states the Americans can take advantage of that and concentrate on the toughest opponent. In the "corn war" it was clearly France which was hardest hit by the American uproar over the Spanish problem. France is the third largest exporter of corn after the United States and Argentina.[42] Before the enlargement France had almost a 60 percent share of the entire EC corn production.[43] As a consequence of the enlargement, French corn producers had counted on preferential access to the Spanish market. Given this strong interest of French farmers in the conflict the repeated French requests in the Council of Foreign Ministers for adopting a tough European stance against the Americans is logical. The Americans were probably equally aware of this situation and chose France as their prime target of attack. About a quarter of

---

42 USDA, *Agricultural Statistics*, 1985.

43 EC Commission, *The Agricultural Situation in the Community,1985 Report*, Luxembourg, 1986, p. 200. Italy and Greece, with about 30 percent and 10 percent respectively, produced most of the rest.

French exports to the US were hit by the announced tariff increases of December 1987, the main products being brandy and white wine. Out of the affected trade volume of about $400 million brandy took up $150 million and white wine $100 million.[44] As a result, during the final stages of the negotiation over the preliminary agreement France, on the one hand, had a strong interest in defending its future share of the Spanish feed grain market while at the same time it obviously had an almost equally strong interest in protecting French cognac producers from the damaging effects of the American retaliatory measures.

The French desire for a "let's get tough with Americans" approach was further weakened by its failure to find support for this attitude among the other member states. They, and especially Germany, were more concerned about a spillover of the conflict into the industrial sector which of course would have been very harmful to German exports. The umbrella organization of European industries, the Union of the Industries of the European Community (UNICE), had pointed to this danger from the beginning of the "corn war" and had tried to draw the attention of the press and the Commission to it.[45] Together with the British the Germans placed themselves on the moderate wing in the negotiations with the Americans. What in fact was reached through the agreement of January 1987 was a return to the pre-enlargement situation. The Europeans gave up the 15.5 percent share of the Portuguese cereals market and the Americans were granted access to the Spanish feed grains market for the next four years. France and the French corn growers could not effectively defend their interests. American farm lobby groups were more successful because they enjoyed the advantage of an aggressive initiating role and a special political effect before the Senate elections. In addition the Americans worked hard on one important member state, France, in particular, that would have needed more support to defend its tough line in the "corn war."

---

44 *White House press release*, see note 30.

45 L'UNICE s'oppose à une guerre commerciale entre la CEE et les Etats-Unis, *Press Release*, 15 April 1986.

CONCLUSION

The above analysis showed the important role American farm lobby groups played in this transatlantic trade conflict. As explained at the outset, these trade conflicts are mainly due to the common problem of surplus production both in the US and the EC and divergent views on agricultural policies. The CAP will remain a prime target of American attack as the American farmers continue to fight for their market shares. On a larger scale, the "corn war" proved that, despite the great American interest in the enlargement and in European unification in general, the US is not willing to accept consequences which jeopardize their economic interests.

Future agricultural trade conflicts are to be expected and are probably unavoidable as long as these principal conditions remain unchanged. However, while European politicians have little influence on the strength of American farm lobby groups, there are still ways to hamper transatlantic tension, e.g. in the case of a future enlargement. One way is a more careful calculation of the effect of such an enlargement on specific sectors in the US. This effect can only be adequately judged with a thorough knowledge of the partner's problems (and therefore vulnerable points) at the time of the enlargement. In the mid-80s, the US struggled with an ever growing trade deficit which would trigger protectionist proposals in Congress in the following years. The traditional US surplus in agricultural trade with the EC was cut in half. Already sensitive because of this general decline of export markets, not to speak of debts due to high investments in previous years and the declining value of land, US farmers reacted especially forcefully. As a result of their pressure, the US would not consider the global solution of counting gains in the industrial field against agricultural losses. The US would not even consider compensation in a field other than the very subsectors at stake: feed grains, cereals and oilseeds.

A careful observation of these agricultural forces in the US might have anticipated this stubborn reaction. Once such sensitive points in the partner's texture are detected cautious preliminary actions might be undertaken. One of the more astonishing facets of the "corn war" is the apparent ignorance on both sides. While the admission of Spain and Portugal was not prepared secretively and the Treaty of Accession was negotiated over a long period, the

Americans only seemed to realize the consequences after the Treaty's provisions became effective. The Europeans on the other hand could not have been completely unaware of the fact that the Americans were eligible for compensation. While it can be justified under GATT to say, as the Commission did, that compensation only had to be granted after the enlargement is completed, tentative offers or even speculations about how to solve an upcoming conflict could have eased the situation. The sooner these precautions are taken the less likely it is that a costly trade war would be precipitated. Such precautions, however, should not keep the Europeans from forming a "club" of their own and from admitting members according to their own rules.

11

The Power of Strategic Initiatives in the Federal Republic of Germany

David Rubenson

INSTITUTIONAL POWER AND STRATEGIC POLICY

One evening in early 1989, a German colleague told me about his on-going study of the SDI debate in the United States. I was surprised to hear that he was still studying SDI in 1989. He insisted that the SDI debate had an important impact on the Federal Republic which had to be better understood. He had concluded that the FRG should place a special team of strategic analysts in Washington in order to influence new initiatives like SDI. I laughed because my study of the SDI debate in the Federal Republic had led me to the opposite conclusion; that Germans ought to have a self-imposed moratorium on commenting on US strategic initiatives until they see which ones survive the technical, financial, and bureaucratic obstacles that are part of the US security policy decision making process.[1]

1 The following analysis is based largely on the author's personal experiences following the security policy debates in the Federal Republic of Germany and in the United States as well as in working with a number of German security policy analysts. The views presented in this article represent those of the author alone and do not reflect the views of any institution or organization.

The US security policy system is simultaneously configured to develop new strategic initiatives[2] and to block their implementation. The existence of these powerful, yet counterbalancing, forces is difficult to perceive without day to day experience working in our system. As a result many Europeans falsely interpret new initiatives as representing initial steps toward the formulation of new policies.

Nowhere is this difficulty more important than in the Federal Republic of Germany, where history and geostrategic position produce an intense security policy debate. However, much of this debate has a narrow focus on issues related to strategy and deterrence. There is a tendency to ignore issues related to implementation, and to treat the strategic implications of new initiatives as current problems. There is insufficient focus on the forces that act to retard, alter, or negate new initiatives. The result is a failure to accurately discriminate true shifts in American policy from transitory discussion.

One purpose of this paper is to argue that German anxieties about American initiatives are often premature. A retrospective look reveals that most initiatives were doomed by the very forces that created them. A second objective is to argue that American concerns about the implied inconsistencies are minimized by familiarity with the system. The cohort of analysts with bold but unrealistic visions is complemented by a set of hardened bureaucrats with excellent instincts for predicting the evolution of new initiatives. German analysts tend to debate the ideas of the bolder group, not fully appreciate the influence of the latter group, and be disturbed by the consistencies implied by the countervailing forces.

It is still too early to know how these forces will behave in an era of rapid strategic change. However, in looking toward the future, it will be important for Germans to remember that institutional forces, not strategic issues, dominated US security policy in the 1980s. It is only by understanding this behavior will Germans be prepared to accurately assess US policies in the 1990s.

---

2 Strategic initiatives being defined as new policies or military programs rather than the narrow definition of programs affecting intercontinental weapons.

THE POWER OF CONTRADICTORY FORCES IN THE US SYSTEM

Since most controversial military initiatives originate in the United States, the thesis implies that Americans propose ideas they do not really mean, and Germans do not understand this. A complete explanation of this unique phenomenon is both beyond the scope of this paper and the capabilities of the author. The following discussion describes two components of the US system that contain these contradictory impulses: the "study culture" and institutional diversity. Both have played a role in the development of initiatives and in differentiating German and US reactions. The effect of these factors on specific debates will be discussed in the following section.

The Power of the "Study Culture"

Perhaps the single most important factor that encourages new ideas is the large number of studies that are conducted. Each of the armed services utilizes private think tanks, as do the Joint Chiefs of Staff and the Office of the Secretary of Defense. These think tanks produce large numbers of policy studies and technical analyses. Within the Pentagon a large number of offices perform studies as do the national laboratories and other Federally Funded R&D centers. This is only the tip of the iceberg. The Pentagon is supported by a large number of private study consulting firms as are most of the regional military commands. The extent and breadth of this study industry is unique to the United States and has no counterpart in the FRG.

By themselves, the large number of studies provide a stimulus for new ideas. Even in a static strategic and technical environment, such a large number of studies is likely to produce some controversial ideas. A slowly changing technical or strategic environment will produce a disproportionate number of interesting new initiatives. With the appearance of unlimited budgets in the early Reagan years there were few limits on what might be proposed.

This same "study culture" also acts to insure that change occurs slowly. Given the large number of institutions involved, any interesting study will give rise to studies of the study. These second generation studies will invariably flush out the detailed problems of implementation and provide contradictory arguments. The large number of studies also acts to diminish the importance of any individual study. That a new study has proven a point is of little consequence in the US community.

The longevity of individuals in the "study industry" also reduces the credibility of studies. After a few years an individual will begin to revisit failed initiatives. Having been through a study cycle on a particular idea, it is easy to anticipate technical and financial problems and be skeptical about a repeat of the process. There are many jokes within the community about dusting off the old studies and changing a few acronyms to make them current. During one briefing on Soviet strategic forces the speaker remarked that he could add a 1, in front of the 9, on SS-9, and use the same charts he had used 15 years earlier.

Finally it should be mentioned that many of the studies are less profound than their coverage in the European press may imply. An American analyst may hear about a new study and spend several months attempting to get access, during which excitement for the initiative builds. It is not uncommon to find that the study was not even a study, but xerox copies of briefing charts with little or no supporting text or analysis. It is not surprising that such initiatives have little chance of moving beyond the study phase.

The Power of Institutional Diversity

The fluid institutional interactions within the American security policy community are also a source of contradictory incentives. The armed services, the executive branch, the think tanks, civilian Pentagon bureaucrats, the Congress, congressional staffs, the Arms Control and Disarmament Agency (ACDA), the defense industry, and the national laboratories, all have influences on security policy. Given these diverse interests, and the competition for budgets and turf, it is surprising that any decisions are implemented.

Equally important to the obfuscatory power of these institutions is their connection to policy makers. The typical top level Pentagon decision maker will have had a variety of careers. Some will be former military officers, some will come from industry, others from the think tanks. These labels are also heterogeneous. A think tank member may be a former military officer or have worked in industry. A member of a congressional staff might have had a diverse Department of Defense background. The movement of individuals is constant and forms a complex web linking the institutions that comprise the security policy system.

One effect of this movement is to stimulate new initiatives. By combining experience in technology, policy, and military operations, analysts are well equipped "to think up" technical concepts that have battlefield applications. Industry managers with governmental experience will have an excellent understanding of what might sell. Think tank analysts with industry experience can create new ideas from concepts that never left the aerospace company briefing room. Multi-disciplinary experience is the key element to creating the "zeroth order" analyses that form the basis of many new ideas.

Multi-disciplinary experience also produces analysts who are conscious of the difficulties in implementing such initiatives. Even if trained as an historian or political scientist, the American security policy analyst may have had significant exposure to weapon system acquisition and development. Such an analyst may have worked in industry, in a Pentagon project control office, or seen dozens if not hundreds of contractor briefings. He would have experience with cost overruns, schedule slippages, and bloated claims of technical performance. This experience increases awareness of implementation obstacles and makes some analysts more skillful at using these obstacles to block initiatives inconsistent with their own institutional interests.

In contrast, security policy analysts in the FRG are subject to a less heterogeneous set of influences. The community of civilian security policy analysts within the Ministry of Defense (MOD) is smaller and is based on a system offering less opportunity to work in other institutional settings. Analysts at the institutes, such as the Hessische Stiftung Friedens- und Konfliktforschung (HSFK), Stiftung Wissenschaft und Politik (SWP), Konrad Adenauer, or Friedrich Ebert Stiftung, tend to have scholarly backgrounds with little formal connection to the defense industry or the bureaucracy. Compared to American security policy analysts, these scholars have an impressive understanding of strategy, and the historical and geopolitical basis for strategy. However, they have less understanding of weapon system acquisition and Pentagon politics. German analysts have an exceptional ability to describe the inconsistencies of US initiatives, but are less in touch with the factors that will determine if those inconsistencies are real problems.

THE POWER OF STRATEGIC IDEAS IN THE 1980s

The forces that encourage new strategic ideas were extremely active in the 1980s. Numerous ideas never entered the European debate and better publicized ones, such as SDI, anti-tactical ballistic missiles (ATBM), Follow-on-Forces-Attack (FOFA), Discriminate Deterrence, and Reykjavik, aroused serious strategy debates in the FRG. However, the major impact of even these initiatives were the debates themselves. The forces that inhibit implementation were generally successful. Such an outcome was not universally predicted in the United States and there were many who believed in the concepts. However, within the grouping sensitive to implementation obstacles, there was substantial skepticism. With the benefit of hindsight, we can see many factors that supported their predictions.

In contrast, the German debate tended to evaluate the positive and negative aspects of the initiatives while treating their implementation as an unknown, or perhaps a 50-50, prospect. Without the "homegrown" knowledge of US institutions, Germans concentrated on the ideas implied by the initiatives. This focus obscured the greater power of bureaucracy, finances, and technology in influencing the course of security policy.

The Power of Strategic Ideas vs. the Power of the Bureaucracy

Perhaps the best illustration of this differing perspective (though not necessarily the most important) arose with the recent Department of Defense study "Discriminate Deterrence"[3]. To many German analysts this study was the long awaited announcement of America's turn away from Europe. Conducted by influential policy-makers,

---

3 Commission on Integrated Long Term Strategy, Chairmen, F. Iklé and A. Wohlstetter, *Discriminate Deterrence*, 1988.

Europeans were disappointed and shocked at the apparent change in American strategy. The study seemed to confirm that America would not trade New York for Hamburg and that Washington's commitment to flexible response was questionable.

As an American analyst I was surprised to find German newspapers reporting Discriminate Deterrence on the front page. For an American security policy analyst Discriminate Deterrence was just another study in an institutional bureaucracy that produces an inordinate number of studies, almost all of which have little or no impact. That the study was conducted by influential defense analysts also seemed of little consequence. The names collected on the Discriminate Deterrence study were impressive, but represented only a very small portion of the influential voices in US security policy.

Treating Discriminate Deterrence as a major new American policy also failed to account for the institutional interest in the defense of Europe. For the US armed services, the defense of Europe means large elements of force structure which cannot be justified in other theaters. American industry is the prime financial beneficiary of this force structure requirement. Civilian Defense Department bureaucrats and private think tanks have built up enormous intellectual capital understanding European defense strategy. Even American liberals support the defense of Europe enthusiastically. It provides a military mission that validates their interest in military security and whose resources requirements provide an effective means of arguing against adventures like SDI or involvement in Central America.

The Discriminate Deterrence study was unlikely to have significant impact because it was only a study, and because it ran contrary to vested interests. The ideas behind the study may have played upon European fears, and no doubt the authors anticipated such reactions, and may have intended to arouse them. Nonetheless, the study had minimal impact on decision making. The European reaction was more a misreading of the American system than an accurate observation of American policy.

The Reykjavik discussions provide a similar example. Whereas the SPD may have hailed the proposal to eliminate nuclear weapons, and the CDU\CSU saw it as a betrayal, many American defense analysts viewed it as neither. The primary American fear was that Europeans would take these discussions seriously and that the ensuing debate would damage the credibility of nuclear deterrence.

The calmer US reaction was primarily due to the clearer understanding that Reykjavik did not mean the US was contemplating the abandonment of nuclear weapons. Had the President and Mr. Gorbachev reached agreement, an array of representatives from the security policy apparatus would have come forward to defend nuclear deterrence. Without such a proposal working its way through the bureaucratic institutions, and gaining support along the way, there is little chance of it becoming policy. Such institutional support, as also evidenced by SDI, is far more important than stimulus provided by even a popular president.

The Power of Strategic Ideas vs. the Power of Technology

There is little doubt that Germans were challenged by the power of the strategic ideas in SDI and felt the need to protect German interests against them. One illustration was the argument that SDI might produce an effective shield against ICBMs, but could never effectively defend Europe against short range missiles. For the SPD it meant SDI must be stopped, for the government it implied no deployment, and for the German right it meant an independent European version of SDI.

From the European perspective decoupling would seem to have been a valid concern. The US had embarked on a major technology initiative which did not address the question of short range missiles with equal vigor. American scientists were divided about SDI feasibility, hence the possibility of it being successful seemed like a contingency which had to be anticipated.

Within the United States there are still debates about SDI feasibility, but there is a growing tendency to play down the significance of the initiative. Certainly many segments of the US community predicted a negative outcome from the beginning and a retrospective look provides significant basis for this prediction. Although scientists were divided, many scientific advocates clearly had a vested interest in advocacy. Without such voices, scientific opinion was far less evenly split. Some American analysts had experience with other satellite programs and could see that 26 billion dollars was an insignificant sum of money for what was being contemplated. There was also awareness that SDI technologies had been under development prior to SDI and that 26 billion dollars would not cause a significant acceleration. Finally many US analysts had participated in the earlier anti-ballistic missile debates and understood the enormous technical and financial challenges implied.

It was also clear that SDI lacked the required institutional support. Gathering momentum at a time while defense budgets were peaking, the armed services saw SDI as competition for other elements of force structure. Even those responsible for military space systems were unenthusiastic since it seemed to trivialize traditional space missions. Contrary to SPD or Green views, industry was also unenthusiastic. While producing a windfall of short run study money, SDI elevated system technical requirements thus delaying more lucrative production orders.

Institutional, technical, and financial obstacles led some Americans to minimize the importance of SDI and discount European concerns about decoupling. There was more American concern about the decoupling debate than decoupling itself. There was a relatively greater recognition that neither a defense against ICBMs nor short range missiles had any significant engineering or financial basis. Given the lack of technical definition, no serious strategic debate was possible.

To the extent that Europeans did look beyond the strategic implications of SDI, there was great concern about the technological challenge that had to be met. Americans kept hearing (though mostly from the French rather than the Germans) that 26 billion dollars on R&D had to produce something and that a technological revolution would be the likely result. For those working in the American aerospace industry, the argument of the Europeans was not impressive. In the words of one American colleague, "26 billion can't produce anything? That's business as usual."

The Power of Strategic Ideas vs. the Power of Scientific Theory

The story of the deployment and ultimate removal of the INF forces is somewhat different in that the initiatives were not purely American and both deployment and removal actually occurred. However different perceptions of the contradictory forces described above contributed to the more dramatic reaction in the FRG than in the United States.

The American community obviously played the major role in dramatizing the importance of INF for meeting NATO's requirements. American analysts were overwhelmingly convinced that the ability to strike the Soviet homeland from European soil was essential for NATO strategy. For some US analysts INF deployment represented the triumph of strategic logic over public emotion. Removal of the weapons was just as much an inconsistency for these analysts as it was for German analysts. It resulted from the failure to anticipate that the Soviets would accept the zero-zero initiative rather than any change in belief about the need for these weapons.

Although both communities saw the inconsistency, Germans were far more shaken by it. To Germans the inconsistency indicated a lack of American interest in European security. However, this fails to account for the vested interests in maintaining our presence in Europe. Instead, the German reaction may reflect a greater emphasis on the need for a consistent strategy. Certainly American analysts also desire consistency, but they are accustomed to falling short of goals and to tolerating inconsistencies. Most American analysts have dealt with weapon system requirements that have little basis in actual needs, must be altered when proven unattainable, and exist only to help move a program through the system. Strategy itself is often a tool of convenience. To perform in the U S system, an analyst must be prepared to say, that what might have been critical yesterday, is less so today. American analysts are well conditioned to accepting inconsistencies, even if basic views remain unaltered.

Thus from the American viewpoint NATO strategy existed prior to INF and exists now that it has been removed. NATO strategy remains flexible response and can still be implemented by a variety of means. Many are discouraged by the inconsistency and the failure to incorporate military strategy in the arms control process. Nonetheless, the inconsistency itself does not represent a reason to abandon the status quo or prohibit the ability to be consistent in a general way.

In contrast, the German debate treated INF as if it were analogous to a test of Einstein's laws of gravitation. Both the left and the right seemed to view INF as a necessary condition for "NATO theory" to exist. Without it, the entire theory seemed to be invalid. The German right began to advocate removal of other nuclear weapons and the SPD was vindicated for its doubts about NATO and the Americans. Chancellor Kohl, often accused of not understanding security policy, was one of the few voices who seemed to grasp the non criticality of INF withdrawal. Appropriately balancing his concerns with the needs of his vacation, the chancellor returned to Germany to announce in effect that NATO strategy could continue without INF. Not surprisingly, few Germans believed him.

COPING WITH OUR SYSTEM IN THE 1990s

American Analysis vs. the Power of Rationale Thinking

"Why do you take us so seriously?" has been my question to German analysts for several years. The answer seems to be that, "We have to take you seriously." After all, any conflict waged on German soil could be a death sentence for the nation. Anything affecting the likelihood of such a conflict must be evaluated seriously.

The answer is compelling but fails to place these initiatives in the context of other risks and opportunities. Germans assumed that INF was either a great danger or an essential instrument of peace. Germans might have pointed to the thousands of nuclear weapons in the world, and in Germany, and argued that INF might not matter one way or the other. Germans elevated INF above a wide range of political, economic, sociological, and environmental factors that might also lead to East-West tensions and ultimately threaten the security of the Federal Republic.

Undoubtedly one reason for this focus is the United States. The French might deploy neutron bombs, or other controversial weapons, but the impact is less significant. Germans have what may be an inappropriate respect for the seriousness of US initiatives. Much of this results from a respect for the American defense analytical community and the belief that decades of experience provides us with a level of expertise that must be taken seriously.

As argued above, elements of the American community do have a better opportunity to anticipate the evolution of new initiatives.

However, this advantage is not due to expertise in areas where Germans are most concerned. More realistic US assessments are due largely to more diverse experience with bureaucracy rather than any greater knowledge of strategic policy, force levels, classified information, or basic science.

Increasing the Power of German Analysis

What then should Germans do to increase their ability to discern the true motives and forces behind American security policy initiatives? Part of the problem may be self-correcting. The INF experience may make Germans more skeptical about the seriousness of US initiatives. The changing character of the security policy relationship may also have an effect. The emergence of the FRG as an economic superpower is likely to increase German self-confidence in dealing with the United States. This is likely to reduce the perceived power of initiatives emerging from the United States. In the future Germans may be less likely to believe that the typical Pentagon study will have an important effect on their lives.

Nonetheless Germans remain self-conscious about a perceived lack of depth in strategic affairs. Many German analysts point with pride at university programs that are now training a future stock of strategic analysts. Similarly my friend's recommendation to send a team of analysts to Washington to work with US strategists reflects interest in expanding the depth of strategic knowledge in the FRG.

Unfortunately such programs are likely to exacerbate German reactions to US initiatives rather than to place them in a more realistic context. The growth of a cohort of young strategic analysts, who have gained a detailed knowledge of nuclear strategy, but bring little to the table in terms of institutional or engineering experience, is likely to increase the seriousness with which strategic policy initiatives are treated. German knowledge of strategy is already adequate and the US is unlikely to be heavily influenced by German concerns about strategy. Germans would be better off trying to understand how strategy interacts with US industry and institutions. Rather than send a team of German analysts to study US strategy, such a team would be better sent to work in the bowels of the Pentagon or in the budget offices of a US aerospace firm.

The Strategic Initiatives of the 1990s

What then will be the strategic initiatives of the 1990s that Germans will need to evaluate? Obviously prediction is difficult in such a fluid strategic environment. Certainly the budget euphoria of the early 1980s has passed and fewer ideas will emerge from a system suffering declining budgets. The change of administrations will also slow down the flow of new initiatives. Top level Bush administration security experts are more heavily weighted toward the group invested in the status quo than the more adventurous concept developers.

Ironically, the new strategic era may lead to closer cooperation between these two groups. Arguments about limits on conventional force reductions and the continued role of flexible response, even after estimated conventional imbalances are eliminated, seem to utilize the creative forces while supporting the status quo. There is also increased discussion about the growing need to examine the role of US forces outside Europe. Given the possibility that defense requirements in Europe will change, despite interest in the status quo, new threats could serve the interest of both segments. In any event, it will continue to be this institutional interaction which dominates US security policy and which will continue to obscure true US intentions to the outsider. Those seeking to better understand our country should focus their attention on how these institutions behave rather than the ideas emerging from them.

12

A New Transatlantic Bargain? An Essay on US Policy toward European Defense Cooperation

Stanley R. Sloan[1]

INTRODUCTION

A few years ago, at a European-American conference on security policy in Bonn, West Germany, the discussion turned to the issue of European defense cooperation. After several hours of stimulating debate and speculation, one European participant - a member of the Dutch parliament - decided to test the official American reaction to the prospect of a more sturdy European pillar for the alliance. During the reception at the US Minister's residence that followed the day's discussion, the Dutch parliamentarian singled out two high level American diplomats to ask each independently the same question: what is the American attitude toward European defense cooperation? Approaching the first diplomat, the Dutch member of parliament asked his question and was told quite decisively that the United States had always supported the process of European integration and continued to do so, including European defense cooperation. "It's great!" this American concluded, as he headed for the buffet. The Dutch parliamentarian then caught the attention of

1 The author is the Specialist in U.S. Alliance Relations for the Congressional Research Service of the Library of Congress. These views are not necessarily those of CRS or the Library of Congress.

another American diplomat and asked his question. The second American official responded with what appeared initially to be a similar reply. "Of course we support European defense cooperation," he declared. But, after a slight pause, the second official added "just so long as they don't go off in the corner and gang up on us."

The Dutch parliamentarian's two simple inquiries had revealed a fundamental and profound truth about the US attitude toward European defense cooperation. Yes, the United States does support European defense cooperation. On the other hand, the United States has not come to terms with all the implications of such cooperation and may not yet be prepared to cope successfully with the likely consequences.

Recent progress toward intensified European defense cooperation raises a number of important questions for the NATO alliance and for US policy. How has the United States reacted to the early stages of the renaissance of European defense cooperation? What is likely to affect the manner in which it reacts in the future? What choices and decisions will the United States face and how should it attempt to influence the process?

NATO AS AN UNNATURAL BUT INTRACTABLE RELATIONSHIP

Before discussing these issues, it is only fair to the reader that the author reveal some of his prejudices concerning the Western alliance, its past, present and future. NATO is, and perhaps always has been, an unnatural relationship among sovereign, independent nations. This alliance relationship is of course more normal than that between the Soviet Union and its Warsaw Pact allies, but it still is awkward for independent nations to depend so heavily on an ally for the ultimate guarantee of their national security as the Europeans depend on the United States.

However, even though one would expect an unnatural or unbalanced relationship to be unstable, NATO remains a relatively intractable relationship. It is so intractable that no alternative to the alliance has appeared sufficiently feasible or desirable to stimulate revolutionary change. It is so intractable that the burden of proof has rested, and continues to rest, on the advocates of change.

A number of factors account for NATO's relative stability. First, while the Russian Bear may appear more friendly under Mikhail Gorbachev than it ever has in the post-war era, it still is a very big bear. Soviet power concentrated in Central Europe and supported by strategic nuclear forces and a growing global intervention capability is a major incentive for continuity in the West. In the absence of unilateral Soviet moves to diminish their own military power or of arms control agreements accomplishing that end, both the United States and West Europe are inspired to hold the alliance together.

From the US perspective, withdrawal from the alliance has been judged consistently by US administrations and a large majority in the US Congress and in American public opinion as a step that would bestow on the Soviet Union an immense increment in political influence that, ultimately, could be translated into military and strategic global advantages at great cost to US national security interests. From the perspective of most West Europeans, the best chance of remaining free and independent is to stay allied to the United States, so that US resources and strategic power can help balance Soviet power in Europe.

A second factor that tends to make the alliance relationship intractable is the fact that Germany remains divided. The Western alliance has provided a central part of the contemporary formula for dealing with the "German problem." The inclusion of West Germany in the Western alliance may not be a solution to the German problem but it has proven to be a most effective tool for managing the German problem. While many Germans may be uncomfortable with this formula as an indefinite solution, there is no consensus on alternatives to this approach.

The Soviet Union does not believe that a reunified Germany is in its interest. The East German leadership, for their part, see the German Democratic Republic's future as an autonomous international entity, not as a junior partner in a reunified Germany. For the forseeable future, it would appear that the Soviet Union would tolerate a reunified Germany only under conditions that would be unacceptable to the West. Moscow seems unlikely to tolerate any form of reunification that could produce a future threat to the Soviet Union. From a Western perspective, how would a Germany, so constrained that it could not threaten the Soviet Union, be sufficiently free of Soviet control to be acceptable to the West? As of today, such questions remain unanswered, accounting in part for NATO's persistence.

Thirdly, West Europe does not exist as a coherent political/military entity. Some would even argue whether it exists as a coherent economic entity, but at least in this area the European Community has much to show for the labors of the last thirty years. West Europe is not greater than the sum of its parts and, in many ways, it may even be less than the apparent sum of those parts.

Partly as a consequence of these factors, NATO remains a remarkably resilient alliance. This American-European coalition has survived close to forty years of military challenges, political differences and economic strains. On many occasions over those four decades, the alliance has been in political "crisis," and on just as many occasions has emerged strong and relatively united. It has survived in part because the arrangement responded to some vital common American and West European interests and no alternative has proved sufficiently compelling to replace it. Perhaps most importantly, the alliance has proven that it is capable of being adjusted to changing international circumstances.

FACTORS OF CHANGE

Over many years, however, a fundamental change has occurred in the US-European relationship, reflecting the gradual relative reduction in the international power and influence of the United States. As a consequence, the task of alliance leadership has become far more complex for the United States than it was in the 195Os. Strong determination in the hands of effective diplomats frequently carried the day for the United States in relations with its allies during NATO's early years, even when the allies had second thoughts about the wisdom of US policies. But US power has declined relative to that of America's European allies, and they have recovered much of the confidence in national judgment that they lost as a consequence of World War II. Grateful memories of US wartime and post war assistance have dimmed with the passing of time and the less flattering images of the United States growing out of Vietnam, Watergate, Iran, and US policies in Central America and elsewhere, have become more salient.

As one consequence, the time is past when the European allies will quietly defer to the United States on issues affecting the entire alliance. No European country today feels it necessary to hide its interpretation of national or alliance interests. At the same time, the alliance still requires American leadership, and the United States requires the support of its allies to achieve its international objectives. The strength of the alliance as ever depends on the extent of the consensus achieved among the members.

US leadership of the alliance, if it is to be effective, more than ever needs to take into account European perspectives. When US policies toward the alliance are designed to attract broad party and public support in West Europe, the alliance generally is strengthened. Policies that polarize political reactions either within Europe or between Europe and the United States tend to weaken support for NATO, and make it vulnerable to Soviet efforts to divide the allies.

In the last decade, judging by West European reactions to US policies and measured against the goal of enhancing consensus in NATO, the United States has not been a particularly effective alliance leader. From the European perspective, the Carter administration failed to provide consistent and predictable leadership. The allies found the Reagan administration more consistent, but the substance of administration policies did not prove in all cases to be a basis around which a broad European consensus would form.

In reaction to this perception of inadequate American leadership, no European country or grouping of countries emerged to fill the gap. Most analysts would argue that no one European country is capable of filling that gap. Most would also agree that the Europeans, acting together, could contribute more in terms of leadership and military efforts if their assets were better coordinated at the European level. But dramatic improvement in such coordination would require a much more substantial level of European intergration than exists, or perhaps is likely to exist in the foreseeable future.

In some ways, the limits on European cooperation are consciously self-imposed. Most European statesmen do not believe that even a coordinated European effort could replace the political leadership and deterrent power of the United States. Some Europeans are concerned that any serious European attempt to play a much greater role could serve as the excuse for the United States to withdraw from involvement in the defense of Europe. European policies therefore have generally sought to strike a balance between the danger of inspiring a US withdrawal either out of disgust with too little European effort or, on the other extreme, out of unwarranted confidence in European self-reliance capabilities.

Another consequence of the decline in relative American power is the resurgence in the US Congress of efforts to reduce the level of US contributions to NATO. This issue of defense burden-sharing and the US contribution to European defense, after being quiescent throughout the mid-to-late 197Os, gained new life in 1979 when the need for defense improvements became an issue in the debate over ratification of the SALT II treaty negotiated by President Jimmy Carter's administration with the Soviet Union. Before the Soviet invasion of Afghanistan, it appeared that the treaty might be ratified based on a political consensus that the United States would have to improve other areas of its defense capabilities in parallel with limiting its strategic nuclear forces. This consensus led both conservatives and liberals in the US Congress to ask what the allies were doing in the way of defense spending and improvements. Members continued to focus on this issue into the 198Os, many reaching the conclusion that a special push was required to get the allies to "do more."

Senator Sam Nunn provided a substantial push in 1984 when he submitted legislation threatening US troop reductions in Europe unless the allies met certain spending or defense improvement criteria. The measure barely failed to pass the Senate, and it sent a strong message to Europe. The Nunn initiative and the sentiment that it symbolized undoubtedly contributes to the willingness of the members of the Western European Union (WEU)[2] to re-launch this organization with the Rome Declaration issued by WEU foreign and defense ministers meeting on October 27, 1984.[3]

---

2 The members of the WEU are France, Great Britain, West Germany, Italy, Belgium, the Netherlands, and Luxembourg and, since 1988, Spain and Portugal.

3 The text of the Rome Declaration is published as Atlantic Document No. 56, in *Atlantic News*, Number 1329, 27 October 1984.

THE DOUBLE IMPACT OF INF

Perhaps the single most significant factor that has stimulated political activity in the defense cooperation area has been the INF missile saga. The many barriers to European defense cooperation - material, military, historical, political and psychological - have throughout most of the last 4O years been the source of substantial inertia. The last eight years of experience with the issue of intermediate range nuclear forces, however, appear to have provided the critical mass required to begin to move the process ahead. For the first few years of the INF debate, events pushed the European left in the direction of cooperation on the European level in security policy. The apparent end of the INF saga has pushed European conservative parties in the same general direction. This might not have been the ideal circumstance under which to stimulate positive change in the alliance, but now that the pot has been stirred up, the question is whether the alliance can produce a good stew.

In 1979, very few observers would have imagined that the INF story, as it unfolded, would stimulate both the left and the right in Europe to support intensified defense cooperation. The left coalesced in opposition to the deployment of the new INF missiles. One important symbol of the effect on the left was the formation of the "Scandilux" grouping of European socialist and social democratic parties. Beginning in 1981 as a low profile consultation on security policy among left parties in the Scandinavian and Benelux NATO countries, it was transformed into a forum including "observers" from other West European socialist parties. Throughout the 198Os, the Scandilux group has been a central focus for the formation of common perspectives on security policy issues among West Europe's socialist parties. One of the points of general consensus has been that the European countries should have greater influence over NATO's policies.

Given the early INF effect on the left, it is particularly ironic that the US-proposed "zero-option," originally vilified by the left as non-negotiable with the Soviet Union, ultimately, under new Soviet leadership, provided the basis for US-Soviet agreement, producing an outcome that the European left has to regard as far better than they could have reasonably hoped in the early 198Os.

On the other hand, the INF outcome stunned many on the political right in Europe. For these observers and politicians, the approach had been ill conceived in terms of NATO's strategic interests and the accord demonstrated that Europe's strategic interests were not at the top of the American political agenda. The American attitude had been signaled by US actions at the US-Soviet pre-summit in Reykjavik in October 1986 where not only the INF zero option was agreed in principle but where President Reagan proposed eliminating all ballistic nuclear missiles. This surprise initiative stunned Europeans who believed that ballistic missiles would continue to be the most reliable vehicle for American and European deterrent capabilities for the foreseeable future. More out of regret than anger, the political right in Europe turned strongly toward European defense cooperation as a necessary insurance policy against what became increasingly seen as an "inevitable" further US reduction in its contribution to European defense.

In 1987, conservative parties were in power in most European countries, and their concern could therefore be translated almost immediately into governmental actions. France and Germany agreed to form a "European brigade" and, in September 1987, the two countries conducted a major joint military exercise in Germany with combined French and German forces operating under French command. This first-ever major French-German military exercise had been in planning for several years, but the timing tended to highlight the clear trends in political thinking.

Perhaps most notably, the Western European Union countries in October 1987 issued a "Platform on European Security Interests" that constituted the most explicit and far-reaching European statement to date on common approaches to European security issues. The document emphasized the continuing importance for Western security interests of both nuclear weapons and American involvement in European defense.[4] Because European fears of a Soviet attack certainly are not on the rise, it is quite clear that the recent steps toward European defense cooperation are more in response to the perceived American threat of a reduced commitment to European defense than to concern that Warsaw Pact forces will invade West Europe any day soon.

---

4 The WEU declaration is published as Atlantic Document 561 in *Atlantic News*, 31 October 1987. For the complete text, see the Annex.

US POLICY

Since the Second World War, the United States has consistently declared its support for the process of European integration and the ultimate objective of European unity. Marshall Plan assistance to Europe in the important post-war reconstruction period was premised on a cooperative European approach to using that assistance. This encouragement supported the establishment of the European Community which has fundamentally transformed many aspects of relations among the West European countries. But in the early 195Os, European defense cooperation was an idea whose political time had not yet arrived. The European Defense Community proposal failed in the French National Assembly in 1954 largely because of French fears that the United States would withdraw from Europe once the defense community were established, leaving France exposed to a resurgent Germany.

In spite of this early setback, the United States continued to support the idea of a united Europe and to hope that integrated European defense forces could one day play a much larger role in balancing Soviet power in Europe. American attitudes toward European integration, however, have suffered from the maladies of inflated expectations about the process of European cooperation followed by excessive cynicism when the process did not move as expeditiously as hoped. The high hopes for European integration in some American policy circles in the 195Os and 196Os were followed in the 197Os by considerable skepticism about the process, as the European Economic Community got bogged down in mountains of surplus butter, budget debates, and endless battles among the members over the maze of community rules and regulations. Most American officials appeared to believe that the European "idea" had lost its way, and that the process had lost all political impetus.

Ironically, at a time when views in the United States had become most skeptical about European cooperation, the members of the European Community in the early 197Os initiated the process of European Political Cooperation that, in historical perspective, can be seen as laying some of the groundwork for future European defense cooperation. But the EC members carefully excluded "military aspects of cooperation" from their mandate to avoid conflict with NATO's prerogatives. The majority of American officials and politicians remained virtually unaware of the process. Other cooperative European ventures focused on cooperation in defense production, but the successes of this process (managed mainly through the Independent European Program Group - IEPG) were few and far between. From 1954 until recently, therefore, most of the initiatives toward European defense cooperation appeared unambitious and therefore neither threatening nor reassuring from an American perspective.

This situation began to change in the 198Os, as more Americans began to take note of the trends in Europe toward increased cooperation. At least one European scholar who has looked at this question in detail remained skeptical about the ability of the United States to accept the phenomenon of European cooperation that infringed on American political and security policy leadership. Following extensive interviews with US policy-makers and foreign policy "elites," Baard Bredrup Knudsen in 1982 concluded that "A number of significant changes of American foreign policy as well as of the dominant American mind-set are required if the United States is to cooperate with West Europe on the basis of an equal partnership." In Knudsen's judgment, "... it would take far greater statesmanship to arrest and reverse the political and societal trends in the United States which seem to make America incapable of adjusting to a transformed international environment in a constructive way than what the nation has fostered in recent years."[5]

The initial official American reactions to the revitalization of the Western European Union suggested that Knudsen might have been right. Following the 1984 Rome Declaration that signaled the political resuscitation of the WEU, the WEU members decided to try to formulate a coordinated European perspective on the US Strategic Defense Initiative (SDI). Early in 1985, the US State Department reportedly sent cables to ambassadors in WEU member capitals instructing the US representatives to discourage the WEU countries

5 Baard Bredrup Knudsen, *The 'European Challenge' versus the 'American Problem': Europe and American Foreign Policy in the 198Os* (A manuscript prepared as part of a research project conducted under the auspices of the Institute of Political Science, University of Oslo and the School of International Service, The American University entitled "Political Union in Western Europe and the Atlantic Alliance: Compatible Elements or Increased Strain?"), November 1982, p.V.

from trying to shape a common attitude toward SDI.[6] The WEU members then backed away from the project. It is difficult to know whether this US message had a more profound effect than simply crushing the idea of a coordinated European position on SDI, but it may have been more than a coincidence that in the two years that followed, the WEU revitalization project seemed to lose forward momentum. In private conversations, West Germans complained that the French - the main political motor for the WEU revitalization undertaking - seemed to have lost interest. It may also be true that the American signal was interpreted - rightly or wrongly - in Europe as a call for slowing the process to a pace more tolerable to Washington.

In any case, the Reykjavik summit stunned the European governments so deeply that any reticence about moving forward appeared to have been removed. And, importantly, the official American reaction to these trends in 1987 appears to have changed substantially from the approach taken just two years earlier. In two major speeches late in 1987, President Reagan explicitly supported the process of European defense cooperation and the construction of a European pillar in the Atlantic alliance.

In a speech to the cadets of the US Military Academy at West Point, President Reagan observed that

> ... we have seen the emergence among some of our European allies of a willingness, even an eagerness, to seek a larger, more closely coordinated role for Western Europe in providing its own defense. We Americans welcome this.[7]

Reagan went on to note that the United States has for many years been the "senior partner" in the alliance, but that "now the alliance should become more and more among equals, indeed, an alliance between continents."

---

6 Elizabeth Pond, Europe seems to lose interest in its newly revived security forum, in *Christian Science Monitor*, 23 April 1985, p.1O.

7 Ronald Reagan, The Agenda of U.S.-Soviet Relations, Address to the Corps of Cadets of the U.S. Military Academy, West Point, New York, 28 October 1987, as reprinted by the U.S. Department of State, Bureau of Public Affairs, in *Current Policy*, No. 1O21, p. 3.

It became clear that this was not just a one-time phenomenon but a conscious choice of the President's advisors when Reagan, speaking to a Washington audience on 14 December 1987 pledged to sustain the American commitment to European defense in the wake of the INF treaty but repeated the language from the West Point speech calling for an alliance "more among equals."[8]

It therefore appears that the Reagan administration decided to try to turn the unintended effect of the INF treaty in positive directions, encouraging the process of European defense cooperation. While, in theory, this approach should be welcomed by the Europeans, the reaction will no doubt be qualified. Some Europeans inevitably will interpret the approach as further evidence of long term trends in the United States leading to an American withdrawal. This again illustrates the damned-if-you-do-and-damned-if-you-don't aspect of the US-European alliance relationship. Such difficulties and concerns will continue as does the process of transformation of the alliance toward a "more equal" relationship.

THE FUTURE

Over the longer term, political trends in alliance countries suggest that re-establishing a more solid consensus may require fundamental changes in the structural relationship between the United States and the West European allies and among the European allies themselves. To ensure continued US support for the alliance, the allies will come under increasing pressure to demonstrate their willingness to assume progressively greater shares of the NATO defense burden. Under current resource constraints, they may be able to do so only by rationalizing their efforts and intensifying defense cooperation among themselves. To ensure a broader European political base of support for the alliance, the United States will likely be called on to share more fully leadership responsibilities and political influence in NATO with the Europeans. This process of realignment cannot be expected to occur overnight. But current political and economic trends suggest increased tensions in alliance

---

8 Gene Grabowski, Reagan ties strings to next accord on missiles, in *Washington Times*, 15 December 1987, p. 1.

relationships during the 1990s in the absence of movement in these directions.

Shaping a New Transatlantic Bargain

In the wake of the INF accord, it has become increasingly popular for analysts and politicians to argue that NATO should undertake a "new Harmel exercise." In the mid-1960s, at an earlier time of transition and change in the transatlantic relationship, the NATO allies selected Belgian Foreign Minister Pierre Harmel to lead a study of NATO's purposes. Harmel's report, adopted by NATO in December 1967, recommended that the alliance subsequently be seen as a Western instrument not just for defense and deterrence, but also for pursuing détente with the East.

The Harmel report's "defense and détente" combination provided an intellectual and political framework for NATO policies which accommodated the growing split in the alliance between left and right. By bridging two different views of the East-West politico-military situation, it broadened the potential base of support for NATO. Subsequently, instead of providing a focus for polarization among Western politicans, the alliance served as a fulcrum for balancing divergent perspectives on the requirements for the West's security policy in Europe.

The defense, deterrence and détente formula remains remarkably relevant for the NATO alliance in the late 1980s. But some new gaps have opened that may need to be closed to sustain NATO's viability in the future. The seemingly-endless debate in the alliance about defense burden-sharing has worn its way through a decade of reports and objectives that have, in fact, changed very little the structure of relationships within the alliance. The debate now may be turning away from gimmicks and bureaucratic gadgetry toward some fundamental political decisions about the future directions of the alliance.

Under the circumstances, a new "Harmel" exercise would quite likely focus on the perceived need for a shifting of burdens and responsibilities in the alliance toward a more substantial and unified European role. The outcome might well be a formula calling for NATO policies of defense, détente, and devolution toward a new transatlantic bargain.[9] Such a decision might provide the necessary political impetus and policy framework to ensure that, over time, alliance burdens and responsibilities would come to rest more equally on European and American pillars of the alliance.

Expanding NATO's policy framework in this manner would likely depend on the allies making a number of new, or renewed, political commitments. A new administration in the United States might be called on to affirm its intent to continue a strong American contribution to the alliance, including a substantial troop presence in Europe and nuclear forces structured and deployed in ways that would strengthen deterrence for the entire alliance. Without such a commitment as part of the bargain, the European allies might be reluctant to reach for their new role in the alliance, fearing that it would provoke an American withdrawal.

In return, the European allies would pledge to intensify defense cooperation among themselves while ensuring that such cooperation increased the West's defensive capabilities while not undermining its political cohesion. Such a high-level political commitment would be necessary to overcome the political and bureaucratic inertia that has frustrated many plans for stimulating European defense cooperation.

Finally, the allies could jointly agree that all future alliance force posture, infrastructure, programmatic and arms control decisions would take into consideration the agreed need for the European allies progressively to assume a greater share of NATO burdens and responsibilities.

This new policy framework would capture a blend of continuity and change, just as the Harmel formula that it would replace did two decades earlier. It might provide the basis on which the United States and its European allies could revitalize their relationship by bridging some of the differences that currently trouble transatlantic malaise about burdens and responsibilities within the alliance.

---

9 For the author's analysis of the need for such a new bargain see Stanley R. Sloan, *NATO's Future: Toward a New Transatlantic Bargain* (Washington, D.C.: National Defense University Press 1985 and London: Macmillan 1986).

Continuing Reliance on US Leadership

The perceived need for major evolutionary change should not obscure the fact, however, that until such changes have a chance to mature, the United States will continue to bear the principal weight of making NATO work. A great variety of domestic and international factors other than the goal of strengthening the NATO consensus influences US policy decisions. But in so far as the United States still places a high priority on NATO consensus, its policies and rhetoric would be called on to respond effectively to the Harmel Report's formula of maintaining a strong defense, an effective deterrent posture, and an active pursuit of improved relations with the East, while at the same time facilitating the transition toward a new bargain with its European allies.

ANNEX

Documents

Treaty between the French Republic and the Federal Republic of Germany concerning Franco-German Cooperation (Paris, 22 January 1963)

Preamble to the Act of the Federal German Government ratifying the Franco-German Treaty of Cooperation (approved by the Bundestag, 16 May 1963)

Protocol to the Treaty of 22 January 1963 between the Federal Republic of Germany and the French Republic on Franco-German Cooperation (Paris, 22 January 1988)

Western European Union Platform on European Security Interests (The Hague, 27 October 1987)

Single European Act (Luxembourg, 17 February 1986 and The Hague, 28 February 1986) (Excerpts)

Joint Declaration on the Establishment of Official Relations between the European Economic Community and the Council for Mutual Economic Assistance (Luxembourg, 25 June 1988)

European Council Meeting of the Heads of State and Government (Rhodes, 2-3 December 1988) (Excerpts)

European Council Meeting of the Heads of State and Government (Madrid, 26-27 June 1989) (Excerpts)

Institutions for European Security Cooperation

European Political Cooperation

Western European Union

Independent European Program Group

Eurogroup

DOCUMENTS

TREATY BETWEEN THE FRENCH REPUBLIC AND THE FEDERAL REPUBLIC OF GERMANY CONCERNING FRANCO-GERMAN COOPERATION

(Paris, 22 January 1963)*

In connection with the joint declaration of the President of the French Republic and the Federal Chancellor of the Federal Republic of Germany of 22 January 1963,[1] concerning the organization and principles of cooperation between the two States, the following provisions have been agreed upon:

I. ORGANIZATION

1. The Heads of State and Government shall issue as and when necessary the requisite directives and shall regularly follow the implementation of the programme specified below. They shall meet as often as may be necessary for this purpose and in principle at least twice a year.

2. The Ministers for Foreign Affairs shall ensure the implementation of the programme as a whole. They shall meet at least

* Federal Republic of Germany, *Documents 1962* (Bonn: Press and Information Office, 1962). The Treaty came into force on 2 July 1963, the date by which each of the two Governments had notified the other that its domestic requirements had been fulfilled, in accordance with part III, article 5.

1 Federal Republic of Germany, *Documents 1962* (Bonn: Press and Information Office, 1962).

every three months. Without prejudice to normal contacts through the Embassies, the senior officials of the two Ministries of Foreign Affairs responsible for political, economic and cultural affairs shall meet each month, alternately at Paris and at Bonn, to determine the status of current problems and to prepare for the meeting of the Ministers. In addition, the diplomatic missions and consulates of the two countries, and their permanent missions to international organizations, shall establish such contacts as may be necessary concerning problems of mutual interest.

3. There shall be regular meetings between responsible authorities of the two countries in the fields of defense, education and youth affairs. Such meetings shall in no way affect the operations of pre-existing organs - the Franco-German Cultural Commission, the Permanent Military Staff Group - whose activities shall, on the contrary, be expanded. The Ministers for Foreign Affairs shall be represented at such meetings in order to ensure the overall coordination of cooperation.

(a) The Minister of the Armed Forces and the Minister of Defense shall meet at least once every three months. The French Minister of Education shall likewise meet, at the same intervals, the person designated on the German side to follow the implementation of the programme of cooperation in the cultural field.

(b) The Chiefs of Staff of the two countries shall meet at least once every two months; if they are unable to attend a meeting, they shall be replaced by their responsible representatives.

(c) The French High Commissioner for Youth and Sport shall meet, at least once every two months, the Federal Minister for Family and Youth Affairs or his representative.

4. In each of the two countries, an interministerial commission shall be appointed to follow problems of cooperation. It shall be presided over by a senior official of the Ministry of Foreign Affairs and shall include representatives of all the departments concerned. Its function shall be to coordinate the action of the Ministries concerned and to report to its Government at regular intervals on the status of Franco-German cooperation. It shall also have the function of submitting such suggestions as may be appropriate concerning the implementaion of the programme of cooperation and its possible extension to new fields.

II. PROGRAMME

A. Foreign affairs

1. The two Governments shall consult each other, prior to any decision, on all important questions of foreign policy, and particularly on questions of mutual interest, with a view to achieving as far as possible an analogous position. Such consultations shall cover, *inter alia*, the following subjects:

- Problems concerning the European communities and European political cooperation;
- East-West relations, in both the political and the economic fields;
- Matters dealt with in the North Atlantic Treaty Organization and the various international organizations which are of interest to the two Governments, particularly in the Council of Europe, the Western European Union, the Organization for Economic Cooperation and Development, the United Nations and its specialized agencies.

2. The collaboration already established in the field of information shall be continued and developed between the departments concerned in Paris and Bonn and between the missions in third countries.

3. As regards aid to developing countries, the two Governments shall systematically compare their programmes with a view to maintaining close coordination. They shall study the possibility of undertaking activities jointly. Inasmuch as several ministerial departments are competent in respect of such matters on both the French and the German sides, it shall be the responsibility of the two Ministries of Foreign Affairs to determine jointly the practical bases for such collaboration.

4. The two Governments shall study jointly the means of strengthening their cooperation in other important sectors of economic policy, such as agricultural and forestry policies, energy policies, communication and transport problems and industrial development, within the framework of the Common Market, and export credit policies.

B. Defense

1. The objectives pursued in this field shall be the following:

a) As regards strategy and tactics, the competent authorities of the two countries shall endeavour to align their theories with a view to achieving common approaches. Franco-German operational research institutes shall be established.

b) Exchanges of personnel between the armed forces shall be increased; they shall involve, in particular, instructors and students of the Staff Colleges; they may include the temporary detachment of entire units. In order to facilitate such exchanges, both sides shall endeavour to provide practical language instruction for the personnel concerned.

c) As regards armaments, the two Governments shall endeavour to organize joint teamwork as from the stage of formulation of appropriate armament projects and of preparation of the financing plans.

For this purpose, Mixed Commissions shall study, and shall undertake a comparative review of, the research in progress on such projects in both countries. They shall submit proposals to the Ministers, who shall review them during their quarterly meetings and shall issue the necessary directives for the implementation thereof.

2. The Governments shall study the conditions in which Franco-German collaboration may be established in the field of civil defense.

C. Education and youth affairs

As regards education and youth affairs, the proposals contained in the French and German memoranda of 19 September and 8 November 1962 shall be studied in accordance with the procedures indicated above.

1. In the field of education, efforts shall be directed primarily to the following points:

(a) Language instruction:

The two Governments recognize that knowledge in each of the two countries of the language of the other is of vital importance to Franco-German cooperation. They shall accordingly endeavour to take positive action to increase the number of French schoolchildren learning German and of German schoolchildren learning French.

The Federal Government shall consider with the Governments of the Länder, which are competent in the matter, how it is possible to introduce regulations enabling this objective to be achieved.

Practical instruction in the French language should be organized in all institutions of higher education in Germany and in the German language in all such institutions in France and should be open to all students.

(b) Problem of equivalence:

The competent authorities of both countries shall be requested to expedite the adoption of provisions concerning the equivalence of periods of school attendance, examinations and university degrees and diplomas.

(c) Cooperation in the field of scientific research:

Research agencies and scientific institutes shall develop their contacts with each other, beginning with more thorough exchanges of information; concerted research programmes shall be established in those disciplines in which this proves to be possible.

2. The youth of the two countries shall be offered every opportunity to strengthen the ties which exist between them and to deepen their mutual understanding. Group exchanges shall, in particular, be increased in number.

An agency to develop such opportunities and to promote exchanges, headed by an autonomous governing council, shall be set up by the two countries. The agency shall have at its disposal a Franco-German common fund to be used for meetings and exchanges of schoolchildren, students, young craftsmen and young workers between the two countries.

III. FINAL PROVISIONS

1. The requisite directives shall be issued in each country for the immediate implementation of the foregoing. The Ministers for Foreign Affairs shall determine, at each of their meetings, what progress has been achieved.

2. The two Governments shall keep the Governments of the other member states of the European communities informed of the development of Franco-German cooperation.

3. With the exception of the provisions concerning defense, this Treaty shall also apply to Land Berlin, provided that the Government of the Federal Republic of Germany has not delivered a contrary declaration to the Government of the French Republic within three months from the date of entry into force of the Treaty.

4. The two Governments may make such adjustments as may prove desirable for the implementation of this Treaty.

5. This Treaty shall enter into force as soon as each of the two Governments has notified the other that the domestic requirements for its entry into force have been fulfilled.

PREAMBLE TO THE ACT OF THE FEDERAL GERMAN GOVERNMENT RATIFYING THE FRANCO-GERMAN TREATY OF COOPERATION

(approved by the Bundestag, 16 May 1963)*

CONVINCED that the treaty concluded on 22 January 1963[1] between the Federal Republic of Germany and the French Republic will intensify and develop the reconciliation and friendship between the German and the French peoples.

STATING that this treaty does not affect the rights and obligations resulting from multilateral treaties concluded by the Federal Republic of Germany,

RESOLVED to serve by the application of this treaty the great aims to which the Federal Republic of Germany, in concert with the other States allied to her, has aspired for years, and which determine her policy,

TO WIT the preservation and consolidation of the unity of the free nations and in particular of a close partnership between Europe and the United States of America, the realization of the right of self-determination for the German people, and the restoration of German unity, collective defense within the framework of the North Atlantic Alliance and the integration of the armed forces of the States bound together in that Alliance, the unification of Europe by following the course adopted by the establishment of the European Communities, with the inclusion of Great Britain and other States wishing to accede, and the further strengthening of those Communities, the elimination of trade barriers by negotiations between the European Economic Community, Great Britain, and the United States of

---

* Federal Republic of Germany, *The Bulletin*, May 21, 1963 (Bonn: Press and Information Office, 1963).

1 For the text of the treaty, see the previous document.

America as well as other States within the framework of the General Agreement on Tariffs and Trade,

CONSCIOUS that a Franco-German cooperation inspired by such aims will benefit all nations and serve the peace of the world and will thereby also promote the welfare of the German and French peoples,

the Bundestag enacts the following Law...

PROTOCOL TO THE TREATY OF 22 JANUARY 1963 BETWEEN THE FEDERAL REPUBLIC OF GERMANY AND THE FRENCH REPUBLIC ON FRANCO-GERMAN COOPERATION

(Paris, 22 January 1988)*

The Federal Republic of Germany and the French Republic,

- convinced that European unification will remain incomplete as long as security and defense are not included,
- determined for this purpose to expand and intensify their cooperation on the basis of the Treaty of 22 January 1963 on Franco-German cooperation, whose translation into practice was manifested in particular by the declarations of 22 October 1982 and 28 February 1986,
- convinced of the need, in conformity with the declaration issued by the ministers of the Member States of the Western European Union at The Hague on 27 October 1987, to develop a European identity in the field of defense and security which, in accordance with the obligations of solidarity assumed under the modified Brussels Treaty, effectively gives expression to the community of fate linking the two countries,
- resolved to ensure that, in consonance with Article V of the modified Brussels Treaty, their determination to defend all States parties to that treaty at their frontiers is made visible and is strengthened by the necessary means,
- convinced that the strategy of deterrence and defense, on which their security rests and which is designed to prevent any war, must continue to be based on a suitable combination of nuclear and conventional forces,
- determined to maintain, in unison with their other partners and with due regard for their own options in the North Atlantic Alliance,

---

* Federal Republic of Germany, *Documents 1988* (Bonn: Press and Information Office, 1988).

an adequate military contribution with a view to preventing any aggression or attempt at intimidation in Europe,

- convinced that all nations of our continent have the same right to live in peace and freedom and that strengthening both of the foregoing is the prerequisite for progress towards a just and lasting peaceful order in the whole of Europe,
- determined to ensure that their cooperation serves these goals,
- conscious of their common security interests and resolved to harmonize their views on all matters concerning the defense and security of Europe,

have to this end agreed as follows:

Article 1

To give expression to the community of fate linking the two countries and to develop their cooperation in the field of defense and security, a Franco-German Defense and Security Council shall be established in conformity with the goals and provisions of the Treaty of 22 January 1963 between the Federal Republic of Germany and the French Republic on Franco-German Cooperation.

Article 2

The Council shall consist of the Heads of State or Government and the foreign and defense ministers. The chief of staff of the Bundeswehr and the chief of staff of the French Armed Forces shall take part ex officio.

The Committee of the Council shall comprise the foreign and defense ministers. Senior civil servants and members of the military responsible for bilateral cooperation in the field of defense and security may be called upon to participate in its work.

Article 3

The Franco-German Defense and Security Council shall meet at least twice a year alternately in the Federal Republic of Germany and in France.

Its work shall be prepared by the Committee of the Council, which shall be assisted by the Franco-German Defense and Security Commission.

Article 4

The work of the Franco-German Defense and Security Council shall in particular serve the following purposes:

- elaboration of common concepts in the field of defense and security;
- increasing coordination between the two countries in all matters concerning Europe's security, including the sphere of arms control and disarmament;
- decision-making in respect of the mixed military units set up through mutual agreement;
- decision-making regarding joint maneuvers, the training of military personnel and support arrangements designed to strengthen the capacity of both countries' armed forces to cooperate with each other both in peacetime and in the event of a crisis or war;
- improvement of the interoperability of the equipment of both countries' armed forces;
- development and intensification of armaments cooperation with due regard for the need to maintain and strengthen an adequate industrial and technological potential in Europe for the purpose of ensuring common defense.

Article 5

The Secretariat of the Franco-German Defense and Security Council and of the Committee of the Council shall be headed by representatives of both countries. The Secretariat shall be based in Paris.

Article 6

This Protocol shall be annexed to the Treaty of 22 January 1963 between the Federal Republic of Germany and the French Republic on Franco-German Cooperation and shall form an integral part of that treaty.

It shall enter into force as soon as the two Governments have informed each other that the respective national requirements for such entry into force have been fulfilled.

Done at Paris on 22 January 1988 in duplicate in the German and French languages, both texts being equally authentic.

WESTERN EUROPEAN UNION PLATFORM ON EUROPEAN SECURITY INTERESTS

(The Hague, 27 October1987)*

1. Stressing the dedication of our countries to the principles upon which our democracies are based and resolved to preserve peace in freedom, we, the Foreign and Defence Ministers of the member states of WEU, reaffirm the common destiny which binds our countries.

2. We recall our commitment to build a European union in accordance with the single European act, which we all signed as members of the European Community. We are convinced that the construction of an integrated Europe will remain incomplete as long as it does not include security and defense.

3. An important means to this end is the modified Brussels Treaty. This treaty, with its far-reaching obligations to collective defense, marked one of the early steps on the road to European unification. It also envisages the progressive association of other states inspired by the same ideals and animated by the like determination. We see the revitalisation of WEU as an important contribution to the broader process of European unification.

4. We intend therefore to develop a more cohesive European defense identity which will translate more effectively into practice the obligations of solidarity to which we are committed through the modified Brussels and North Atlantic Treaties.

5. We highly value the continued involvement in this endeavour of the WEU Assembly which is the only European parliamentary body mandated by treaty to discuss all aspects of security including defense.

---

* Western European Union, *The Reactivation of WEU. Statements and Communiqués 1984-1987* (Great Britain: Newsomeprinters Ltd., 1988).

I. Our starting point is the present conditions of European security:

1. Europe remains at the centre of East-West relations and, forty years after the end of the second world war, a divided continent. The human consequences of this division remain unacceptable, although certain concrete improvements have been made on a bilateral level and on the basis of the Helsinki final act. We owe it to our people to overcome this situation and to exploit in the interest of all Europeans the opportunities for further improvements which may present themselves.

2. New developments in East-West relations, particularly in arms control and disarmament, and also other developments, for example in the sphere of technology, could have far-reaching implications for European security.

3. We have not yet witnessed any lessening of the military build-up which the Soviet Union has sustained over so many years. The geostrategic situation of Western Europe makes it particularly vulnerable to the superior conventional, chemical and nuclear forces of the Warsaw Pact. This is the fundamental problem for European security. The Warsaw Pact's superior conventional forces and its capability for surprise attack and large-scale offensive action are of special concern in this context.

4. Under these conditions the security of the Western European countries can only be ensured in close association with our North American allies. The security of the alliance is indivisible. The partnership between the two sides of the Atlantic rests on the twin foundations of shared values and interests. Just as the commitment of the North American democracies is vital to Europe's security, a free, independent and increasingly more united Western Europe is vital to the security of North America.

5. It is our conviction that the balanced policy of the Harmel report remains valid. Political solidarity and adequate military strength within the Atlantic Alliance, arms control, disarmament and the search for genuine détente continue to be integral parts of this policy. Military security and a policy of détente are not contradictory but complementary.

II. European security should be based on the following criteria:

1. It remains our primary objective to prevent any kind of war. It is our purpose to preserve our security by maintaining defense readiness and military capabilities adequate to deter aggression and intimidation without seeking military superiority.

2. In the present circumstances and as far as we can foresee, there is no alternative to the western strategy for the prevention of war, which has ensured peace in freedom for an unprecedented period of European history. To be credible and effective, the strategy of deterrence and defense must continue to be based on an adequate mix of appropriate nuclear and conventional forces, only the nuclear element of which can confront a potential aggressor with an unacceptable risk.

3. The substantial presence of United States conventional and nuclear forces plays an irreplaceable part in the defense of Europe. They embody the American commitment to the defense of Europe and provide the indispensable linkage with the United States strategic deterrent.

4. European forces play an essential role: the overall credibility of the western strategy of deterrence and defense cannot be maintained without a major European contribution not least because the conventional imbalance affects the security of Western Europe in a very direct way.

The Europeans have a major responsibility both in the field of conventional and nuclear defense. In the conventional field, the forces of the WEU member states represent an essential part of the alliance. As regards nuclear forces, all of which form a part of deterrence, the cooperative arrangements that certain member states maintain with the United States are necessary for the security of Europe. The independent forces of France and the United Kingdom contribute to overall deterrence and security.

5. Arms control and disarmament are an integral part of western security policy and not an alternative to it. They should lead to a stable balance of forces at the lowest level compatible with our security. Arms control policy should, like our defense policy, take into account the specific European security interests in an evolving situation. It must be consistent with the maintenance of the strategic unity of the alliance and should not preclude closer European

defense cooperation. Arms control agreements have to be effectively verifiable and stand the test of time. East and West have a common interest in achieving this.

III. The member states of WEU intend to assume fully their responsibilities:

A. In the field of western defense

1. We recall the fundamental obligation of Article V of the modified Brussels Treaty to provide all the millitary and other aid and assistance in our power in the event of armed attack on any one of us. This pledge, which reflects our common destiny, reinforces our commitments under the Atlantic Alliance, to which we all belong, and which we are resolved to preserve.

2. It is our conviction that a more united Europe will make a stronger contribution to the alliance, to the benefit of western security as a whole. This will enhance the European role in the alliance and ensure the basis for a balanced partnership across the Atlantic. We are resolved to strengthen the European pillar of the alliance.

3. We are each determined to carry our share of the common defense in both the conventional and nuclear field, in accordance with the principles of risk- and burden-sharing which are fundamental to allied cohesion:

- in the conventional field, all of us will continue to play our part in the on-going efforts to improve our defenses;
- in the nuclear field also, we shall continue to carry our share: some of us by pursuing appropriate co-operative arrangements with the United States; the United Kingdom and France by continuing to maintain independent nuclear forces, the credibility of which they are determined to preserve.

4. We remain determined to pursue European integration including security and defense and make a more effective contribution to the common defense of the West.

To this end we shall:

- ensure that our determination to defend any member country at its borders is made clearly manifest by means of appropriate arrangements,

- improve our consultations and extend our co-ordination in defense and security matters and examine all practical steps to this end,

- make the best possible use of the existing institutional mechanisms to involve the defense ministers and their representatives in the work of WEU,

- see to it that the level of each country's contribution to the common defense adequately reflects its capabilities,

- aim at a more effective use of existing resources, *inter alia* by expanding bilateral and regional military cooperation, pursue our efforts to maintain in Europe a technologically advanced industrial base and intensify armaments cooperation,

- concert our policies on crises outside Europe in so far as they may affect our security interests.

5. Emphasising the vital contribution of the non-WEU members of the alliance to the common security and defense, we will continue to keep them informed of our activities.

B. In the Field of arms control and disarmament

1. We shall pursue an active arms control and disarmament policy aimed at influencing future developments in such a way as to enhance security and to foster stability and cooperation in the whole of Europe. The steadfastness and cohesion of the alliance and close consultations among all the allies remain essential if concrete results are to be brought about.

2. We are committed to elaborate further our comprehensive concept of arms control and disarmament in accordance with the alliance's declaration of 12th June 1987 and we will work within the framework of this concept as envisaged particularly in paragraphs 7 and 8 of this declaration. An agreement between the United States and the Soviet Union for the global elimination of land-based INF missiles with a range between 5OO and 5 5OO km will constitute an important element of such an approach.

3. In pursuing such an approach we shall exploit all opportunities to make further progress towards arms reductions, compatible with our security and with our priorities, taking into account the fact that work in this area raises complex and interrelated issues. We shall evaluate them together, bearing in mind the

political and military requirements of our security and progress in the different negotiations.

C. In the field of East-West dialogue and cooperation

1. The common responsibility of all Europeans is not to preserve the peace but to shape it contructively. The Helsinki final act continues to serve as our guide to the fulfillment of the objective of gradually overcoming the division of Europe. We shall therefore continue to make full use of the CSCE process in order to promote comprehensive cooperation among all participating states.

2. The possibilities contained in the final act should be fully exploited. We therefore intend:

- to seek to increase the transparency of military potentials and activities and the calculability of behaviour in accordance with the Stockholm document of 1986 by further confidence-building measures;
- vigorously to pursue our efforts to provide for the full respect of human rights without which no genuine peace is possible;
- to open new mutually beneficial possibilities in the fields of economy, technology, science and the protection of the environment;
- to achieve more opportunities for the people in the whole of Europe to move freely and to exchange opinions and information and to intensify cultural echanges, and thus to promote concrete improvements for the benefit of all people in Europe.

It is our objective to further European integration. In this perspective we will continue our efforts towards closer security cooperation, maintaining coupling with the United States and ensuring conditions of equal security in the alliance as a whole.

We are conscious of the common heritage of our divided continent, all the people of which have an equal right to live in peace and freedom. That is why we are determined to do all in our power to achieve our ultimate goal of a just and lasting peaceful order in Europe.

SINGLE EUROPEAN ACT
(Luxembourg, 17 February 1986 and The Hague, 28 February 1986)
Excerpts*

TITLE I: COMMON PROVISIONS

Article 1

The European Communities and European Political Cooperation shall have as their objective to contribute together to making concrete progress towards European unity.

The European Communities shall be founded on the Treaties establishing the European Coal and Steel Community, the European Economic Community, the European Atomic Energy Community and on the subsequent Treaties and Acts modifying or supplementing them.

Political Cooperation shall be governed by Title III. The provisions of the Title shall confirm and supplement the procedures agreed in the reports of Luxembourg (1970), Copenhagen (1973), London (1981), the Solemn Declaration on European Union (1983) and the practices gradually established among the Member States.

Article 2

The European Council shall bring together the Heads of State or of Government of the Member States and the President of the Commission of the European Communities. They shall be assisted by the Ministers for Foreign Affairs and by a Member of the Commission.

The European Council shall meet at least twice a year.

---

* Bulletin of the European Communities, *Single European Act* (Supplement 2/86) (Luxembourg: Office for Official Publications of the European Communities, 1986).

Article 3

The institutions of the European Communities, henceforth designated as referred to hereafter, shall exercise their powers and jurisdiction under the conditions and for the purposes provided for by the Treaties establishing the Communities and by the subsequent Treaties and Acts modifying or supplementing them and by the provisions of Title II.

The institutions and bodies responsible for European Political Cooperation shall exercise their powers and jurisdiction under the conditions and for the purposes laid down in Title III and in the documents referred to in the third paragraph of Article 1.

TITLE II: PROVISIONS AMENDING THE TREATIES ESTABLISHING THE EUROPEAN COMMUNITIES

. . .

Chapter II: Provisions amending the Treaty establishing the European Economic Community

. . .

Section II: Provisions relating to the foundations and the policy of the Community

Subsection I - Internal market

Article 13

The EEC Treaty shall be supplemented by the following provisions:

"Article 8 A

The Community shall adopt measures with the aim of progressively establishing the internal market over a period expiring on 31 December 1992, in accordance with the provisions of this Article and of Articles 8 B, 8 C, 28, 57 (2), 59, 70 (1), 83, 99, 100 A and 100 B and without prejudice to the other provisions of this Treaty.

The internal market shall comprise an area without internal frontiers in which the free movement of goods, persons, services and capital is ensured in accordance with the provisions of this Treaty."

Article 14

The EEC Treaty shall be supplemented by the following provisions:

"Article 8 B

The Commission shall report to the Council before 31 December 1988 and again before 31 December 1990 on the progress made towards achieving the internal market within the time limit fixed in Article 8 A.

The Council, acting on a qualified majority on a proposal from the Commission, shall determine the guidelines and conditions necessary to ensure balanced progress in all the sectors concerned."

Article 15

The EEC Treaty shall be supplemented by the following provisions:

"Article 8 C

When drawing up its proposals with a view to achieving the objectives set out in Article 8 A, the Commission shall take into account the extent of the effort that certain economies showing differences in development will have to sustain during the period of establishment of the internal market and it may propose appropriate provisions.

If these provisions take the form of derogations, they must be of a temporary nature and must cause the least possible disturbance to the functioning of the common market."

Article 16

1. Article 28 of the EEC Treaty shall be replaced by the following provisions:

"Article 28

Any autonomous alteration or suspension of duties in the common customs tariff shall be decided by the Council acting by a qualified majority on a proposal from the Commission."

2. In Article 57 (2) of the EEC Treaty, the second sentence shall be replaced by the following:

"Unanimity shall be required for directives the implementation of which involves in at least one Member State amendment of the existing principles laid down by law governing the professions with respect to training and conditions of access for natural persons."

3. In the second paragraph of Article 59 of the EEC Treaty, the term "unanimously" shall be replaced by *"a qualified majority"*.

4. In article 70 (1) of the EEC Treaty, the last two sentences shall be replaced by the following:

"For this purpose the Council shall issue directives, acting by a qualified majority. It shall endeavor to attain the highest possible degree of liberalization. Unanimity shall be required for measures which constitute a step back as regards the liberalization of capital movements."

5. In Article 84 (2) of the EEC Treaty, the term "unanimously" shall be replaced by *"a qualified majority"*.

6. Article 84 of the EEC Treaty shall be supplemented by the following paragraph:

"The procedural provisions of Article 75 (1) and (3) shall apply."

Article 17

Article 99 of the EEC Treaty shall be replaced by the following provisions:

"Article 99

The Council shall, acting unanimously on a proposal from the Commission and after consulting the European Parliament, adopt provisions for the harmonization of legislation concerning turnover taxes, excise duties and other forms of indirect taxation to the extent that such harmonization is necessary to ensure the establishment and the functioning of the internal market within the time limit laid down in Article 8 A."

Article 18

The EEC Treaty shall be supplemented by the following provisions:

"Article 100 A

1. By way of derogation from Article 100 and save where otherwise provided in this Treaty, the following provisions shall apply for the achievement of the objectives set out in Article 8 A. The Council shall, acting by a qualified majority on a proposal from the Commission in cooperation with the European Parliament and the Economic and Social Committee, adopt the measures for the approximation of the provisions laid down by law, regulation or administrative action in Member States which have as their object the establishment and functioning of the internal market.

2. Paragraph 1 shall not apply to fiscal provisions, to those relating to the free movement of persons nor to those relating to the righs and interests of employed persons.

3. The Commission, in its proposals laid down in paragraph 1 concerning health, safety, environmental protection and consumer protection, will take as a base a high level of protection.

4. If, after the adoption of a harmonization measure by the Council acting by a qualified majority, a Member State deems it necessary to apply national provisions on grounds of major needs referred to in Article 36, or relating to protection of the environment or the working environment, it shall notify the Commission of these provisions.

The Commission shall confirm the provisions involved after having verified that they are not a means of arbitrary discrimination or a disguised restriction on the trade between Member States.

By way of derogation from the procedure laid down in Articles 169 and 170, the Commission or any Member State may bring the matter directly before the Court of Justice if it considers that another Member State is making improper use of the powers provided for in this Article.

5. The harmonization measures referred to above shall, in appropriate cases, include a safeguard clause authorizing the Member States to take, for one or more of the non-economic reasons referred to in Article 36, provisional measures subject to a Community control procedure."

Article 19

The EEC Treaty shall be supplemented by the following provisions:

"Article 100 B

1. During 1992, the Commission shall, together with each Member State, draw up an inventory, of national laws, regulations and administrative provisions which fall under Article 100 A and which have not been harmonized pursuant to that Article.

The Council, acting in accordance with the provisions of Article 100 A, may decide that the provisions in force in a Member State must be recognized as being equivalent to those applied by another Member State.

2. The provisions of Article 100 A (4) shall apply by analogy.

3. The Commission shall draw up the inventory referred to in the first subparagraph of paragraph 1 and shall submit appropriate proposals in good time to allow the Council to act before the end of 1992."

. . .

Subsection V - Research and technological development

Article 24

A Title VI shall be added to Part Three of the EEC Treaty, reading as follows:

"Title VI

Research and technological development

Article 130 F

1. The Community's aim shall be to strengthen the scientific and technological basis of European industry and to encourage it to become more competitive at international level.

2. In order to achieve this, it shall encourage undertakings including small and medium-sized undertakings, research centres and universities in their research and technological development activities; it shall support their efforts to cooperate with one another, aiming in particular, at enabling undertakings to exploit the Community's internal market potential to the full, in particular through the opening up of national public contracts, the definition of common standards and the removal of legal and fiscal barriers to that cooperation.

3. In the achievement of these aims, particular account shall be taken of the connection between the common research and technological development effort, the establishment of the internal market and the implementation of common policies, particularly as regards competition and trade.

Article 130 G

In pursuing these objectives the Community shall carry out the following activities, complementing the activities carried out in the Member States:

(a) implementation of research, technological development and demonstration programmes, by promoting cooperation with undertakings, research centres and universities;

(b) promotion of cooperation with third countries and international organizations in the field of Community research, technological development, and demonstrations;

(c) dissemination and optimization of the results of activities in Community research, technological development, and demonstration;

(d) stimulation of the training and mobility of researchers in the Community.

Article 130 H

Member States shall, in liaison with the Commission, coordinate among themselves in policies and programmes carried out at national level. In close contact with the Member States, the Commission may take any useful initiative to promote such coordination.

Article 130 I

1. The Community shall adopt a multiannual framework programme setting out all its activities. The framework programme shall lay down the scientific and technical objectives, define their respective priorities, set out the main line of the activities envisaged and fix the amount deemed necessary, the detailed rules for financial participation by the Community in the programme as a whole and the breakdown of this amount between the various activities envisaged.

2. The framework programme may be adapted or supplemented, as the situation changes.

Article 130 K

The framework programme shall be implemented through specific programmes developed within each activity. Each specific programme shall define the detailed rules for implementing it, fix its duration and provide for the means deemed necessary.

The Council shall define the detailed arrangements for the dissemination of knowledge resulting from the specific programmes.

Article 130 L

In implementing the multiannual framework programme, supplementary programmes may be decided on involving the participation of certain Member States only, which shall finance them subject to possible Community participation.

The Council shall adopt the rules applicable to supplementary programmes, particularly as regards the dissemination of knowledge and the access of other Member States.

Article 130 M

In implementing the multiannual framework programme, the Community may make provision, with the agreement of the Member States concerned, for participation in research and development programmes undertaken by several Member States, including participation in the structures created for the execution of those programmes.

Article 130 N

In implementing the multiannual framework programme, the Community may make provision for cooperation in Community research, technological development and demonstration with third countries or international organizations.

The detailed arrangements for such cooperation may be the subject of international agreements between the Community and the third parties concerned which shall be negotiated and concluded in accordance with Article 228.

Article 130 O

The Community may set up joint undertakings or any other structure necessary for the efficient execution of programmes of Community research, technological development and demonstration.

Article 130 P

1. The detailed arrangements for financing each programme, including any Community contribution, shall be established at the time of the adoption of the programme.

2. The amount of the Community's annual contribution shall be laid down under the budgetary procedure, without prejudice to other possible methods of Community financing. The estimated cost of the specific programmes must not in aggregate exceed the financial provision in the framework programme.

Article 130 Q

1. The Council shall, acting unanimously on a proposal from the Commission and after consulting the European Parliament and the Economic and Social Committee, adopt the provisions referred to in Articles 130 I and 130 O.

2. The Council shall, acting by a qualified majority on a proposal from the Commission, after consulting the Economic and Social Committee, and in cooperation with the European Parliament, adopt the provisions referred to in Articles 130 K, 130 L, 130 M, 130 N and 130 P(1). The adoption of these supplementary programmes shall also require the agreement of the Member States concerned."

. . .

TITLE III: PROVISIONS ON EUROPEAN COOPERATION IN THE SPHERE OF FOREIGN POLICY

Article 30

European Cooperation in the sphere of foreign policy shall be governed by the following provisions:

1. The High Contracting Parties, being members of the European Communities, shall endeavor jointly to formulate and implement a European foreign policy.

2. (a) The High Contracting Parties undertake to inform and consult each other on any foreign policy matters of general interest so as to ensure that their combined influence is exercised as effectively as possible through coordination, the convergence of their positions and the implementation of joint action.

(b) Consultations shall take place before the High Contracting Parties decide on their final position.

(c) In adopting its positions and in its national measures each High Contracting Party shall take full account of the positions of the other partners and shall give due consideration to the desirability of adopting and implementing common European positions.

In order to increase their capacity for joint action in the foreign policy field, the High Contracting Parties shall ensure that common principles and objectives are gradually developed and defined.

The determination of common positions shall constitute a point of reference for the policies of the High Contracting Parties.

(d) The High Contracting Parties shall endeavor to avoid any action or position which impairs their effectiveness as a cohesive force in international relations or within international organizations.

3. (a) The Ministers for Foreign Affairs and a member of the Commission shall meet at least four times a year within the framework of European Political Cooperation. They may also discuss foreign policy matters within the framework of Political Cooperation on the occasion of meetings of the Council of the European Communities.

(b) The Commission shall be fully associated with the proceedings of Political Cooperation.

(c) In order to ensure the swift adoption of common positions and the implementation of joint action, the High Contracting Parties shall, as far as possible, refrain from impeding the formation of a consensus and the joint action which this could produce.

4. The High Contracting Parties shall ensure that the European Parliament is closely associated with European Political Co-operation. To that end the Presidency shall regularly inform the European Parliament of the foreign policy issues which are being examined within the framework of Political Cooperation and shall

ensure that the views of the European Parliament are duly taken into consideration.

5. The external policies of the European Community and the policies agreed in European Political Cooperation must be consistent.

The Presidency and the Commission, each within its own sphere of competence, shall have special responsibility for ensuring that such consistency is sought and maintained.

6. (a) The High Contracting Parties consider that closer cooperation on questions of European security would contribute in an essential way to the development of a European identity in external policy matters. They are ready to coordinate their positions more closely on the political and economic aspects of security.

(b) The High Contracting Parties are determined to maintain the technological and industrial conditions necessary for their security. They shall work to that end both at the national level, and where appropriate, within the framework of the competent institutions and bodies.

(c) Nothing in this Title shall impede closer cooperation in the field of security between certain of the High Contracting Parties within the framework of the Western European Union or the Atlantic Alliance.

7. (a) In international institutions and at international conferences which they attend, the High Contracting Parties shall endeavor to adopt common positions on the subjects covered by this Titel.

(b) In international institutions and at international conferences in which not all the High Contracting Parties participate, those who do participate shall take full account of positions agreed in European Political Cooperation.

8. The High Contracting Parties shall organize a political dialogue with third countries and regional groupings whenever they deem it necessary.

9. The High Contracting Parties and the Commission, through mutual assistance and information, shall intensify cooperation between their representations accredited to third countries and to international organizations.

10. (a) The Presidency of European Political Cooperation shall be held by the High Contracting Party which holds the Presidency of the Council of the European Communities.

(b) The Presidency shall be responsible for initiating action and coordinating and representing the positions of the Member States in relations with third countries in respect of European Political Cooperation activities. It shall also be responsible for the management of Political Cooperation and in particular for drawing up the timetable of meetings and for convening and organizing meetings.

(c) The Political Directors shall meet regularly in the Political Committee in order to give the necessary impetus, maintain the continuity of European Political Cooperation and prepare Ministers' discussions.

(d) The Political Committee or, if necessary, a ministerial meeting shall convene within forty-eight hours at the request of at least three Member States.

(e) The European Correspondents' Group shall be responsible, under the direction of the Political Committee, for monitoring the implementation of European Political Cooperation and for studying general organizational problems.

(f) Working groups shall meet as directed by the Political Committee.

(g) A Secretariat based in Brussels shall assist the Presidency in preparing and implementing the activities of European Political Cooperation and in administrative matters. It shall carry out its duties under the authority of the Presidency.

11. As regards privileges and immunities, the members of the European Political Cooperation Secretariat shall be treated in the same way as members of the diplomatic missions of the High Contracting Parties based in the same place as the Secretariat.

12. Five years after the entry into force of this Act the High Contracting Parties shall examine whether any revision of Title III is required.

JOINT DECLARATION ON THE ESTABLISHMENT OF OFFICIAL RELATIONS BETWEEN THE EUROPEAN ECONOMIC COMMUNITY AND THE COUNCIL FOR MUTUAL ECONOMIC ASSISTANCE

(Luxembourg, 25 June 1988)*

The European Economic Community, of the one part, and the Council for Mutual Economic Assistance, of the other part, having regard to the acts establishing the European Economic Community and the Council for Mutual Economic Assistance, and in particular the Treaty of Rome, on the basis of the Final Act of the Conference on Security and Cooperation in Europe, and taking account of the results of the subsequent stages of the CSCE process, desirous of contributing, by the activities they pursue within their fields of competence, to the further development of international economic cooperation, an important factor in economic growth and social progress, declare as follows:

1. The European Economic Community and the Council for Mutual Economic Assistance establish official relations with each other by adopting this Declaration.

2. The Parties will develop cooperation in areas which fall within their respective spheres of competence and where there is a common interest.

3. The areas, forms and methods of cooperation will be determined by the Parties by means of contacts and discussions between their representatives designated for this purpose.

4. On the basis of the experience gained in developing cooperation between them, the parties will, if necessary, examine the possibility of determining new areas, forms and methods of cooperation.

5. As regards the application of this Declaration to the Community, it shall apply to the territories in which the Treaty

---

* *Official Journal of the European Communities* No. L 157/35 (24 June 1988).

establishing the European Economic Community is applied and under the conditions laid down in that Treaty.

6. This Declaration is drawn up in duplicate in the Bulgarian, Czech, Danish, Dutch, English, French, German, Greek, Hungarian, Italian, Mongolian, Polish, Portuguese, Romanian, Russian, Spanish and Vietnamese languages, each text being equally authentic.

Done at Luxembourg, on the twenty-fifth day of June one thousand nine hundred and eighty-eight.

EUROPEAN COUNCIL MEETING OF THE HEADS OF STATE AND GOVERNMENT

(Rhodes, 2-3 December 1988)
Excerpts of Communiqué*

...

II. DECLARATION OF THE EUROPEAN COUNCIL ON THE INTERNATIONAL ROLE OF THE EUROPEAN COMMUNITY

Reaffirming its commitment to achieve concrete progress towards European unity on the basis of the Single European Act,

determined to strengthen and expand the role of the European Community and its member states on the international political and economic stage, in cooperation with all other states and appropriate organizations,

and aware that the completion of the internal market in 1992, which is already inspiring a new dynamism in the Community's economic life, will equally affect the Community's political and economic role in the world,

the European Council reaffirms that the single market will be of benefit to Community and non-Community countries alike by ensuring continuing economic growth. The internal market will not close in on itself. 1992 Europe will be a partner and not a "fortress Europe." The internal market will be a decisive factor contributing to greater liberalization in international trade on the basis of the General Agreement on Tariffs and Trade (GATT) principles of reciprocal and mutually advantageous arrangements. The Community will continue to participate actively in the GATT Uruguay Round, commited as it is to strengthen the multilateral trading system. It will also continue to pursue, with the U.S., Japan

---

* European Community News, *E.C.Summit Leaders Assess Progress of 1992 Program* (No. 32/88) (Washington, D.C.:EC Office of Press and Public Affairs, 1988)

and the other Organization for Economic Cooperation and Development partners, policies designed to promote sustainable noninflationary growth in the world economy.

The Community and its member states will continue to work closely and cooperatively with the United States to maintain and deepen the solid and comprehensive transatlantic relationship. Closer political and economic relations with Japan and the other industrialized countries will also be developed. In particular, the Community wishes to strengthen and to expand relations with EFTA countries and all other European nations which share the same ideals and objectives. Open and constructive dialogue and cooperation will be actively pursued with other countries or regional groups of the Middle East, and the Mediterranean, Africa, the Caribbean, the Pacific, Asia and Latin America, with special emphasis on interregional cooperation.

The European Council emphasizes the need to improve social and economic conditions in less-developed countries and to promote structural adjustment, both through trade and aid. It also recognizes the importance of a continuing policy to tackle the problems of the highly indebted countries on a case by case basis. It looks forward to the successful conclusion of the negotiations for the renewal of the Convention between the European Community and its 66 African, Caribbean and Pacific partners during the coming year.

The European Community and its member states are determined to play an active role in the preservation of international peace and security and in the solution of regional conflicts in conformity with the United Nations Charter. Europe cannot but actively demonstrate its solidarity to the great and spreading movement for democracy and full support for the principles of the Universal Declaration on Human Rights. The Twelve will endeavor to strengthen the effectiveness of the United Nations and to actively contribute to its peace-keeping role.

Against the background of improved East-West relations, the European Council welcomes the readiness of the European members of the Council of Mutual Economic Assistance to develop relations with the European Community and reaffirms its willingness to further economic relations and cooperation with them, taking into account each country's specific situation, in order to use the opportunities available in a mutually beneficial way.

The European Council reaffirms its determination to act with renewed hope to overcome the division of our continent and to promote the Western values and principles which member states have in common.

To this effect, we will strive to achieve:

- full respect for the provisions of the Helsinki Final Act and further progress in the Conference on Security and Cooperation in Europe process, including an early and successful conclusion of the Vienna follow-up meeting;
- the establishment of a secure and stable balance of conventional forces in Europe at a lower level, the strengthening of mutual confidence and military transparence and the conclusion of a global and verifiable ban on chemical weapons;
- promotion of human rights and fundamental freedom, free circulation of peoples and ideas and the establishment of more open societies; promotion of human and cultural exchanges between East and West;
- the development of political dialogue with our Eastern neighbors.

The European Community and the Twelve are determined to make full use of the provisions of the Single European Act in order to strengthen solidarity among them, coordination on the political and economic aspects of security, and consistency between the external policies of the European Community and the policies agreed in the framework of the European Political Cooperation. They will strive to reach swift adoption of common positions and implementation of joint action.

The European Council invites all countries to embark with the European Community as world partner on an historic effort to leave to the next generation a continent and a world more secure, more just and more free ...

EUROPEAN COUNCIL MEETING OF THE HEADS OF STATE AND GOVERNMENT

(Madrid, 26-27 June, 1989)

Excerpts of Communiqué*

...

EXTERNAL RELATIONS

In keeping with the Rhodes Declaration on the international role of the European Community, the European Council reviewed developments in relations between the Community and a number of its partners:

(1) The European Council noted with satisfaction the progress made in cooperation with the European Free Trade Association (EFTA) countries following the Summit of the Heads of Government in Oslo and the joint meeting of Ministers for Foreign Affairs, which were held in March.

In this context, it emphasized the importance which it attached to the rapid identification of the best ways of developing these relations in a more structured way.

It hoped to be apprised at its next meeting of concrete results obtained in the meantime in this area.

(2) The European Council noted that satisfactory progress had been made in establishing an appropriate policy towards the East European countries ensuring consistency between Community policies and those agreed within political cooperation, in accordance with Article 30 (5) of the Single Act. In this context, it noted the progress made towards the conclusion of trade and cooperation agreements with a number of those countries, at the same time emphasizing the common will to contribute to the efforts made, by

---

* European Community News, *E.C. Summit Brings Agreement on Monetary Union* (No. 21/89) (Washington, D.C.: EC Office of Press and Public Affairs, 1989).

Poland and Hungary in particular, to open up their economies and put them back on a sound footing.

(3) The European Council restated the importance it attached to the successful conclusion of the multilateral negotiations under the Uruguay Round, which should make it possible to set up an international system able to meet the challenge arising on a world scale not only for trade in goods, but also for services, for the protection of intellectual property and for action on the special situation of the developing countries. It reaffirmed the Community's determination to oppose any recourse to unilateral measures which might jeopardize such an international system.

(4) The European Council reaffirmed its commitment to a close and comprehensive transatlantic relationship, and noted with satisfaction the cooperative relations which had already been established with the new United States Administration.

(5) The European Council stressed the importance it attached to the consolidation of the long-established privileged links between the Community and the African, Caribbean and Pacific (ACP) States. It welcomed the progress made in renegotiating the ACP-EEC Convention and called for the negotiations to be concluded by the end of the year.

(6) The European Council likewise confirmed the significance it attached to strengthening and extending relations with the countries associated with the Community.

(7) The European Council paid particular attention to examining the situation of middle-income countries facing the problem of indebtedness. Their situation was extremely worrying, especially in Latin America, where a solution to this problem was of particular importance for the consolidation and strengthening of democracy.

The European Council confirmed that the Member States of the Community had a responsibility to play an active part in finding realistic solutions, in the appropriate fora, given the historical links and cultural and political affinities linking them with the countries in question.

The European Council and the Member States accordingly confirmed the conclusions reached by the Ministers at the Meeting of the Economic and Financial Council in March and stressed the willingness of the Member States to consider solutions involving voluntary reductions in debt and debt servicing, taking into account the global measures adopted recently by France and Belgium, with the participation of the International Monetary Fund (IMF) and the World Bank.

The European Council emphasized that it was not possible to delay a solution to this problem. It called upon commercial banks and debtor countries to evolve the practical mechanisms required for a solution to this matter, which posed serious economic and political problems.

The European Council took note of the Spanish proposal, summarized in Annex II, to set up a European Guarantee Fund for the purpose of ensuring a special European contribution to the strengthening and balance of the international effort in this area. This proposal will be examined by the Economic and Financial Council of Ministers.

...

ANNEX II
ELEMENTS OF THE SPANISH PROPOSAL CONCERNING THE CREATION OF A EUROPEAN GUARANTEE FUND (EGF) FOR OPERATIONS TO REDUCE THE PAYMENT AND LEVEL OF THE FOREIGN DEBT OF HEAVILY INDEBTED COUNTRIES

1. The system would address the problem of the debt of middle-income countries. It would cover not only Latin America, but North African, Far Eastern and East European countries too.

2. For this system to be launched three conditions must be satisfied:

(a) the debtor countries must reach agreement with the IMF on the economic program to be pursued over the three following years;

(b) the banking sector must accept the reductions which the IMF and the EGF consider appropriate;

(c) the creditor countries which are not members of the EGF must make a contribution on a case-by-case basis, equivalent to that made by the countries participating in the above Fund.

3. The creation of the EGF would strengthen the multilateral aspect envisaged for dealing with the debt problem.

4. The Fund would allow a more balanced distribution of the efforts to be made by ensuring that the commercial banks shoulder their share of responsibility.

5. As the EGF is to be a guarantee system, it is not envisaged that the participating countries would pay initial contributions.

6. The EGF would be formed on an intergovernmental basis; all interested European countries could take part in it.

***

EUROPEAN POLITICAL COOPERATION

1. East-West relations, including Conference on Security and Cooperation in Europe (CSCE)

The European Council recognizes the importance of the profound changes now taking place in the USSR and Central and Eastern European countries, while regretting that serious violations of human rights still occur in some of those countries, in particular against members of ethnic and religious minorities. It has reaffirmed the determination of the Community and its Member States to play an active role in supporting and encouraging positive changes and reform.

The European Council has reaffirmed the full validity of the comprehensive approach integrating political, economic and cooperation aspects which the Community and its Member States follow in their relations with the USSR and with Central and Eastern European countries. It has assessed positively the concrete steps which the Community and its Member States, following the Rhodes Declaration, have taken in these fields.

The European Council looks forward to an intensification of relations between East and West in all fields. It reaffirms its belief that progress in arms control and disarmament, respect for human rights and the free circulation of ideas, information and persons remain necessary elements for this improved East/West atmosphere to materialize into further tangible results.

The European Council is convinced that the CSCE process provides the appropriate framework to achieving greater progress in all these fields, enabling Europe to look forward to a day when its present divisions become a matter of history.

The Twelve Member States, who are gradually strengthening their cooperation as a contribution to preserving their security, seek to enhance stability and security through lower levels of forces and armaments as well as through greater transparency and predictability in military matters and thus to promote progress in rapprochement and in the dialogue among all the peoples in Europe. In this framework, they attach great importance to the negotiations on conventional forces in Europe and on confidence and security building measures currently underway in Vienna and will strive for their early and satisfactory conclusion. The resumed Geneva negotiations on reductions in strategic nuclear weapons and the negotiations on chemical weapons also offer prospects for greatly reduced military confrontation and an improved climate of relations between East and West ...

INSTITUTIONS FOR EUROPEAN SECURITY COOPERATION*

---

* Source: Catherine McArdle Kelleher and Gale A. Mattox, eds., *Evolving European Defense Policies* (Lexington: D.C. Heath and Company, 1987), pp. 54-57. This information has been revised and updated by the editor.

EUROPEAN POLITICAL COOPERATION

Founded in 1970

Current Members

Belgium[1]
Denmark[2]
France
West Germany
Greece[4]
Ireland
Italy
Luxembourg
Netherlands
Portugal[3]
Spain
United Kingdom

Security Mandate

1. The Single European Act of 1987 provided a formal treaty basis for the consideration of the "economic and political aspects of security." The Twelve are committed to security consultation within the framework of European Political Cooperation (EPC). For details see Thomas Grunert's chapter in this volume.
2. European Political Cooperation was launched as an intergovernmental cooperation at the The Hague Summit in 1969. It has progressively established a habit of consultation, or a "coordination reflex" among the member states. In particular, Title III of the Single European Act strengthened the Twelve's commitment to seek a common line on foreign policy questions. (See the Annex, Documents).
3. The need to strengthen further European Political Cooperation and to achieve consistency between the external policies of the European Community and the policies agreed in the framework of the European Political Cooperation was underlined by the Heads of

---

1 Membership in the European Community (EC) and European Political Cooperation (EPC) is identical. The original members of EPC in 1970 were Belgium, France, the Federal Republic of Germany, Italy, Luxembourg and the Netherlands.

2 Denmark, Ireland and the United Kingdom joined EPC in 1973.

3 Portugal and Spain entered EPC in 1986.

4 Greece was admitted to EPC in 1981.

Government at the December 1988 European Council meeting in Rhodes, Greece. (See the Annex, Documents).

Methodology

1. EPC operates solely on the basis of consensus. There is a small permanent secretariat in Brussels which coordinates the activities of groups of experts meeting on major foreign policy areas, i.e. Eastern Europe.
2. The European Council, bi-annual meetings of the Heads of State and Government, considers EPC as well as EC matters.
3. Foreign ministers hold some six to eight formal meetings and two informal weekend meetings a year, and also discuss EPC issues at the EC Foreign Affairs Council.
4. A Political Committee comprising political directors, meets monthly, as does a working level committee of EPC "correspondents."
5. There is also a range of geographical and functional working groups associated with EPC, covering inter alia: Africa, Asia, Latin America, the Middle East, Eastern Europe, the Euro-Arab dialogue, the Mediterranean, the United Nations, UN disarmament, CSCE and Non-proliferation.

WESTERN EUROPEAN UNION

Founded in 1954

Current Members

Belgium[5]
France
West Germany
Italy
Luxembourg
Netherlands
Portugal[6]
Spain
United Kingdom

Security Mandate

1. The parties will afford any members subjected to an armed attack "all the military and other aid and assistance in their power."
2. The parties, while promoting unity among West European countries, will work in close cooperation with NATO. Recognizing the undesirability of duplicating the military staffs of NATO, the WEU Council and its agency will rely on the appropriate military authorities of NATO for information and advice on military matters.
3. The treaty sets limits on the maximum size of the forces that the parties will place under SACEUR in peacetime on the mainland of Europe.
4. The United Kingdom will maintain four divisions and a tactical air force on the mainland of Europe.
5. West Germany will not manufacture atomic, biological or chemical weapons. Restrictions concerning the production of conventional arms have been gradually removed.
6. The Agency for the Control of Armaments (ACA) has been monitoring fulfillment of the treaty's provisions on the size of forces, on West German manufacture of weapons, and on stocks of weapons held by member states on the mainland of Europe.

---

5 The original members of the WEU were Belgium, France, the Federal Republic of Germany, Italy, Luxembourg, the Netherlands and the United Kingdom.

6 Portugal and Spain acceded to the WEU in 1988.

7. The Standing Armaments Committee (SAC) has been seeking to improve cooperation on the development, standardization, production and procurement of armaments.

Methodology

1. A council meets at ministerial and permanent representative levels. In former years ministerial meetings have been held annually: since 1984 they are twice-yearly, (one of them informal) and will involve both foreign and defense ministers. The Permanent Council meets about ten times a year in London. It is chaired by the secretary general, and comprises London-based ambassadors plus a British Foreign and Commonwealth Office Assistant Under Secretary of State. The Council is responsible for confirming the continued adherence of members to the treaty, supervising the work of the Agencies, and responding to the WEU assembly of parliamentarians. The presidency rotates annually.
2. Following the Rome Declaration of 1984 three new Agencies were created in Paris, on arms control and disarmament; security and defense; armament cooperation (including subgroups). The Ministerial Council of WEU decided on 13 November 1989 to create a "WEU Institute for Security Studies" located in Paris.

INDEPENDENT EUROPEAN PROGRAM GROUP

Founded in 1976

Current Members

Belgium[7]
Denmark
France
West Germany
Greece
Italy
Luxembourg
Netherlands
Norway
Portugal
Spain
Turkey
United Kingdom

Security Mandate

1. To act as the principal means of extending equipment cooperation among the European members of NATO.
2. To increase standardization and interoperability of equipment.
3. To ensure the maintenance of a healthy European defense industrial and technological base.
4. To foster closer and more balanced armaments cooperation with North America.

Methodology

1. The first meeting of IEPG at full defense minister level was held in November 1984.
2. State secretaries meet annually, and national armaments directors twice a year. Chairmanship rotates bi-annually.
3. A staff group meets regularly (every 6-8 weeks).
4. Recently, at a meeting in Lisbon, the establishment of a permanent secretariat was decided upon.

There are, in addition, three expert groups:

---

7 The original members of the IEPG were Belgium, Denmark, France, West Germany, Greece, Italy, Luxembourg, the Netherlands, Norway, Turkey and the United Kingdom.

a) Panel I: Searches for cooperative possibilities; prepares an annual equipment replacement schedule.
b) Panel II: Coordinates efforts once a cooperative program is underway.
c) Panel III: A procedural and policy group.

EUROGROUP
Founded in 1968

Current Members

Belgium[8]
Denmark
West Germany
Greece
Italy
Luxembourg
Netherlands
Norway
Portugal
Spain
Turkey
United Kingdom

Security Mandate

1. To help strengthen the whole NATO alliance by ensuring that the European contribution to the common defense is as strong, cohesive, and effective as possible.
2. To provide through its subordinate groups a means by which members can coordinate their defense efforts and thus make the maximum use of available resources.
3. To provide a forum for the harmonization of European views on political and strategic questions affecting the defense of NATO Europe.

Methodology

1. Defense ministers meet twice a year, immediately before NATO's Defense Planning Committee meetings. Chairmanship rotates annually.
2. The NATO Permanent Representatives of Eurogroup countries meet as necessary during the interim period to implement decisions and prepare advice.
3. A staff group meets regularly at NATO headquarters to conduct routine work.

---

8 The original members of the Eurogroup were Belgium, Denmark, West Germany, Greece, Italy, Luxembourg, Netherlands, Norway, Turkey and the United Kingdom.

4. The United Kingdom provides a small secretariat from its delegation to NATO.

5. There are in addition several expert subgroups, including:

a) Eurolongterm: Prepares joint concepts of operations and outlines specifications for equipment.

b) Eurocom: Works on interoperability of battlefield communications equipment.

c) Euromed: Works on close cooperation in the military medical field.

ABBREVIATIONS

ABM — anti-ballistic missile
ACDA — Arms Control and Disarmament Agency
ACE — avion de combat européen
ACP — African, Caribbean and Pacific states
ASA — American Soybean Association
ASEAN — Association of South-East Asian Nations
ATBM — anti-tactical ballistic missile
AWACS — Airborne Warning and Control Systems

BRITE — Basic Research in Industrial Technologies

CAP — Common Agricultural Policy
CARICOM — Caribbean Community
CDE — Conference on Disarmament in Europe
CDU — Christdemokratische Union
CFE — Conventional Forces in Europe
CMEA — Council for Mutual Economic Assistance
COCOM — Coordination Committee (for Multilateral Export Controls)
COGECA — Comité de la Coopération Agricole de la Communauté Economique Européenne
COPA — Committee of Agricultural Organizations in the EEC
COREPER — Committee of Permanent Representatives to the European Communities
CSCE — Conference on Security and Cooperation in Europe
CSI — Cours Supérieures Interarmées

EAGGF — European Agricultural Guidance and Guarantee Fund
EC — European Communities
EAEC — European Atomic Energy Community
EEC — European Economic Community
ECSC — European Coal and Steel Community
ECU — European Currency Unit
EDC — European Defense Community

EFA	European Fighter Aircraft
EGF	European Guarantee Fund
EIB	European Investment Bank
EMS	European Monetary System
EMU	Economic and Monetary Union
EP	European Parliament
EPAC	Empresa Publica de Abastecimento de Cereais
EPC	European Political Cooperation
ERDF	European Regional Development Fund
ESA	European Space Agency
ESF	European Social Fund
ESPRIT	Strategic Program for Research Development in Information Technologies
EUREKA	European Research Cooperation Agency
FAR	Force d'Action Rapide
FDP	Freie Demokratische Partei
FOFA	Follow on Forces Attack
FOTL	Follow-On To Lance
GATT	General Agreement on Tariffs and Trade
GSP	General System of Preferences
HSFK	Hessische Stiftung Friedens- und Konfliktforschung
ICBMs	Intercontinental Ballistic Missiles
IEPG	Independent European Program Group
IHEDN	Institut des Hautes Etudes de Défense Nationale
IMF	International Monetary Fund
INF	intermediate range nuclear forces
ISA	International Studies Association
LDCs	Less Developed Countries
MAD	Mutual Assured Destruction
MAS	Mutual Assured Security
MFN	most-favored-nation treatment
MINEX	Mineral Export Earnings Stabilization

MOD	Ministry of Defense
MTNs	Multilateral Tariff Negotiations
NACISA	NATO Communications and Information Systems Agency
NATO	North Atlantic Treaty Organization
NICs	Newly Industrializing Countries
NICS	NATO Integrated Communications System
NNA	Neutral and Non-Aligned Countries
NPG	Nuclear Planning Group
NTBs	non-tariff barriers
OECD	Organization for Economic Cooperation and Development
OPEC	Oil and Petroleum Exporting Countries
PLO	Palestine Liberation Organization
PS	Parti Socialiste
RACE	Research Program in Advanced Technologies
R&D	Research and Development
RPR	Rassemblement pour la République
SACEUR	Supreme Allied Command Europe
SADCC	Southern African Development Coordination Conference
SALT	Strategic Arms Limitation Talks
SDI	Strategic Defense Initiative
SEA	Single European Act
SED	Sozialistische Einheitspartei Deutschlands
SNF	short range nuclear forces
SPD	Sozialdemokratische Partei Deutschlands
S&T	Science and Technology
STABEX	Stabilization of Export Earnings
SWP	Stiftung Wissenschaft und Politik
TPSC	Trade Policy Staff Committee
UN	United Nations
UDF	Union pour la Démocratie Française

UNICE	Union of Industries of the European Community
USDA	United States Department of Agriculture
USTR	United States Trade Representative
WEU	Western European Union

CONTRIBUTORS

David Allen is Senior Lecturer in Politics, Department of European Studies, Loughborough University, England. He is the author of a number of articles on European foreign policy-making and the European Community, and edited (with R. Rummel and W. Wessels) *European Political Cooperation* (1982) and (with A. Pijpers) *European Foreign Policy-Making and the Arab-Israeli Conflict* (1985).

Vera Erdmann-Keefer received her Master's degree in Western European Studies from Washington University in St. Louis, Missouri in 1985, and her doctorate in Political Science from Eberhard-Karls-Universität in Tübingen, West Germany. Her thesis is on "Agricultural Trade Conflicts between the U.S. and the E.C." Her contribution to this volume is a revised version of a paper given at the Sixth International Conference of Europeanists in Washington, D.C. in the Fall of 1987 and the 29th Annual Convention of the International Studies Association in St. Louis in the Spring of 1988.

David Garnham is Professor of Political Science at The University of Wisconsin-Milwaukee. His research focuses on international conflict and defense policy. Professor Garnham is the author of *The Politics of European Defense Cooperation: Germany, France, Britain and America* (1988) as well as numerous articles and book chapters.

Roy H. Ginsberg, formerly an official with the United States International Trade Commission, has been Assistant Professor of Government at Skidmore College since 1986. He received his doctorate in Political Science from The George Washington University in 1985. Mr. Ginsberg serves on the Executive Board of the European Community Studies Association and is co-editor of its *Newsletter*. He is author of *Foreign Policy Actions of the European Community: The Politics of Scale* (1989) and is currently co-authoring a book on United States-European Community relations.

Thomas Grunert is a research officer in the Political Affairs Division of the Secretariat of the European Parliament in Luxembourg. He has served as a Kennedy Fellow at the Center for European Studies, Harvard University, and as a research fellow at the European University Institute in Florence. Dr. Grunert has also been the Director of the Economic Committee at the General secretariat of the North Atlantic Assembly in Brussels. His publications include numerous articles on West European integration, international relations and security policy.

Christopher Hill is a Lecturer in International Relations at the London School of Economics. Dr. Hill has also been a Research Fellow at the Royal Institute of International Affairs, and a Guest Scholar at the Woodrow Wilson International Center for Scholars in Washington, D.C.. He is the editor of *National Foreign Policies and European Political Cooperation* (1983) as well as a contributor to many other books and scholarly journals. His main interests are in foreign policy analysis, British foreign policy, and European Political Cooperation.

David Rubenson is a security policy analyst in Southern California. As described in his article, Mr. Rubenson is typical of many U.S. security policy analysts in that he has participated in analyses of a wide range of issues affecting security policy including: the development of space surveillance strategies; SDI; ATBM; and a variety of topics related to arms control and European security policy.

Reinhardt Rummel is a member of the research staff of the Stiftung Wissenschaft und Politik, Ebenhausen, and a Professorial Lecturer at the Paul H. Nitze SAIS Bologna Center of the Johns Hopkins University. He has been a visiting scholar at Harvard University and a fellow at the Woodrow Wilson International Center for Scholars. Dr. Rummel's publications include *European Political Cooperation* (1982) which he co-edited.

Peter Schmidt is a Research Associate at the Stiftung Wissenschaft und Politik, Ebenhausen (Federal Republic of Germany). He studied economics, political science and pedagogy at the University of Heidelberg and the University of Mannheim, where he earned his doctorate. Dr. Schmidt has been a Visiting Fellow at the Rand Corporation, Santa Monica, USA, as well as at the Fondation pour les études de Défense nationale, Paris.

Stanley R. Sloan is the specialist in U.S.-Alliance Relations for the Congressional Research Service, Washington, D.C.. Previously he served as head of the Europe/Middle East/Africa Section, Congressional Research Service; as Deputy National Intelligence Officer for Western Europe (CIA); and as a member of the U.S. delegation to the M.B.F.R. negotiations. Mr. Sloan is the author of *NATO's Future: Toward a New Transatlantic Bargain* (1985), and the editor of *NATO in the 1990s* (1989) as well as numerous studies on NATO, arms control and other international security topics.

Michael Smith is Senior Lecturer in International Relations at Coventry Polytechnic. His special research interests are in foreign policy analysis, British-American and European-American relations. He has written many articles, edited several volumes on United States-European Community relations and is the author of *Western Europe and the United States: The Uncertain Alliance* (1984).